# PIRACY AND INTELLECTUAL PROPERTY IN LATIN AMERICA

*Piracy and Intellectual Property in Latin America* is the first sustained effort to present an alternative framework for understanding piracy and contemporary challenges to global discourses on intellectual property (IP) in the Americas.

While piracy might just look like theft and derivative reproduction from the perspective of many right-holders, the contributors to this volume go beyond this economic-driven logic and show how practices of copying are in fact practices of reinvention that reflect the rich social networks and forms of creativity, authorship, commerce, and consumption that characterize informal economies. From a perspective informed by contemporary scenarios in Mexico, Brazil, Chile, Argentina, Peru, Guatemala, and the United States, they engage in a discussion of alternatives that—predicated on the importance of protecting culture—allow for other ways of conceiving prosperity at local, national, regional, and global levels. Examples discussed include video games, clothing, trinkets, music, film, TV, and books.

Designed to help understand the broader implications of IP and piracy for the field of Latin American studies, this book will be a major contribution to Global South studies, as well as to the growing bibliography on globalization, informal markets, and piracy.

**Víctor Goldgel-Carballo** is an Associate Professor in the Department of Spanish and Portuguese at the University of Wisconsin-Madison.

**Juan Poblete** is Professor of Latin/o American Literature and Cultural Studies at the University of California Santa Cruz.

"The essays in this collection expertly localize unauthorized use in Latin America, integrating on-the-ground production with globalizing discourses of circulatory legitimacy. The book should be required reading for those interested in the increasingly important role of digital textuality in emerging economies."

**Alexander S. Dent**, *Associate Professor of Anthropology, The George Washington University*

# PIRACY AND INTELLECTUAL PROPERTY IN LATIN AMERICA

## Rethinking Creativity and the Common Good

*Edited by Víctor Goldgel-Carballo and Juan Poblete*

Routledge
Taylor & Francis Group
NEW YORK AND LONDON

First published 2020
by Routledge
52 Vanderbilt Avenue, New York, NY 10017

and by Routledge
2 Park Square, Milton Park, Abingdon, Oxon OX14 4RN

*Routledge is an imprint of the Taylor & Francis Group, an informa business*



*Library of Congress Cataloging-in-Publication Data*
A catalog record for this title has been requested

ISBN: 978-0-367-42401-5 (hbk)
ISBN: 978-0-367-42399-5 (pbk)
ISBN: 978-0-367-82395-5 (ebk)

Typeset in Bembo
by Taylor & Francis Books

Víctor dedicates this book to all the people whose unpaid labor makes books and sharing knowledge possible.

Juan dedicates this book to the memory of his beloved father-in-law, Joe Mahay (1946–2019): a great bushwhacking Adirondack environmental pioneer, and a better person.

# CONTENTS

# ILLUSTRATIONS

## Figures

## Tables

# ACKNOWLEDGMENTS

We are grateful to our contributors for their patience, kindness, and professionalism and to each other *por la muy buena onda*. It has been a pleasure. We would also like to thank the participants in the Latin American Studies Association workshops on piracy cultures that we organized in New York and Lima in 2016 and 2017. Natalja Mortensen and Charlie Baker, our great editors at Routledge, generously welcomed this project and gave us valuable guidance in this long process. Thanks too are due to the editorial team at Routledge for the material production of this book, and to Richelle Wilson for her help with the preliminary editing of some of the chapters. Víctor would like to thank Cristian De Nápoli, Guadalupe Salomón, and Damián Ríos for their interest in piracy and their invaluable comments, as well as Sarah Ann Wells for her insights on the theoretical dimensions of this project. As usual Juan wants to thank Micah Perks, without whom, nothing.

# CONTRIBUTORS

**Rosana Pinheiro-Machado** is a lecturer of international development at the Department of Social and Policy Sciences at the University of Bath. Previously, she was a lecturer at the Department of International Development at the University of Oxford and held visiting positions at the University of São Paulo and Harvard University. She is the author of *Counterfeit Itineraries in the Global South* (Routledge, 2017) and *Made in China* (Hucitec, 2011). Funded by the Australian Research Council, she is part of a team that investigates new consumer practices in the Global South. Pinheiro-Machado is also a columnist for *The Intercept* (Brasil).

**Kedron Thomas** is Associate Professor of Anthropology at Washington University in St. Louis. She is the author of *Regulating Style: Intellectual Property Law and the Business of Fashion in Guatemala* (University of California Press, 2016) and co-editor of *Securing the City: Neoliberalism, Space, and Insecurity in Postwar Guatemala* (Duke University Press, 2011). Her current research examines policy, practice, and debate regarding labor ethics and environmental sustainability along globalized fashion and footwear supply chains.

**Phillip Penix-Tadsen** is Associate Professor of Spanish and Latin American Studies at the University of Delaware. He holds a PhD from Columbia University and is a specialist in Latin American cultural studies, focusing on the intersections between politics, economics, new media, and visual culture in the region today. His first book, *Cultural Code: Video Games and Latin America* (MIT Press, 2016), offers a synthetic theorization of the relationship between video games and culture through case studies related to Latin America. Professor Penix-Tadsen is also the editor of the anthology *Video Games and the Global South* (ETC Press, 2019).

**Santiago Alfaro Rotondo** is a sociologist and Professor at the Pontificia Universidad Católica del Perú (PUCP). He is the author of many articles and book chapters, including: "Peruwood: la industria del video digital en el Perú" (LARR, 2013), "La música andina como mercado de consumo" (PUCP, 2015), and "Crecimiento con desigualdad: brechas y retos de la economía de las industrias culturales y creativas del Perú" (Universidad Miguel Hernández, 2018, co-authored). His research areas include cultural policies, ethnicity, and the economics of cultural and creative industries. He has also been the deputy manager of performing arts and cultural industries at the Metropolitan Municipality of Lima and general director of cultural industries and arts at the Ministry of Culture.

**Jennifer Ashley** is Assistant Professor of Global Affairs at George Mason University. She has a PhD in Anthropology from Brown University. Her work focuses on media and political subjectivity and has been published in journals such as *American Ethnologist, Popular Communication*, and *Television & New Media.*

**Juan Llamas-Rodriguez** is Assistant Professor of Transnational Media in the School of Arts, Technology, and Emerging Communication at the University of Texas at Dallas. His research and teaching mobilize media theories to critically analyze social phenomena on a global scale. His areas of specialization include media theory, border studies, infrastructure studies, and Latin American film and television. He has published in *Feminist Media Histories, Film Quarterly, Flow, Jump Cut*, and the *Journal for Cinema and Media Studies.* He is a member of the Global Internet TV Consortium, a network of media studies scholars seeking to understand the implications of Internet-distributed television around the world.

**Fábio Tozi** is Assistant Professor of Political and Economic Geography at the Universidade Federal de Minas Gerais (UFMG). He was a National Council for Scientific and Technological Development postdoctoral fellow at the Universidade Estadual de Campinas (UNICAMP). He holds a PhD in human geography from the Universidade de São Paulo and a master's degree in geography from UNICAMP. He did a doctoral internship at the École des Hautes Études en Sciences Sociales in Paris. His main areas of his research are socio-spatial inequalities, territorial planning, piracy, counterfeiting and forgery, urban and popular economy, innovation, digital platforms, and intellectual property.

**Juan Poblete** is Professor of Latin/o American Literature and Cultural Studies, University of California, Santa Cruz. He is the author of *Hacia una historia de la lectura y la pedagogía literaria en América Latina* (Cuarto Propio, 2019), *La Escritura de Pedro Lemebel como proyecto cultural y político* (Cuarto Propio, 2019), and *Literatura chilena del siglo XIX: entre públicos lectores y figuras autoriales* (Cuarto Propio, 2003); editor of *New Approaches to Latin American Studies: Culture and Power* (Routledge, 2017) and *Critical Latin American and Latino Studies* (University of Minnesota Press,

2003); and co-editor of *Sports and Nationalism in Latin America* (Palgrave, 2015), *Humor in Latin American Cinema* (Palgrave, 2015), *Desdén al infortunio: Sujeto, comunicación y público en la narrativa de Pedro Lemebel* (Cuarto Propio, 2010), *Andrés Bello* (IILI, 2009), and *Redrawing The Nation: National Identities in Latin/o American Comics* (Palgrave, 2009).

**Víctor Goldgel-Carballo** is Associate Professor in the Department of Spanish and Portuguese at the University of Wisconsin, Madison. He is the author of *Cuando lo nuevo conquistó América. Prensa, moda y literatura en el siglo XIX* (Siglo XXI, 2013), awarded the Premio Iberoamericano by the Latin American Studies Association. His research and teaching focus on Latin American literature, media history, visual culture, and race. A recipient of fellowships and grants from the American Council of Learned Societies, the Social Science Research Council, and the Mellon Foundation, he is currently a fellow at the National Humanities Center.

**Zac Zimmer** is Assistant Professor of Literature at UC Santa Cruz and faculty affiliate with Legal Studies and Latin American and Latino Studies. He received his PhD from the Department of Romance Studies, Cornell University. His research explores questions of literature, aesthetics, politics, and technology in Latin America. Previous publications have appeared in *Latin American Research Review, Chasqui, Modern Language Notes, Technology & Culture*, and *Revista de Crítica Literaria Latinoamericana.*

**Matías Dewey** is a senior researcher at the Institute of Sociology at the University of St. Gallen, Switzerland. He has also worked at the Max Planck Institute for the Study of Societies in Cologne (Germany) and has been a visiting scholar at the Extra-Legal Governance Institute at the University of Oxford, at MaxPo in Paris, and most recently at the Department of Sociology at the University of Texas at Austin. He has published extensively on social theory, economic sociology, illegal markets, and qualitative research. With Jens Beckert, he recently edited the volume *The Architecture of Illegal Markets: Towards an Economic Sociology of Illegality in the Economy* (Oxford University Press, 2017). His forthcoming book, *Making It at Any Cost: Aspiration and Politics in a Counterfeit Clothing Marketplace*, will be published by the University of Texas Press. His articles have appeared in *Socio-Economic Review, Latin American Research Review, Journal of Latin American Studies*, and *Current Sociology*.

# INTRODUCTION

*Juan Poblete and Víctor Goldgel-Carballo*

> ~~My personal view is that digital culture brings with it a new idea of intellectual property, and that this new culture of sharing can and should inform government policies.~~
>
> ~~*Gilberto Gil*~~

Gilberto Gil, Brazil's minister of culture from 2003–2008 and one of his country's most influential musicians, stated the following in a 2007 interview with the *New York Times*: "My personal view is that digital culture brings with it a new idea of intellectual property, and that this new culture of sharing can and should inform government policies" (Rohter). We had wanted to include this quote as an opening epigraph where you now see strike out text, but we were informed by our editor that it is Routledge policy not to publish any epigraph quotes less than 150 years old because epigraphs do not fall into the same fair-usage guidelines as quotes in the main body of the text since they are deemed to be more decorative than analytical. We obviously do not share this anecdote to complain about our editor, who, like us, works under certain constraints. Rather, we wanted to begin by illustrating visually the follies and exaggerations that the current regime of intellectual property (IP) enforcement has brought on all of us, and why our volume is timely.

*Piracy and Intellectual Property in Latin America: Rethinking Creativity and the Common Good* participates in the current global effort to rethink IP and its relation to creativity and the common good. From a perspective informed by contemporary Latin American scenarios, we engage in a discussion of alternatives that—predicated on the importance of safeguarding culture from the reductive logic of property and commodification— may allow for other ways of conceiving prosperity at local, national, regional, and global levels. Through a number of case studies, we discuss the ways in which different actors (individual and collective, legally recognized or traditionally established) engage with current IP regimes, paying attention to how knowledge-based products are created, used, exchanged, and transformed. Above all, we share an interest in the lived experiences of Latin/x Americans as they negotiate, through multiple forms of participation in the market, their needs and desires in contexts often dominated by the hegemonic discourse of IP but also open to all kinds of appropriation. While the multiple articulations of piracy make fully comprehensive accounts impossible, our volume addresses a variety of crucial realms, including video games, music, books, film, TV, trinkets, and clothing. All of this across diverse regional contexts, such as Mexico, Brazil, Chile, Argentina, Peru, Guatemala, and the United States.

While we provide a fuller discussion of the key terms and issues in our "Primer on Intellectual Property" in the Appendix at the end of this volume, a basic definition of IP may be in order. According to the World Intellectual Property Organization (WIPO):

> Intellectual property (IP) refers to creations of the mind, such as inventions; literary and artistic works; designs; and symbols, names and images used in commerce. IP is protected in law by, for example, patents, copyright and trademarks which enable people to earn recognition or financial benefit from what they invent or create. By striking the right balance between the interests of innovators and the wider public interest, the IP system aims to foster an environment in which creativity and innovation can flourish. (WIPO)

On the other hand, as Christopher May and Susan K. Sell observe in their *Intellectual Property Rights: A Critical History*, IP "constructs a scarce resource from knowledge or information that is not formally scarce. Unlike material things, knowledge and information are not necessarily rivalrous, and therefore coincident usage seldom detracts from social utility" (5). Artificial scarcity, they argue, is "introduced to ensure that a price can be obtained for use" (6). IP protection, in the form of patents and copyright, is meant to strike a balance between public interest and private rewards for a determined period of time, while stimulating creativity and new knowledge.

Piracy is often defined as a criminal activity that involves the unauthorized reproduction or distribution of copyrighted works, patented inventions, or branded goods—a definition that is as straightforward as it is partial, abstract, and vague. As a number of scholars have argued, piracy "is almost certainly better understood as a product of enforcement debates than as a description of specific behavior" (Karaganis 2). And if its legal meaning has varied historically and geographically, its social, cultural, economic, and political valences are even more heterogeneous. A pirate can be a counterfeiter who produces thousands of Dior bags, a smuggler who gets a few of them into the country in her luggage, or a teenager who downloads a couple of songs or video games. Piracy has been linked in media coverage and public discourse with drug trafficking and terrorism, but also with students trying to get a hold of the texts required for their classes and with activists who proclaim the need to guarantee the free circulation of knowledge. Questions of power and geopolitics lie at the core of the problem, as a number of global and state-sanctioned forces police production, exchange, and consumption of IP-rich products, while at a grassroots level people try to gain and extend access to these products. States that act in defense of the health needs of their populations have been called pirates by more powerful nations who act as global guarantors of the intellectual property rights (IPRs) system, as was famously the case with South Africa and Brazil in relation to patent-protected AIDS medicines (David and Halbert 2); or by intra-national minorities, like indigenous people, when central governments protect the interest of transnational companies to the detriment of native communities (David and Halbert ch. 4; von Lewinski).

This geopolitical dimension helps to explain why any intellectually serious approach to piracy must avoid the simplistic and often false dichotomy between legality and illegality. Furthermore, another positive case for what could paradoxically be called the advantages of *protecting piracy* from anti-piracy efforts is also sometimes made: rather than as theft, pirated products can be understood as a way to help companies and artists bolster the value of their brands, as they involve free advertising and often constitute a first step toward the purchase of the "original." As Eduardo Peñalver and Sonia Katyal have observed in their *Property Outlaws*, pirates, like squatters and other social actors who put social justice before the prerogatives of ownership, can help to challenge and improve the systems they simultaneously question (7). Similarly, in his contribution to this volume (Chapter 4), Santiago Alfaro Rotondo shows that piracy affects the formal market in both negative and positive ways. As he demonstrates, piracy does not necessarily hinder innovation or reduce the revenue of creators. The criminalization of consumers, moralistic educational campaigns, and increased law enforcement, therefore, may ultimately prove less successful than an economic approach that fosters competitive pricing among businesses vying for the pirates' customer base.

As the IP wars emerged in the 1970s, social understandings of piracy have corresponded more and more with definitions advanced by big right-holders and industries. The expansive aim and reach of information-based capitalism—and, more particularly, what Adrian Johns has called the "intellectual property defense industry" (498)—however, confronts a number of obstacles. These include what David and Halbert call the three paradoxes of IP discourses (see the Appendix "Primer on Intellectual Property") but also the persistence of geoculturally situated practices and local spaces for accommodation and modes of subsistence within capitalism. The history of copyright and of the much broader IP global regime has been charged with a number of conflicts between the rights of property owners, national strategic interests, the desire to foster creativity, and the common good. While complex and global in scope, these conflicts are familiar to almost everybody. Short of a very small portion of the world's population who can afford to avoid the hassle, we are all pirates to the extent that we regularly watch, download, upload, or otherwise use IP-protected products in ways that fall outside the technically defined legal realm. Piracy is thus at once a fully extended practice at the social level and a crime at the juridical one. There is then, at the individual level, something akin to what Balázs calls "situational piracy" at the level of the nation (more on this later). We internally justify certain common personal behaviors while, externally, when faced with social sanctions or the practice of others, we are quick to call other people pirates. In his research on piracy in Brazil, Alexander Dent refers to a different form of internally conflictive discourse: a certain double consciousness that affects the provider and consumer of so-called pirated goods. Studying what he calls a neoliberal subjectivity in Brazil as it relates to piracy, Dent analyzes the contradictory affective economy of consumption and piracy. On the one hand, consumers seem "torn between getting a good deal and receiving a fully consummated commodity experience" (32), while, on the other, providers of pirated goods strive for quality and good service. They also display, simultaneously, a daring position of rebellion vis-à-vis transnational corporations—justified by what they see as the latter's exploitation of national consumers—while they are fully aware of their illegitimacy before the law and strive for formalization.

As racism created race, and as prisons often create criminals, IP regimes create piracy. If something is found to infringe IP laws, we have been taught and trained to believe that it is piracy. IP law, however, is a relatively recent invention, dating back to the mid-nineteenth century. The debates that surrounded its creation are still very much with us, in ways that are as increasingly global as they are persistently local. And what piracy does, our volume shows, is precisely to challenge conventional (mostly Western and hegemonically global) narratives of creativity and the knowledge economy, foregrounding alternative conceptions of authorship, inventorship, usership, and property. The question of what constitutes a legitimate copy, for example, might receive a straightforward response from the abstraction of laws, but it is never simple in practice, as social actors across heterogeneous cultures engage with the question differently and in ways that are historically dynamic. Philosopher Byung-Chul Han, for example, has reflected on the Chinese neologism "shanzhai," or "fake." While initially referring to knockoffs such as "Samsing" telephones, the term also describes a particular form of creativity through which an "original" (a term that, again, might work well in the realm of Platonic ideas but gets a lot trickier in practice) is playfully modified and repurposed. Maoism, Han suggests, can be understood as a shanzhai form of Marxism. In the context of the Western-centered figure of the individual author, piracy is often reductively described as a servile, lavish, or uncreative reproduction. However, as Kedron Thomas and Matías Dewey show in their contributions to this volume (Chapters 2 and 11), copying a piece of clothing may also transform it into something new. The same can be said of other pirated products, such as books (Goldgel-Carballo, Chapter 9; Poblete, Chapter 8) and music (Tozi, Chapter 7); even a change of context, as Jennifer Ashley argues in her essay (Chapter 5), can alter a given cultural object in significant ways.

The question of legitimacy—of legitimate copies, but also of legitimate forms of circulation—is at the heart of nearly all cultural understandings of reproduction and piracy. As Alexander Dent has argued, piracy is "the foil against which the enjoyment of legitimately circulated commodities becomes both possible and necessary" (32). If the exact same t-shirt (made by the same hands and with the same materials at the same shop) becomes "pirated" when the seamstress who made it for the brand sells a few of them in the informal market (Gago 40), the experience of buying the "original" t-shirt at full price at a shopping mall is defined negatively, at least in part, in relation to the pirate market. Conversely, as Llamas-Rodriguez shows in Chapter 6, "feeling pirate" can be at the heart of consumption practices that are constitutive of certain identities.

## Latin America and the Global South

This volume is the first sustained effort to articulate a specific framework for understanding these phenomena in Latin America. While piracy might just look like theft and derivative reproduction from the perspective of many right-holders, the contributors to this volume go beyond this economic-driven logic—based almost exclusively on the protection of property—and show that the myriad cultures of the copy active in the hemisphere involve a multiplicity of creative social practices that, in turn, are at the base of different media ecologies and markets in which corporations are just one among many social actors. While attentive to global factors, this volume puts an emphasis on local forms of reproduction and commerce, on vernacular conceptualizations of what constitutes a legitimate copy or a legitimate mode of circulation, and on the forms of creativity and aesthetics that emerge in the context of so-called informal economies. If, as scholars have consistently argued, the global media landscape "is characterized by a deep interdependency between formal and informal economies" (Lobato and Thomas 4–5), our contributors show how salient such interaction is in Latin America. Responding to the piracy debate, which has been and is still shaped by industry-sponsored studies, neoliberal discourse, and international free trade agreements (FTAs), the chapters included in this volume move beyond the usual antinomies (more access vs. loss of revenue, for example) to focus on the rich social networks, regional differences, and heterogeneous practices of creativity, authorship, commerce, and consumption that characterize Latin American cultures of the copy. In doing so, they show that, when looked at from the perspective of specific communities, "piratical" practices disrupt the very categories on which the industry-shaped piracy debate is based, such as property, capitalism, and personhood (Sundaram 111), as well as illegality and criminality.

Walter Mignolo and Boaventura de Sousa Santos have reflected on the totalizing ambitions of what they call, respectively, global designs and globalized localism to refer to how a local perspective on an issue imagines and imposes itself as global. The IP regime is a clear example of this phenomenon, as we try to show with the historical case of the United States in the next section. We believe, as Adrian Johns has argued for the Euro-American context, that thinking historically and comparatively is the best way to overcome these geopolitically generated epistemological obstacles and understand what piracy may mean in multiple geocultural contexts. Legal and philosophical discussions of IP are usually marked by a simplification and a level of abstraction that is very much in tension with the complexity of actual practices of creativity, authorship, and cultural circulation in different contexts (Johns 517). If piracy, as Johns and other scholars have argued, is always an attribute of territory and a manifestation of geopolitics (Johns 13 and 51; Lobato and Thomas 99), the contributions in this volume will help readers interested in the Americas to understand the markedly different shapes it takes among Maya men in Guatemala, audiovisual street merchants in Peru, residents in a poor neighborhood in Santiago de Chile, Mexican immigrants in the southwestern United States, and even within national borders (Brazil's northern and southern regions, for example).

Our volume participates in this broader effort to understand piracy from the perspective of the Global South, where most people regularly access the flow of goods and information undergirding modernity in ways that do not conform to the kinds of IP regulations that metropolitan industries try to enforce. The daily life of the vast majority of the world population, in other words, shows the limits of Eurocentric models of property and authorship. As Lawrence Liang has argued, "porous legalities are often the only modes through which people can access and create avenues of participation" ("Porous Legalities" 8). Because, indeed, piracy involves not only consumption but also production and transformation. In some cases, as Brian Larkin has argued in his study of Nigerian video production, pirate networks and infrastructure become the material foundation for whole new "legitimate" industries (291). Drawing from Ravi Sundaram's influential study of Delhi, Lars Eckstein and Anja Schwarz chose *Postcolonial Piracy* as the title for an edited volume that, like ours, examines the phenomenon from the perspective of the Global South. They argue, and we agree, that the modern notions of authorship, ownership, and property that are invoked to sustain the globally enforced IP regimes are far from universal, and modernity itself is revealed to be the product of imperialism and colonization when we look at it from a tricontinental perspective (Asia, Africa, Latin America). As they point out, any study of piracy in the Global South demands "a composite picture of locally grounded critiques which attend to distinct local histories and epistemologies as much as to the global designs of 'property, wealth, citizenship' which inform the capitalist world system" (Eckstein and Schwarz 12). The contributions to our volume aim to do precisely that.

While the above-mentioned works and a number of others published in the last ten years—such as Joe Karaganis's *Media Piracy in Emerging Economies*, Manuel Castells and Gustavo Cardoso's *Piracy Cultures*, and Ramón Lobato and Julian Thomas's *The Informal Media Economy*—have made substantial contributions to the understanding of piracy and IP in a global context, ours is the first book fully devoted to Latin America. As such, it complements and extends, from the specific perspective of piracy and IP, the recent trend of examining contemporary Latin American informal economies, of which Verónica Gago's *Neoliberalism from Below* constitutes a good example. Gago's concept of "proletarian microeconomies" has advanced new understandings of contemporary forms of labor and revealed the transnational logic that underlies Latin American "illegal" markets where pirated products are sold (33). As many of the contributors to this volume show, these forms of labor combine the innovation and entrepreneurial spirit so touted in neoliberal discourse with the informality, precarity, and criminalization that constitute the darker side of neoliberal globalization, contributing to their ambivalent status as both invisible and hypervisible. For readers unfamiliar with Global South contexts, the chapters that follow will show how different IP regimes and practices of copying look when we focus on these forms of neoliberalism from below or on the ways in which capitalist premises are often questioned, while those who are interested in other regions of the Global South will find numerous opportunities for comparison.

## The View from the Americas

When it comes to IPRs, the US trajectory is illustrative of the distance between an international or global discourse and the national realities of specific countries as they develop economically. Edward Samuels, a self-described sympathizer of contemporary American-style strong IPRs, summarizes this trajectory in the following terms:

> The role of the United States in the international copyright community has gone from that of outlaws to outsiders to "strangers at the feast" to leading members of the club. When we finally decided, in recent years, to fully join in the feast, we pushed ourselves to the front of the line with the moral bravado of newcomers. All in all, it's a pretty embarrassing history. (230)

Similarly, in his "Coda: A Short History of Book Piracy," Bodó Balázs comments on this "embarrassing story" in this way: "For roughly a century, American copyright law was a clear-cut case of situational piracy—of behavior legalized under US law but widely condemned abroad" (408).

When knowledge and written works mostly flowed from Europe to the Americas, the United States—from the first Copyright Act of 1790, through reforms in the 1830s to the 1880s—protected only US authors. The works of foreign writers could be freely reproduced in the US during this whole century, as the practice was considered advantageous and even necessary for the development of the nation. Piracy, in fact, played a role in the birth of the country, as US book publishers believed that reprinting British texts was not just a form of defiance and insurrection but also a means to shape their own unique literary culture—one in which "smaller, cheaper, more portable formats defined a public realm befitting a dispersed republic rather than a centralized aristocracy" (Johns 179). That history, originating in the late eighteenth century, helps to explain why in 1886, when the Berne Convention for the Protection of Literary and Artistic Works was signed by many other countries, the United States, which had delegates at the meeting, refused to participate. When the United States finally decided to recognize the IPRs of foreign authors in 1891 it did so in a half-hearted and tricky way: for copyright to be recognized the book had to be materially produced from beginning to end in the United States and "the foreign authors had to register their works and deposit copies in the US on or before the date of publication anywhere in the world" (Samuels 236). Even in 1952 when the United States—which had by then become a major producer of IP (films, music, books)—decided to push for an international treaty, the Universal Copyright Convention, it did so in a way that fit all the particularities of US IP law and protected US interests. It was not until 1988 that the country joined the Berne Convention. As Balázs observes, the United States had good reasons to act this way: its IP policy allowed it to develop a market for cheap books, which in turn became the basis for the country's mass education project.

Reminding her readers that "the first [US] complete mill for spinning yarn" was legally set up in the country in 1793 using British technology by Samuel Slater—called "the Father of American manufacture" by Andrew Jackson—in clear violation of English laws, Vandana Shiva concludes:

> While the US built its economic power and manufacturing capacity by breaking free of British monopolies, the current US Congress and present-day corporations appear unwilling to allow this spirit of freedom, so fundamental to US history/economic development, to exist anywhere else in the world. (34)

Lawrence Lessig, who founded Creative Commons in 2001 and briefly campaigned for the US presidency in 2016, summarizes this history like this: "We may have been born a pirate nation, but we will not allow any other nation to have a similar childhood" (58).

But hypocrisy about IP rights and the occlusion of this long history of situational piracy is not the only—and perhaps not the most important—change in the US position concerning IP. As Siva Vaidhyanathan makes clear, this trajectory—which currently sees US governmental agencies heavily involved in the global enforcement of a singular IP regime for all countries, regardless of their needs or development level—also implies a shift from the original American framers' public policy-oriented effort to balance the interests of society and those of creators (involving only 14 years of protection for the latter's intellectual creations) to a model much more similar to the one animating the original Berne Convention, which places an emphasis on original creators and their patrimonial and moral rights to own their creations for life plus 50 years. With this mutation, the discourse of property became increasingly powerful and began to dominate public discourse to the point of silencing the policy talk and the idea of the common good behind it. With the discourse of property taking center stage, the conversation has been reduced to one about theft and pirates, not about the productive free flow of information or creative expression. Rather than focusing on IP and the expansive enforcement of the IP rights of transnational corporations, Vaidhyanathan argues, we should concern ourselves with intellectual policy (12). In other words, the combined effects of these two changes in US policy are not only detrimental for many developing countries but—in tipping the scale in favor of the rights of the supposedly original creators against the interests best serving the common good—may, in fact, be highly consequential for the present and future free circulation of ideas and information *in* the United States.

Before becoming a key actor in the global efforts to enforce a highly expanded IPRs regime, the United States participated in a different system, alongside Latin America. After independence, some of the new Latin American republics chose the American model based on the idea of fostering scientific and artistic progress (Mexico, Argentina), while others opted for the French model, which emphasized authorial rights (Chile, Peru). However, by the end of the nineteenth century all countries in the Americas, including the United States, came together to create an alternative to the Berne Convention. The first step was the Treaty of Montevideo of 1889, which left the duration of copyright to the discretion of the signatories. Its provisions, which were revised many times, became important for the development of Latin American national publishing industries and remained in place until the 1980s (the first real effort to bridge the gap between the Berne and the Interamerican systems was the United Nations Educational, Scientific and Cultural Organization (UNESCO) sponsored 1952 Universal Copyright Convention, which opened the way for the eventual universalization of the Berne standards [Cerda 37]). They made possible, for example, the flourishing of the Latin American literary boom of the 1960s and 1970s and the establishment of some of the key publishers on the continent, including Eudeba in Argentina and Fondo de Cultura Económica in Mexico. The system was calculated to allow the Americas a path to cultural development and an expansion of what could be considered within the public domain at a national level.

In the last few years, the contradictions and the debates surrounding IP in Latin America have been more alive than ever. Gilberto Gil—whom we quote at the start of this Introduction—proved that alternative state discourses that balance fostering creativity and the common good in national and international contexts with appropriate safeguards for IP rights are not only possible but necessary. In order to achieve this balance, as Gil made clear, the ethnocentric and self-interested forms of understanding IP that have dominated the mainstream conversation need to be challenged, historicized, and politicized. This is one of the main objectives of this volume. Our contributors show how practices of reappropriation, reinvention, and copying may reflect diverse forms of being human marked by specific histories, epistemologies, and regimes of value. This diversity, they contend, has political consequences, as the modes of participating in the global exchange of products and ideas that are often labeled as "piratical" are, in fact, interventions in a broader debate about power at the local, national, and international levels. That is why, as Zac Zimmer argues in Chapter 10, this debate demands an understanding of culture as something that participates simultaneously in the logic of the commons and in that of commodification. *Piracy and Intellectual Property in Latin America*, in short, shows that piracy is a context-dependent, historically evolving practice made up of contradictory actors, subject-positions, and geopolitical stances.

Our volume partakes in the spirit of the critical perspectives on IPRs that have been part of public debates over the last couple of decades. As May and Sell noted in 2006, IPRs have become an object of study for professionals other than lawyers and economists, who bring with them alternative disciplinary approaches. Instead of taking for granted the stability of naturalized concepts such as property or IP, they all invite us to consider the "extensive *political* and *rhetorical* processes and strategies" that subtend them (16). May and Sell further clarify how laws, rather than simply protecting existing property, transform into property that which is deemed in need of protection. Following Karl Polanyi's suggestion that labor, land, and money could only be thought of as commodities once a commodity fiction was put in place, May and Sell argue that the knowledge economy is also dependent on such a fiction, as the discourse of IPRs not only maintains that knowledge is property—like real estate—but also creates the conditions for its profitability by engineering scarcity (18–19). Unlike property, knowledge is usually not rivalrous; it can be accessed and used by anyone without diminishing its value for the creator or other consumers. Once made scarce and rivalrous, however, knowledge can be sold, thereby opening up the possibility of economic profit. In fact, the easier and cheaper copying knowledge becomes, the more IPRs have to be put to work to prop up its scarcity.

While the dominant view of IPRs tends to naturalize scarcity, the historical record shows that scarcity is socially created and has always been a political process between actors with different capacities for agency who engage in struggles that are only provisionally settled. According to the hegemonic view, IPRs make possible the most efficient creation and distribution of resources; they reward the labor of creators, protect their moral standing as originators of knowledge, and allow for an efficient social distribution of their products through market mechanisms by creating incentives to production and ownership. In this way, the historical tension between the rights of creators and the public good is always mediated by market incentives (May and Sell 26). Over the course of the Euro-American-dominated history of copyright, this market mediation has led to a radical shift from the initial protection of 14 years to one that lasts the life of the creator plus 70 years, as we outline in our Appendix "Primer on Intellectual Property." Unfortunately, the dominant discourse of IPRs insists on framing protections as an intrinsic and invariable aspect of the market while, at the same time, continually modifying them to extend their duration and reach, with little or no regard for the common good, and even less for the living conditions and experiences of the Global South.

## This Volume

The Appendix "Primer on Intellectual Property" at the very end of this volume provides a concise but hopefully useful discussion of the key terms and issues involved in the international IP and IPRs debates.

In Chapter 1, "How Trinkets Became Counterfeits: Value and Intellectual Property in a Low-Income Market in Brazil," Rosana Pinheiro-Machado discusses the value and constructed authenticity of "worthless" products within a specific commodity chain that operated between Ciudad del Este, Paraguay, and Porto Alegre, Brazil from the 1970s to the early 2000s. Based on a "longitudinal ethnography" (fieldwork conducted over a long period of time) that followed the routine of street vendors at the camelódromo in Porto Alegre from 1999 to 2014, her chapter examines how low-income traders ascribe value to unbranded products through their personal engagements and interactions in the marketplace. Through this process, she argues, people in this part of Brazil were developing their own notions of authenticity that differed radically from those defined by the European-American IP regime. Examining how major IP politics of value impact and confront local regimes of value including the cultural, social, and temporal milieus through which commodities circulate, Pinheiro-Machado argues that the criminalization apparatus that has enforced laws against smuggling, piracy, and the informal economy in Brazil from 2003 onward fostered radical unintended consequences.

In Chapter 2, "The Piracy Problem: Indigeneity, Hybridity, and the Racial Politics of IP Enforcement in Guatemala," Kedron Thomas explores the relevance of race, class, and indigeneity for how IP piracy is framed, debated, and policed in contemporary Guatemala. Drawing on ethnographic fieldwork with Maya men who manufacture and market knockoff fashions in the highland region as well as on journalism, policy documents, and anti-piracy propaganda, she examines how racial and cultural narratives about who IP pirates are serve to justify stricter enforcement policies. She argues that the shift from what has historically and disparagingly been called the "Indian problem" to emerging narratives about a "piracy problem" in Guatemala and the wider Latin American region reveals a great deal about the changing relationships of indigenous peoples to the state and international market systems, paying special attention to how hybrid identities and social locations are problematized as particularly threatening to national and international legal and economic orders.

In Chapter 3, "Piracy and/as Legitimate Business," Phillip Penix-Tadsen proposes that Latin American hackers and amateur programmers have been modifying and reverse engineering the products of the global software industry for decades, contributing to the long-standing status of gaming as a social phenomenon, while making pirated and shared computer applications and electronic games the standard in the region. While multinational technology firms have sought to secure their IP through legislation and litigation along with software encoding and encryption practices, these same corporations have frequently ignored the Latin American market, or seen their products' prices skyrocket beyond the reach of the region's consumers due to importation taxes. Out of these particular historical and economic circumstances, software modification, or modding, has taken shape in Latin America as a grassroots form of convergence and an exercise of communication power that exceeds the conventional definition of "piracy" as theft of copyrighted material for economic gain. Like hacktivism and electronic civil disobedience, modding is best understood as an act of counterconsumption—one that operates beyond the traditional norms of commercial exchange. By focusing on the concrete practices of modders in several specific cases, this chapter examines how seemingly "peripheral" actors have repurposed the tools of the dominant market, establishing software modification as a counterconsumptive practice that democratizes access to information technology.

In Chapter 4, "Piracy as Media Practice: The Informal Market of Music and Videos in Peru," Santiago Alfaro Rotondo examines the recent technological evolution and the economic and cultural practices of the Peruvian piracy market of music and audiovisual goods. Since 2003, the Peruvian state has been fighting against the physical piracy of audiovisual content by strengthening the punitive legal framework, financing educational campaigns, enforcing the seizure of materials, and developing judicial processes. This effort, however, has failed to reduce the thriving consumer market for pirated audiovisual goods in the country. Based on ethnographic evidence within the informal economy of digital copies of films, documentaries, songs, soap operas, and other audiovisual expressions, the chapter discusses the state's understanding of piracy, the ineffectiveness of the strategies designed to combat it, and the paradoxical flourishing of alternative markets for Peruvian and non-Euro-American audiovisual products, which have generated new business models for moving between the informal and the formal economies.

In Chapter 5, "Context as Content in Chilean Community Media," Jennifer Ashley examines piracy as a means of creative production in the context of Chilean community media. In January 2018, after two decades of operating outside of a legal framework, Chile's first community television station received a license to transmit under the country's new digital television law. Station members received this news with excitement, but also trepidation. Like their national television counterparts, this small station understood production as not only an act of creating their own content but also a way of finding and disseminating interesting content from other producers. This station had become integral to the community through their reporting on neighborhood events, along with their use of one cable subscription to transmit selected programming to the entire low-income neighborhood. The transition from informal to formal and analog to digital, Ashley shows, would also likely mean a change in the station's logic of production and, subsequently, a greater adherence to

IP laws. Analyzing station members' reticence to give up some of their creative license, Ashley argues for a theory of cultural production that considers a shift in context as a component of content creation.

In Chapter 6, "'Feeling Pirate' as Media Affect in Mexican American Experience," Juan Llamas-Rodriguez theorizes the experiential dimension of video stores targeted at Mexican immigrants in the southwestern United States. He explores these "piratical" spaces to foreground how they blur the distinctions established in mainstream media consumption, a blurring that reveals the mediated construction of the counterpublics congregated in these spaces. He further develops the concept of "feeling pirate" as an affective experience characteristic of Mexicans in the United States. "Feeling pirate," he argues, represents a form of worlding wherein the practices of media consumers diffract their own status as members, or nonmembers, of the communities they inhabit. His chapter builds on observations gathered from multiple visits to Mexican-targeted video stores and is informed by scholarship about media piracy, video spectatorship, postcolonial studies, theories of affect, and Latin/x studies. Feeling pirate, he concludes, lays bare the impoverishment of existing norms of legality and exclusion and the urgent need for alternative norms to emerge.

In Chapter 7, "From Piracy as a Crime to Piracy as a Necessity: Territorial Inequalities and the Socially Necessary Market in Brazil," Fábio Tozi examines piracy in the Brazilian context, addressing the lexical range of the word "piracy" in everyday life. Analyzing national and international legal IP frameworks while simultaneously highlighting local historical processes of criminalization of piracy in Brazil, Tozi begins by distinguishing several piratical practices (maritime, counterfeiting, digital). He then offers a history of the debate on geopolitical innovation, in which the relations between Brazil and the United States come to the forefront. He explores how piracy sustains and makes possible the productive spatial circuit for the Tecnobrega musical style in Belém do Pará. Literally translated as "tacky techno," Tecnobrega includes both electronic versions of popular, cheesy songs and Brazilian versions of foreign hits. As Tozi shows, large sectors of the Brazilian population have been abandoned by both the state and the market; in that context, piracy becomes an effective and socially necessary way to enrich their social lives and to make work, study, and knowledge possible.

In Chapter 8, "Book Piracy in Chile and the Proletarianization of Literature in Pedro Lemebel," Juan Poblete analyzes the book piracy discussion in Chile in connection with the work of Chilean crónica writer and performer Pedro Lemebel. Poblete is particularly interested in what could be called the special status of book piracy in the country. He proposes that Lemebel's position on piracy is directly connected to his concept of what literature is and may be, to his self-understanding as a cultural producer, and to his relation with the literary market and its forms of prestige and authority. He further posits that this issue is best understood against the backdrop of the history of mass book publication in Chile and the evolution of the concept of national culture over the last half century in that country. This history of national culture-building goes from the radical and expansive efforts for a state-driven, mass-produced national culture of the Unidad Popular government of Salvador Allende (1970–1973) to the equally radical privatization of publishing, along with social and individual life, under the Augusto Pinochet dictatorship (1973–1990) and in the long post-dictatorship period reaching to the present.

In Chapter 9, "Pirate Book Aesthetics in Contemporary Argentina," Víctor Goldgel-Carballo identifies and examines several characteristics of pirate aesthetics, including "improper" forms of reproduction, anti-elitist access, cheapness, and the perception of the "fake" as real in its own way. Focusing on book production in the context of contemporary Argentine literature, he begins by analyzing piracy in its relation to plagiarism and parody, using *El Aleph engordado* (*The Fattened Aleph*) as a clarifying example. The book was first published in 2009 by Pablo Katchadjian, who intercalated words to, or "fattened," a famous short story by Jorge Luis Borges. In 2015, while Katchadjian was being formally charged with IP fraud, an editor released a new edition of his book. Goldgel-Carballo examines this edition in terms of its materiality (its form, size, binding, etc.) and uses it as a springboard for a broader analysis of pirate aesthetics. Precisely because they are noticeably cheap and pirate, he argues, books like *El Aleph engordado* disrupt the abstract logic of commodity exchange and draw awareness to the fact that IP rights, brands, originals, and single authors are politically and economically motivated social forms that regulate our access to art and knowledge.

In Chapter 10, "Between Abundance and Appropriation: Indeterminate Critiques of Global IP Schemes," Zac Zimmer engages with the discussions of, and resistance to, international norms of IP as they consistently stumble against the unresolved problem of materiality. On the one hand, new technosocial regimes allow for a seemingly unrestrained production of immaterial culture: file sharing, remixes, even 3-D printing. On the other hand, material conditions—whether based on the uneven distribution of hardware, access to resources, or the economic ramifications of the commodification of information—reflect the heightened and growing global inequality that has come to define the twenty-first century. Below this tension pulse the geopolitical problems of biopiracy and the appropriation of traditional knowledges. In opposition to the reductionist models of creativity and cultural circulation codified by the IP sections of FTAs, Zimmer proposes a theorization of cultural production based on the wave-particle duality that is axiomatic for quantum mechanics. Culture, he argues, can be observed to behave like a propagating wave, leading to theories of abundance, cultural commons, and free culture; but it can also be observed to function like a particle, and accordingly becomes an object available for appropriation, commodification, and regulation. The recognition of the fundamentally dual nature of the creative process, Zimmer suggests, could have profound ramifications for the theorization of global IP norms.

In the last chapter, "The Creative Copy: Agency and Fashion at a Market for Counterfeited Garments," Matías Dewey contradicts a broad assumption, fueled especially by mass media, that sweatshop entrepreneurs, located at the margins of society, manufacture copies of original branded garments, provoking losses to legal companies and subverting public values. His chapter, based on several months of ethnographic fieldwork in La Salada marketplace, the main provider of low-cost garments in Argentina, challenges this common perception by advancing the idea of "creative copying," a production process that does not aim to produce an exact copy, but one adapted to the tastes of specific buyers. The chapter also asserts that the process of creative copying entails a specific mode of information gathering that determines the final characteristics of the products.

## Bibliography


Balázs, Bodó. "Coda: A Short History of Book Piracy." *Media Piracy in Emerging Economies*, edited by Joe Karaganis, Social Science Research Council, 2001, pp. 399–413.

Bollier, David. *Think Like a Commoner: A Short Introduction to the Life of the Commons*. New Society Publishers, 2014.

Boyle, James. *The Public Domain: Enclosing the Commons of the Mind*. Yale UP, 2008.

Castells, Manuel, and Gustavo Cardoso. *Piracy Cultures: How a Growing Portion of the Global Population Is Building Media Relationships Through Alternate Channels of Obtaining Content*. Kindle edition. Xlibris, 2013.

Cerda Silva, Alberto J. "Evolución histórica del derecho de autor en América Latina." *Revista lus et Praxis*, vol. 22, no. 1, 2016, pp. 19–58.

David, Matthew, and Debora Halbert. *Owning the World of Ideas: Intellectual Property and Global Network Capitalism*. Sage, 2015.

De Sousa Santos, Boaventura. "Os Processos de globalização." *A Globalização e as Ciencias Sociais*, edited by Boaventura de Sousa Santos, Cortez Editora, 2002, pp. 25–102.

Dent, Alexander. "Piracy, Circulatory Legitimacy and Neoliberal Subjectivity in Brazil." *Cultural Anthropology*, vol. 27, no. 1, 2012, pp. 28–49.

Drahos, Peter, and John Braithwaite. *Information Feudalism: Who Owns the Knowledge Economy?* New Press, 2002.

Eckstein, Lars, and Anja Schwarz, editors, *Postcolonial Piracy: Media Distribution and Cultural Production in the Global South*. Bloomsbury, 2014.

Elyachar, Julia. *Markets of Dispossession: NGOs, Economic Development, and the State in Cairo*. Duke UP, 2005.

Gago, Verónica. *Neoliberalism from Below: Popular Pragmatics and Baroque Economies*. Duke UP, 2017.

Gil, Gilberto. "Discurso do ministro da cultura, Gilberto Gil, em seminario sobre experiências acerca do tema cultura digital." December 14, 2007, http://cultura.gov.br/324387-revision-v1. Accessed September 13, 2019.

Halbert, Debora J. *Resisting Intellectual Property*. Routledge, 2005.

Han, Byung-Chul. *Shanzhai: Deconstruction in Chinese*. Translated by Philippa Hurd. Bilingual edition. MIT Press, 2017.

Johns, Adrian. *Piracy: The Intellectual Property Wars from Gutenberg to Gates*. U of Chicago P, 2009.

Karaganis, Joe, editor, *Media Piracy in Emerging Economies*. Social Science Research Council, 2001.

Larkin, Brian. *Signal and Noise: Media, Infrastructure, and Urban Culture in Nigeria*. Duke UP, 2008.

Lessig, Lawrence. *Free Culture: How Big Media Uses Technology and the Law to Lock Down Culture and Control Creativity*. Penguin, 2004.

Liang, Lawrence. "Beyond Representation: The Figure of the Pirate." *Access to Knowledge in the Age of Intellectual Property*, edited by Gaelle Krikorian and Amy Kapczynski, Zone, 2010, pp. 353–376.

Liang, Lawrence. "Porous Legalities and Avenues of Participation." *Sarai Reader 05: Bare Acts*, edited by Monica Narula, Shuddhabarta Sengupta, Jeebesh Bagchi, Geert Lovink, and Lawrence Liang, Sarai, 2005, pp. 6–17.

Lobato, Ramón, and Julian Thomas. *The Informal Media Economy*. Polity Press, 2015.

May, Christopher, and Susan K. Sell. *Intellectual Property Rights: A Critical History*. Lynne Rienner, 2006.

Mignolo, Walter. *Local Histories/Global Designs: Coloniality, Subaltern Knowledges, and Border Thinking*. Princeton UP, 2000.

Peñalver, Eduardo Moisés, and Sonia K. Kaytal. *Property Outlaws: How Squatters, Pirates, and Protesters Improve the Law of Ownership*. Yale UP, 2010.

Pinheiro-Machado, Rosana. "The Attribution of Authenticity to 'Real' and 'Fake' Branded Commodities in Brazil and China." *Cultures of Commodity Branding*, edited by Andrew Bevan and David Wengrow, Routledge, 2010, pp. 109–129.

Rohter, Larry. "Gilberto Gil Hears the Future, Some Rights Reserved." *New York Times*, March 11, 2007, www.nytimes.com/2007/03/11/arts/music/11roht.html. Accessed September 13, 2019.

Rullani, Enzo. "Le capitalisme cognitif: du déjà vu?" *Multitudes*, vol. 2, no. 2, 2000, pp. 87–94.

Samuels, Edward. *The Illustrated History of Copyright*. Thomas Dunne Books, 2002.

Shiva, Vandana. *Protect or Plunder? Understanding Intellectual Property Rights*. Zed Books, 2001.

Snodgrass Godoy, Angelina. *Of Medicine and Markets: Intellectual Property and Human Rights in the Free Trade Era*. Stanford UP, 2013.

Sundaram, Ravi. *Pirate Modernity: Delhi's Media Urbanism*. Routledge, 2010.

Vaidhyanathan, Siva. *Copyrights and Copywrongs: The Rise of Intellectual Property and How it Threatens Creativity*. New York UP, 2001.

von Lewinski, Silke. *Indigenous Heritage and Intellectual Property: Genetic Resources, Traditional Knowledge and Folklore*. Kluwer Law International, 2004.

World Intellectual Property Organization (WIPO). www.wipo.int/about-ip/en. Accessed September 13, 2019.

# 1

# HOW TRINKETS BECAME COUNTERFEITS

## Value and Intellectual Property in a Low-Income Market in Brazil

*Rosana Pinheiro-Machado*

### Introduction

"We will need to return standing on the bus because the commodities have priority." That is what Chico (aged 33), a Brazilian peddler, told me during a 15-hour return trip from Ciudad del Este, Paraguay, to Porto Alegre, Brazil. For many years, my research interlocutors like Chico have worked as street vendors in a *camelódromo*, or informal marketplace, in Porto Alegre, where they try their best to preserve the merchandise that they buy in Ciudad del Este in order to resell it on the streets. This attitude toward their merchandise was not prompted by a fear of damaging expensive or precious goods, but rather from a need to preserve and, when necessary, create value on some of the twenty-first-century's cheapest and most commonplace trinkets, gadgets, and other Chinese-manufactured products such as electronic devices, small toys, key chains, hats, T-shirts, socks, decorations, and so on. Since the commodities traded on that circuit are mostly unbranded yet still highly stigmatized merchandise viewed in Brazil as shoddy, "smuggled," or "falsified," their market legitimacy has to be established through the sellers' own efforts rather than by the appeal of their goods.

Acts of self-sacrifice like Chico's, where priority is given to the commodities above personal comfort or safety, transform the ordinariness and moral conditions of these objects (Mauss and Hubert 13), resignifying both the commodity fetishism process that obscures social relations (Marx and Engels 46) and market alienation by bringing back the link between the workers' personal engagement and their commodities in the marketplace (Tsing 21). While Robert Foster's ethnography ("The Work" 707) describes a love between people and brands that coincides with the process of fetishization, which sometimes obscures human relations, my ethnography examines the opposite: how people ascribe value to unbranded things through their personal engagements and interactions in the marketplace.

By creating value for their merchandise, the traders were simultaneously developing their own notions of authenticity, which differed radically from those defined by the European-American intellectual property (IP) regime. The IP regime was created and enforced precisely to mediate the contested meanings that arise from popular appropriations (Coombe 8). As Elizabeth Vann notes, several native groups are guided by different ways of thinking about, or contesting, Western concepts of authenticity. She writes, "Although there is now arguably a global set of [IP regime] standards to which most market-oriented countries are held, their development has not followed a linear, 'progressive' path toward homogenization" (289). My interlocutors' economic practices were not driven by the conventional division between the fake and the genuine, the criminal and the legal, but rather by a contextual classification between *coisa boa* (good stuff, meaning those goods that have had their value transformed through personal effort) and *coisa ruim* (bad stuff). Nevertheless, macro-political and economic changes that have taken place in the twenty-first century, such as law enforcement against piracy, have drastically affected the everyday dynamics of the *camelódromo* by removing the traders from the streets and ultimately altering local authenticity and value constructs.

Although the concepts of value and authenticity are closely related, they refer to distinct processes. Value is understood here as a broader process resulting from different forms of exchange—which, in turn, are related to different forms of sociality—and refers to a holistic approach regarding what is proper and desirable in life (Otto and Willerslev 1). More specifically, the concept of value includes the ways in which human participation can lower the commercial value while increasing the symbolic worth of commodities—a process that could be summarized in a phrase often repeated by my interlocutors: "cheap but good." Authenticity, in turn, is a consequence of such a wider value construction. By ascribing value within the context of the increasing criminalization of piracy, the traders are also creating their own notions of authenticity in a relational manner. It is a process by which good begins also to mean real stuff in relation to the bad stuff.

To begin, I examine the value construction of relatively worthless things within a specific commodity chain that has operated between Ciudad del Este and Brazil from the 1970s onward, but that came to an end in the early 2000s. From there, I analyze how major IP politics of value—meaning the process through which various elite actors and global powers try to control and limit the exchange of goods and consumption, while popular forces try to expand them (Graeber 32)—impacted and confronted local regimes of value, such as the cultural, social, and temporal milieus through which commodities circulate (Appadurai 4). I then demonstrate that the criminalization apparatus that has enforced laws against the informal economy, smuggling, and piracy in Brazil from 2003 onward fostered radical unintended consequences. For example, street vendors had long been trading worthless trinkets and copied merchandise in the streets, such as cheap toys, cosmetics, fashion accessories, and electronic devices. While some of these products were fake, most were not. Once their businesses became formalized, these vendors started retailing luxury branded counterfeits, such as Louis Vuitton and Gucci purses.

In the pages that follow, I explore how the enforcement process developed a pedagogical role through which alternative conceptions of authenticity that existed for decades in the streets became aligned with notions of hegemonic IP and the neoliberal discourse that emerged in Brazil and across the globe at the turn of the millennium. Beyond the mere act of selling counterfeits per se, the traders started admiring such products, disdaining their former value classifications that revolved around "good" and "bad" merchandise. This finding coincides with Dent's argument concerning the paradoxical encounter between the strengthening of a neoliberal IP normativity and the rise of neoliberal subjectivities that foster informal markets for counterfeits in Brazil (29). In my fieldwork, it has become clear that contrary to what has been announced in public reports celebrating the success of the IP regime in Brazil, the set of policies aimed at enforcing IP laws failed in its main endeavor, which was to eliminate counterfeit goods. In keeping with Ferguson's influential work on unintended consequences produced by the industry of development in Lesotho (249), the goal of the global and national IP regime apparatuses seems to have been to suppress certain marginalized groups rather than stopping piracy per se. My research adheres to the anthropological approach to methodological critical fetishism (Foster 246) that has tracked commodities in different stages of commodity chains (Bestor 76). Unlike these works, a vast part of the economic practices deployed in the chain I studied occurred in the realm of the informal economy, which meant that the actors had more autonomy in the process of value construction in a self-regulated market.

This chapter is based on a longitudinal ethnography that followed the everyday commercial routine of street vendors at the *camelódromo* in Porto Alegre, capital of Rio Grande do Sul, the southernmost state of Brazil, from 1999 to 2004. During my fieldwork, I observed and participated in their everyday commercial routines and made regular visits to the marketplace located in the downtown area; from 2003 to 2004, I followed my interlocutors on their weekly trips to Ciudad del Este, Paraguay, through the Triple Frontier region at the borders of Brazil, Paraguay, and Argentina. The traders bought their commodities in stores run by Chinese immigrants and faced many risks on the way to and from Ciudad del Este. These trips became increasingly dangerous after 2003, when Brazil adopted a global IP agenda. This included a set of policies that targeted the street markets, the *camelódromos*, and the activities of traders at the Brazil–Paraguay border. I returned to my site in Porto Alegre in 2004 and carried out intensive fieldwork over a three-month period in order to follow the process of formalization that removed the peddlers from the streets and relocated them to a shopping mall. I returned to the field five years later, in 2009, for more intensive fieldwork that aimed to follow up on their adaptation to life in the mall. In addition, I kept in contact with the traders over the course of these years: we regularly called, messaged, and e-mailed one another. In total, I followed their trade routines over a period of 15 years, which enabled me to observe both micro and major transformations that took place in my interlocutors' lives.

## From Marginal to Criminal: *Camelódromos* as a Problem in Brazil

From the eighteenth century onward, informal street markets have struggled for space in the downtown area of Porto Alegre, as well as against systematic attempts by the local government to evict them, a situation that occurs in many large Brazilian cities. Since then, many peddlers have simply been expelled from the streets, sometimes violently, through policies aimed at "cleaning" the city, while others were able to acquire legal authorization to work in designated areas (Pinheiro-Machado 57). Until the 1980s, street markets sold craft products, fruits, and fish. But during that decade, the peddlers' space became disputed when cheap manufactures of Chinese products arrived on the Brazilian market. In 1989, under the Workers' Party Administration (PT) and after several tense negotiations, the local government granted licenses to 420 peddlers under the following conditions: they had to sell legal merchandise and they had to have been working on the streets for more than ten years, as preference was given to those whose parents had also been street vendors. For their part, traders sought official recognition. They asked to be named *camelôs* and that the place where their stands were located be known as the *camelódromo*. This legalization was never fully secured, however, and the *camelôs* lived in perpetual threat of a new eviction, which in fact occurred in 2009.

Although officially registered, the *camelôs* remained a highly stigmatized group, socially perceived as lazy and dangerous and labeled troublemakers and criminals. This was the result of an enduring perception in Brazil that linked poverty and the informal economy with marginality and unproductivity since the nineteenth century (Oliven 23; Perlman 91). Throughout the entire twentieth century, the mainstream media often complained about the disorder—the crowds, noise, smell, and so forth—that the street vendors allegedly caused in the downtown area. This was a place where white middle-class Brazilians could conceivably shop and visit cafés while experiencing a kind of European-style modernity. An example of the reemergence of these preconceptions occurred in 2009, when the *camelôs* were evicted from the central urban area. The city's main newspaper wrote that "now the beautiful and charming people would finally come back to [the] downtown area" (Trezzi).

In the 1980s, this persistent negative portrayal was reinforced after the introduction of Chinese goods (later referred to as "Paraguayan goods"), which were bought by the *camelôs* in the free-trade zone of Ciudad del Este, in Paraguay, on the border with Foz do Iguaçu, Brazil. This frontier region was a South American hub for cheap manufactured goods such as toys, fashion accessories, cosmetics, gadgets, and trinkets. Most of these products were not copies per se but simply unbranded, low-quality merchandise. In colloquial Portuguese, the adjective "Paraguayan" became a pejorative term synonymous with poor quality, falsification, and duplicity. At the same time, the emergence of these goods in Brazil democratized traders' access to manufactured consumer goods for the first time in the country. Yet the social perception of the *camelódromos* across the country not only remained stigmatized—it also became increasingly criminalized as well.

The turn of the twenty-first century represented the peak of such a process. When the enforcement against piracy reached Brazil in 2002, the country was placed on the Priority Watch List (PWL) of the United States Trade Representative (USTR), which brought sanctions to the country's international trade. This was cause for great concern to the authorities, who quickly sent a delegation to Washington, DC. In alignment with US interests, a Parliamentary Inquiry Commission (CPI), the highest instance of a Brazilian criminal inquiry, was set up. The CPI marked the height of the Brazilian state's repression of piracy at informal marketplaces and on its border with Paraguay. Brazil adopted a new set of policies and employed strong police tactics to enforce laws not only against piracy but also smuggling from Paraguay and the informal economy in general. As the CPI report states:

> It is not our point here, nor is it important to define piracy in a restricted sense, since truth be told, piracy is nothing more than a set of illicit situations involving individuals and businesses practicing countless types of crimes. (CPI da Pirataria 26–27)

In fact, the Brazilian authorities were merely echoing the narrative from above. Interpol's public declarations, for example, made little differentiation between different types of illegal and/or informal practices (Pinheiro-Machado 11). The Brazilian state and the mainstream media effectively reduced narco-trafficking, informality, contraband, and piracy to one and the same thing. Following recommendations from Washington, "piracy"—meaning, in other words, smuggling and informality—became seen as a major national problem. The *camelódromos* across the country, including those on the Brazil–Paraguay border, became the main targets for action. There are many reasons why Brazil followed the US rules so strictly. In 2003, the country was an emerging economy eager to be an active player in the international market, and IP was a central issue for commercial relations. Beyond these practical reasons, the process was conducted by wielding the state apparatus against the street vendors, which revealed the long-standing marginalization of the poor and the informal economy in which they operated and showed how Brazilian authorities clearly endorsed this kind of enforcement. Ultimately, the guidelines from above provided a convenient orientation for political and economic elites on both local and national levels to take action, as they have never accepted the presence of the poor in the streets.

## The Value of Worthless Things

The historical and social constructions of marginality on the one hand, and the struggle for space on the other, convey the circumstances in which the *camelôs* lived and ascribe value to their goods. A regime of value was constructed within the so-called Paraguay-pedra system; this refers to the *camelôs*' weekly trips to Ciudad del Este, where the traders spent approximately $600 USD on their goods. The "pedra" in the term means "stone" and signified both the pavement the traders stood while selling their wares and the hard life they led working 15 hours a day, 7 days a week, on the streets. The more society marginalized the *camelôs*' economic activities, the more they came to value their goods through the construction of a narrative around their everyday practices that emphasized the centrality of the cheap, yet good, products they sold.

In Marx's approach to fetishism, commodities in the capitalist marketplace develop certain "mystical" properties, which disguises the human labor and relations through which exchange value is created (Marx and Engels 46). A paramount example of such a process is the market for art. According to Bourdieu (113), high value is created by obscuring the artist's labor and commercial interests so that the work itself takes on certain "magic" properties (or "aura" in Benjamin's terms [23]), thus making it seem untouched by market forces. The case observed in the first part of my ethnography, discussed later in this chapter, reveals another reality, however. It illustrates a kind of "reversed" fetishism, by which I mean an inversion of Marx's concept. Here I demonstrate how commercial interests and labor in this case were not disguised but overestimated by the traders in order to manage a balance between lowering the cost of commodities (to guarantee the cheapest market price) and increasing their symbolic value. This required, for example, telling consumers about their "adventurous" trips to Paraguay, how they would pick up commodities one by one, the sacrifices they made in order to "save" the products from the smuggling crackdowns, and so on. The combination of lowering commercial value with the raising of symbolic value coincides with Tsing's argument about the blurring boundaries between commodities and gifts:

> Things are exchanged for things, and once exchanged, the exchange, and the steps that led to it, can be forgotten; the commodity is available for use or further transactions. Gifts, in contrast, are akin to persons; they bring something personal with them, drawing the receiver into a social field, and serving as a continual reminder of the need for reciprocation. They thus animate different systems of value: Value in a commodity system is in things for use and exchange. Value in a gift system is in social obligations, connections, and gaps. (22)

In her ethnography on the supply chain of mushrooms, Tsing (23) argues that the division between gifts and commodities mentioned above is unreal. My ethnography follows a similar line of argumentation by showing how commercial and personal attributes were intertwined in the traders' practices and narratives. They constructed stories that bonded them with the objects so that they were in control during the exchange process and by means of these narratives revealed the human experiences, such as their living labor and (self-)exploitation, which are otherwise hidden according to Marx's notion of fetishism. Taken together, these properties became transformed into something magical, a kind of "aura" or "brand" around which the final price of such special and good unbranded products was constructed.

Such instances of "reversed" fetishism were founded on four principles that affirmed the process of value construction: the first and foremost was sacrifice. Many of the stories that male *camelôs* told abound with the real and imagined risks that they faced on the border. They portrayed themselves as adventuring heroes who needed to hide in the woods, go without food, or face off with the police. As they used to say, the main thing was protecting their commodities. Losing their goods was described as a tragedy that disrupted their whole monthly plan. When controls at the Brazil–Paraguay border were increased from 2006 onward, Chico had to cross the border with his three bags full of key chains and teddy bears on an unsafe boat under fire from police. This story, like many similar ones, was directly told to me; in this case it was narrated by Chico himself, the hero in a saga of escape from the police.

Although saving the goods from confiscation by the police was a key task, it was not the only thing that mattered. The physical integrity of the commodities was viewed as far more important than the well-being of the traders. On a bus trip that lasted 16 hours, it was uncommon for traders to sleep, as seats were reserved for bags of merchandise. This was not only because of how much cargo they had, but also because they maintained that the goods should not be tightly crammed when traveling. In Porto Alegre, I witnessed several such examples of unusual care taken with merchandise. The *camelôs* were accustomed to using two sunshades: one for the goods (to preserve their color), the other for the client, and none for themselves; they would spend the whole day *na pedra*, "on stone." Carminha (aged 33) and Amir (aged 52), for example, spent the first three hours of the morning arranging their stand and brushing each of the teddy bears and the hats respectively, one by one. When one day a storm suddenly came, the *camelôs* became desperate, and both expended an equal amount of physical effort improvising a roof for their wares, even though Carminha was pregnant at the time.

The second principle was skill. For the *camelôs*, the low prices they received from the goods were not the result of dealing with worthless goods. On the contrary, they stressed that the wholesale market of their quality goods was lowered as a result of their purchasing and handling knowledge. They paid close attention to every single product that they bought and packed. This involved certain learned techniques (as well as a specific vocabulary), such as how to *garimpar* (dig for) commodities in Paraguay, how to pack and remove packages, how to squeeze the products into their luggage without harming them, how to display, and, finally, how to bargain for them. One crucial component of this knowledge was to display a colorful stand, since "colors accomplish work that no other quality of things can, especially in the hands of knowledgeable practitioners; colors animate things in a variety of ways … emitting brilliance, endowing things with an aura of energy" (Young 173). It is not by chance that Carminha's and Rui's stands, the most colorful at the *camelódromo*, were the most visited. In this context, Amir told me that the main inheritance he was passing down to his son was how to sell a product. He taught him how to persuade the consumer by putting the merchandise into their hands, for example. The elders in the *camelódromo* accumulated techniques like these and were proud of their intelligence, bravery, or superior IQ. As Rui (aged 62) told me: "If you have a superior IQ, you know how to dig for good stuff in Paraguay, you know how to display and sell it, and you make money."

The *camelôs* believed that good stuff would always function properly. They perceived the quality and durability of the products as a matter of honor, and honor comprised the third principle by which value was constructed. In Brazil, it is common to joke about the goods bought in Ciudad del Este. For example, if a projector does not work during a meeting or in a classroom, people will immediately say, "It is from Paraguay!" Based on this preconception, the *camelôs*' customers often express a concern that the product they buy might not last. This uncertainty is usually addressed by the *camelôs* during face-to-face negotiations with their customers, where the trader will explain the origin of the product, publicly demonstrate that it works (by turning on a CD player, for example), and using their word as a guarantee. For instance, as Carminha daily repeated: "I promise you that if there is any problem, I'll give you another product."

Finally, the fourth principle was cleanliness, of a legal as well as a hygienic kind. On the one hand, the *camelôs*' goods and practices needed to have their legal status resignified through several symbolic mechanisms that purified the "dirtiness," or social stigma, attributed to their economic activities. On the other, there was also the hourly routine of tidying the stand and spraying it with perfume. Carminha once explained how important it was to "be clean and smell nice" in order for the customers to trust her as a salesperson. The activity of inspectors was also described in terms related to cleanliness. When authorities were nearby, the environment was labeled as "dirty." For instance, one vendor would warn another: "Don't go there, it's dirty." At the same time, the arrival of inspectors would also be announced with cries of "Look at the rain!" While rain might evoke a cleaning process for some, for anyone working in the street it is also a source of confusion and chaos.

The most noteworthy example of this attention to cleanliness is one I observed in August 2004 when I was returning with the traders from Ciudad del Este. On the way back, there were frequent police raids, and the traders would often say "the road is dirty" (referring to the bribery process). Although the total travel time was 36 hours, they were keen to stop halfway through to shower in cold water in a restaurant restroom without heating, though the temperature was only 4° C at the time. I asked why they would not wait a few more hours to shower at home, and they replied: "Because we are clean people." Approaching the restaurant, the *camelôs* began joking with each other: "Who's gonna skip showering?" "I won't travel with dirty people," and so on. There was huge pressure placed on people not to skip a shower. Afterwards Chico told me: "You see? And people think the *camelôs* are dirty! We are much cleaner than most people." The *camelôs*' insistence on cleanliness seemed to be a direct response to the perception of illegality as a kind of "dirtiness" surrounding their activities; the *camelôs*' attention to physical cleanliness reflected their sense of moral integrity.

A large part of these four principles—sacrifice, skill, honor, and cleanliness—was anchored in the legal space in which the traders work, which takes on a distinctive status within the context of the informal economy. These principles not only influenced the traders' behavior and perception of their surroundings, they also impacted the value of their wares, which became closely linked to their identity and notions of self-worth. Another sign of prestige and local distinction was the amalgamated network of regular middle-class consumers who feared buying anything from unauthorized peddlers and only bought products from their trusted *camelô*. Cheap trinkets were thus transformed into *coisa boa* (good stuff) through a process during which the mind, body, social relations, and commodities became increasingly intertwined. *Coisa boa* was a native category created by the traders that indicated products of quality and durability sold in a legal place, but also increasingly referred to authenticity, especially after 2002, when Brazil was placed on the USTR's PWL and started its war against piracy.

## Native Notions of IP

Before discussing the *camelôs*' notions of authenticity, I must first introduce another group of social actors that were part of their everyday life: the *caixinhas*, or the unregistered street vendors that surrounded the *camelódromo* and behaved as competitors. *Caixinhas* were peddlers who arrived on the streets at the turn of the millennium. They worked with improvised and precarious stands (paper boxes), and due to their illegal status as well as their lack of economic capital or space to sell their wares, *caixinhas* sold smaller, cheaper, and even more illicit goods than the *camelôs*, such as fake cigarettes, sunglasses, batteries, and so on. This provoked negative feelings among the *camelôs* who had been busy constructing a moral narrative in order to legitimize not only the commercial but also the moral value of their goods. They were frustrated because, unlike the *caixinhas*, they could not trade in counterfeits due to police inspections. When the authorities came, the *caixinhas* simply closed up their paper boxes and ran away, while the *camelôs* had to stay and prove their legitimacy.

At the beginning of my fieldwork, I arrived at the *camelódromo* with a very critical report from the local newspapers claiming that the downtown street vendors were criminals because they traded pirated goods. I expected that my interlocutors would react negatively to this, but instead Maria simply said, "This is all true. It is the *caixinhas*' fault." She continued: "They cause all this disorder, this chaos. They engage in piracy." Regarding the government inspectors, Amir would say: "I get along really well with the inspectors; we have a relationship of mutual respect. We're not the problem, it's the *caixinhas*." In 2002, during an interview with Terra, an online web portal, the *camelô* Evaristo Mattos said: "The majority of the *camelôs* have had their stands downtown for over 30 years. If you do good work, it's hard to lose your spot. The *caixinhas* are the real problem." In the *camelôs*' view, the reason for the negative press was clearly the *caixinhas* and their shoddy and/or illegal merchandise, and it was these outsiders who were the real culprits and the source of all that would later be labeled piracy. Amir described to me his view of the situation along with his opinions regarding the moral character of the *caixinhas*:

> Some people get in fights, wreak havoc. It's the *caixinhas* who mess things up, disturb our lives. Their appearance was the worst thing that could have happened to us … Most of them have no skills, most are … how should I say it? Lots of bad seeds. It's where you'll find all kinds of awful stuff, bad folks. Most are *cadeieiros* [jailbirds] … It's bad for our image as honest folks, because when they talk about the *camelôs* they're going to be talking about everyone. Thank God, I'm an honest man, a good citizen. I've always worked honestly. I like to do the right thing.

Dalva (aged 65), another elder, had similar views regarding the effects of her *caixinhas* neighbors on the *camelôs*' work:

> We're registered, we've got a city ID. We're in good standing with the union too. And those hangers-on out there? I think they should have their place, but not here, not close to us. They should put them somewhere else because they mess up our sales here.

During this interview, I noticed that Dalva was selling an electric hair clipper that seemed to be exactly the same model as the one sold by the *caixinhas*. She contested this point, however:

> They sell stuff that's no good. The stuff they sell is worse than ours. When people buy them, of course they're going to complain, thinking it's us instead of them. They think it's us and we're the ones with the real stands. The newspapers say "*camelôs*," but they shouldn't say it that way. Newspapers should define what's right and wrong. We have badges, they've got nothing.

> They came and forced their way in and there they are. The stuff we sell is much better. They sell third-class stuff. Take an electric hair clipper. There's good ones out there, but they sell the worst kind, while I sell the best.

It is also worth mentioning that many *camelôs* had been *caixinhas* in the past. Many *camelôs* also sold the goods they bought in Paraguay to *caixinhas*, meaning that the position of superiority they claimed was more of a moral narrative to distinguish themselves from the competition than a sharply defined legal and material categorization between the two groups. Amid these kinds of local disputes, *camelôs*' native notions of IP made sense in a relational context until 2003. Prior to that, the traders did not consider their merchandise to be "fake" goods. The *camelôs*, however, only had a vague idea of what the terms "piracy" or "fake goods" meant. When I asked what piracy was, Dalva answered: "Piracy is everything that the *caixinhas* sell." Whenever the word "piracy" was used among the *camelódromo*, it meant something "bad," "wrong," "dirty," or "shoddy" and always referred to the products of another trader. None of my interlocutors considered the things that they sold to be fake, although technically most of them did sell some fake merchandise, such as counterfeit perfumes and Mickey Mouse dolls.

They did, however, retain their own notions of authenticity that revolved around the dichotomy of good things versus bad things. As the stories that follow will illustrate, good things were those that came with receipts and were dug out one by one from a shopping center in Paraguay, then sold at a permanent stall in Porto Alegre, and that ultimately would work. Bad things, on the other hand, were bought by the *caixinhas* from street vendors in Paraguay and sold at illegal spots around the city. I would come to a better understanding of what good things meant when I traveled with Rui and Chico to Paraguay. One point that was instructive for me in our trips, and that had been mentioned in Amir's and Dalva's statements cited previously, was the importance attributed to labels, paperwork, documents, and IDs. The traders' notions about the authenticity and legitimacy of their goods encompassed both their legal permission to trade them, along with the formality of their clients' stores in Paraguay. In conventional parlance, IP and informality refer to different elements within an economic system; the former generally refers to notions of authorship, ownership, and the origin of the goods, while the latter pertains to the legal nature of labor and economic activities. The *camelôs* clearly draw upon both of these concepts in their authenticity constructs: if they purchased their products in a formalized environment and had the authorization to trade them, then the goods were considered "good" as a consequence.

I watched as Chico rifled through large baskets of stuffed animals—classic Mickey or Minnie Mouse dolls, or characters like Hello Kitty, Nemo, or Shrek—in order to find the nicest-looking ones with the cleanest Disney tags. He told me that the Disney label was important, as it showed potential customers that it was a "good product." When Chico arrived in Porto Alegre, he used a damp cloth to remove the dust from each toy label. His father-in-law, Rui, was a third-generation *camelô*. As one of the most senior, successful, and proudest vendors, the idea that the Mickey Mouse doll he sold could be considered pirated was unthinkable. He had built his reputation by personally digging for the very best products in Paraguay's foremost formalized wholesale outlets. When Rui only received small receipts after his purchases, he asked for bigger ones on A4-sized paper. He carefully folded and kept these papers close to him. While his prices might have been a bit higher than those of his competitors, according to him, this was because everything was "in order." In Rui's case, the combination of his own seniority and the origin of his commodities was an important factor in his claim to authenticity.

Authenticity is a locally constructed concept. Away from the hegemonic circuits there is, in relation to piracy, a complex continuum that separates the acceptable from the unacceptable (Vann 287). The traders' notion of IP was built on contingent moralities within a moral scheme of professional belonging, self-worth, and sacrifice. For many years, this value regime that was built across the Paraguay-pedra system was enough to certify the authenticity and originality of their commodities. Despite existing in an environment of precarity, competition, poor working conditions, and, above all, social stigma that marginalized those involved, this system worked well for many years, especially because the traders believed in the importance of their social role. Both their notions of self-worth and their businesses were built upon a strong belief in honesty. Even though they operated within the informal economy and carried out smuggling activities, they could still be considered honest, well-intentioned people: they offered cheap goods to low-income Brazilians. As a result, the traders thus managed to circumvent the hegemonic concept of piracy and operate within their own categories of value and authenticity.

Yet this native construct gradually came to an end after 2003, when the police raids grew increasingly intense. The crackdowns now benefited from an integrated police force made up of local, state, and federal agents during their raids. These were implemented ostensibly to control the many possible crimes related to the different spheres of activities taking place. The turn of the century had exacerbated long-standing tensions between local inspectors, storeowners, and different groups of *camelôs*, who now faced both national and international pressure. Confrontations of many different kinds placed diverse groups and interests at odds with each other. Nationwide, street vendors who used to be considered marginal now represented more than just urban disorder; they became perpetrators of what Interpol declared the "crime of the twenty-first century," a classification that the Brazilian authorities reaffirmed in their everyday discourse. Cheap commodities became dangerous commodities, and their vendors became criminals. In this new context, the hegemonic concept of piracy was imposed on the *camelódromo*, and the *camelôs* had to learn to negotiate this top-down classification of their activities and reconcile it with their notion of good things.

From 2003 to 2009, *camelôs* were obliged to reclassify good and bad merchandise along the piracy spectrum. They expanded and negotiated the list of meanings for this category as it became more routine. Local authorities played a fundamental pedagogical role in this informal learning process. Within the emergent anti-piracy discourse, certain types of commodities were viewed as worse than others. Although an official list of illegal products was never published, everyone knew what was allowed, thanks to the mediation of border authorities. Traders knew what kinds of goods police were more interested in confiscating. As Chico told me: "They told me cigarettes and CDs are no-nos, the rest is alright." Cigarettes and CDs became the main targets of police raids, especially during the early years of the enforcement against piracy (2003 and 2004), because the tobacco industry began lobbying against the proliferation of counterfeit cigarettes from Paraguay. The same occurred with CDs and DVDs after pressure was exerted by domestic and North American audio-visual companies. As Chico explained, his toys were considered "worthless junk" during the raids. Chico's informal knowledge acquired in practice led him to define piracy in this way in 2004: "Piracy means cigarettes, the stuff *caixinhas* sell. They don't care about my products because they're good."

In summary, until 2003 the main ways the *camelôs* classified authenticity revolved around the notion of good and bad things. After that year, this binary understanding needed to be renegotiated according to what the internationally prompted national enforcement against piracy prioritized, and thus traders learned what goods were permitted through their everyday contact with state agents. By 2009, when the traders were finally removed from the streets and formalized in a low-income shopping mall, the native notion of IP had already been replaced by an alignment with the hegemonic anti-piracy discourse.

## Trading Counterfeits

I finished my fieldwork at the *camelódromo* in 2004 and left Porto Alegre, and it was a number of years until I returned. The news I read about the city reported increasingly tense scenarios in downtown areas as police raids became more frequent and violent. The headlines of local sensationalist daily newspapers painted the scenes as a war zone. I returned to Porto Alegre in 2009, precisely when both *camelôs* and *caixinhas* were finally being removed from the streets and reallocated across 800 little stores in a low-income shopping mall as a result of a public–private policy. The website devoted to the venture stated: "We came to solve traditional problems of the city and its population, opening a dignified space for a new type of entrepreneur, who is able to grow from his/her own effort."[1] This policy was the result of long-standing pressure from local elites, which gained additional support when the global enforcement against piracy reached Brazil. Within the enforcement framework, some cities were designated by the government as being "free of piracy." Removing the *camelódromos* that existed across the country was a fundamental measure in order to receive such an award.

In this new entrepreneurial environment, the traders were forced to abandon the self-designated name "*camelô*" in favor of the term "micro-entrepreneur." The term "*camelódromo*" was banished as well. Now that they were more formalized, the traders had to deal with the standard bureaucracy surrounding bank accounts and credit cards. They received access to micro-credit schemes as well as workshops from national institutions aimed at educating them on how to run a business in a more efficient and law-abiding manner. Many company representatives spoke about the problems of piracy. For instance, a marketing specialist in store-window design instructed the new entrepreneurs that they should discontinue the habit of crowding the space with colorful wares and that they could not extend the space of their shops toward the shopping aisles. All these changes provoked mixed feelings, but the traders were excited with the new opportunities and specially with the possibility of having a roof over their wares.

In 2009, Brazil's recovery from the global financial crisis was aided in part by promoting "financial inclusion" and offering credit to a large portion of low-income groups in order to increase domestic consumption, which decisively contributed to the economic growth peak of 7.4 percent in 2010 under Rousseff's administration. Brazil's economy was gaining momentum, and the business of the traders along with it. It was a moment when the traders were full of hope and dreams for the future. They referred to themselves in a positive way, reflected by terms concerning the worth of property, financialization, and entrepreneurship embedded in the new neoliberal discourse.

During this period of intense financialization of the poor, all of my interlocutors borrowed money from banks to invest in their little shops. Informal credit was also provided by Ricardo (aged 52), a wealthy man and Pentecostal pastor who was one of the managers of the mall and also worked as a bookmaker. He offered credit to any trader who demonstrated a motivation and willingness to leave behind the old practices of the streets. He worked very closely with the traders and employed an evangelical style of language to describe the formalization process. In an interview I conducted, he stated that the *camelôs* were savage animals—dirty, ignorant, rude, lazy, and violent—whose souls needed to be rescued. To him, the traders had to forget their past in order to be reborn and made civilized. Crucial to this process was abandoning "the undomesticated manners of the street." Ricardo offered credit for trips to São Paulo, which, as he saw it, was a way of stopping the *camelôs* from traveling to Ciudad del Este. The aim was to shed the label of "smuggler" and to avoid the negative image surrounding Paraguayan goods. This was considered to be a positive step in the positioning of the mall in the marketplace, though it worked mainly as a response to pressures from the national enforcement against piracy and smuggling alike.

As mentioned earlier, the *camelôs*' regime of value had emerged within a specific Paraguay-pedra system of commodity distribution. When the circulatory system changed, the regime of value also changed. By replacing the routes, the traders became immersed in a totally new framework of goods. Now the four principles that anchored their value construction—sacrifice, skill, honor, and cleanliness—made little sense. Personal effort was less necessary in order to create value, as the trips became safer and "cleaner" because there were no police controls along the routes. Ricardo used to travel with the traders in order to check the quality of the products they bought. "I need to go along to teach them what is appropriate to buy, since they are now entrepreneurs," the pastor told me. In addition, they also found different kinds of commodities in the popular market on 25 de Março Street in São Paulo, which is also run by Chinese migrants.

After some months of formalization Maria (aged 62), a former *camelô*, told me: "Now [that] I am a businesswoman, I can no longer sell those shit hats I traded in the streets." In this way, during the first two years of formalization, I witnessed how many of my interlocutors changed their narrative surrounding their old commodities. What were once good things were now despised as shoddy. They understood that they should no longer trade products that could be associated with the streets. Overall, this dramatic change had a radical, unintended consequence: the traders who had gained economic capital now invested it in fake luxury branded goods and fetishized counterfeits. The process of formalization, which was guided by a pastor who employed a language of both business and spiritual salvation, brought new narratives and mystical properties to the process of value construction. Curiously enough, the path that the traders took to reinvent themselves as more formalized entrepreneurs was by trading goods that were, strictly speaking, even more illegal than the ones they had been selling before.

This unintended consequence occurred for several reasons. The first and most evident was the fact that the traders had immersed themselves in a new trading route. At 25 de Março Street in São Paulo, they came across different commodities than the ones they were used to buying in Paraguay. In Ciudad del Este, the main shopping malls were run by Taiwanese proprietors who created a niche for a certain type of very simple, unbranded manufactured products. Despite the malls' reputation, however, most of the products were not fake per se. In São Paulo, mainland Chinese sellers imported all types of cheap manufactured goods, including counterfeits.

There was also a more pragmatic reason for the former *camelôs*' desire to trade in counterfeits: the logic of the new marketplace itself meant clients wanted to visit the mall in search of fakes. When formalization took place, my interlocutors (mostly elders from the *camelódromos*) understood they were too old to start a completely new venture after decades in the streets. Though they maintained control of the businesses, people like Ruy, Amir, Dalva, and Maria gave more autonomy to their children to implement new business practices. For their part, the new generation was eager to modernize the shops. For example, on her first trip to São Paulo, Miriam spent all her limited capital ($200 USD) on just ten pairs of fake branded jeans, which in the end she was unable to sell in the mall, causing her to run into debt.

Another reason was the new nature of the market competition that arose in the mall. *Caixinhas* and other new traders joined in the space, and they operated alongside each other. The former classification based on authenticity, which was crucially constructed upon a perceived difference between *camelôs* and *caixinhas*, now lost importance. The two groups now mingled, traveled together, and received the same market incentives and opportunities. Yet even more important than this fusion between the two groups were the new traders that appeared in the market: immigrants and refugees from Haiti or African countries like Senegal. They were new in the city, they engaged in other transnational trade routes, and they introduced fake luxury purses, such as Louis Vuitton and Gucci, to the local market. These attracted middle-class buyers to the mall and changed the nature of the competition.

Chico started out selling the same old toys in the mall, but now few people would look at them as the cost of rent and taxes increased the final price of his commodities. Consumers could buy the same toy for a similar price in a middle-class shopping mall. Chico was very curious about the new luxury fakes, though at the same time he maintained a discriminatory narrative about the new traders ("They should trade in their country, not here"). He tried to strike up a friendship with the new arrivals in order to learn how they imported their products. Through this, Chico decided to import directly from a Chinese website, no longer via São Paulo or Paraguay. He spent the limit of his recently acquired credit card in order to buy around 30 units of Gucci purses. Like Miriam, Chico managed to buy only a small number of items, so his price was higher and variety less than his competitors. Chico's purses did not attract clients. Without capital to buy more inventory, his little shop was soon empty. After only a few months of formalization, his new shop presented a very different scenario from his previously abundant stand. He became increasingly indebted and could no longer afford the taxes and rental space, which forced him to buy even more illegal goods like fake medicines. Regarding these counterfeits, he insisted that "these medicines are a temporary measure to raise capital, and then I will buy branded wallets." He was still full of hope. In 2014, during my last visit to the mall, Chico had rented his shop and was working as an employee in his former space, the proprietor of which now sold cell phones.

A further reason for the proliferation of counterfeits was the pedagogical role that the enforcement process ultimately performed. The traders were constantly being harassed by police over goods that they did not sell. Through repression and violence, the traders learned a totally new vocabulary of objects, which increased their desire for counterfeits. During the phase between 2003 and 2009, local authorities were constantly declaring which goods were allowed and which were forbidden. It was during this phase that Chico was arrested several times. In 2009, the newly made entrepreneurs received several lectures, including one given by a Nike employee, explaining how IP worked. In the end, it was the process of enforcement against piracy and smuggling in Brazil that planted the seed and taught street traders, by both formal and informal means, what piracy actually was.

I discovered this when, in 2004, I noticed how the *camelôs* had developed a very accurate and precise knowledge of intellectual property rights (IPRs). Now, they maintained a very legalist narrative, citing the years they could spend in jail based on the penal code for smuggling, IP infringement, or tax evasion. Their narratives were in total alignment with the hegemonic discourse that came from above—from local, national, and global authorities. But the actual effects of this discourse were unintended since, by learning this new vocabulary of punishment and crime, the *camelôs* started to desire trading in fakes. As a result, by being included in the financial system, experiencing new routes, and trading fake branded products, the traders' economic practices and social relations became more alienated from the products they sold Consequently, the products became more commodified in Marx's terms and less "gifted" as a result, since traders no longer needed to put a lot of themselves in the exchange process.

Moreover, traveling to São Paulo, modernizing their businesses, engaging with new competition, and learning about IP were all elements that fostered the trade for luxury brands among my former interlocutors and their children. It is also curious how a large part of this process was described by the pastor manager as a kind of spiritual rebirth. Roberto was desperate to see the mall working well, so he looked the other way when fakes were sold, as long as the traders kept paying their rents and clients visited the mall. By 2014, most of my former interlocutors were either selling fake goods or planning to do so. They talked about them all the time: they described the fakes as products that had a superior materiality. Beta, Maria's neighbor, once came to me and showed me how firm her leather product was. The exposure to the name brands made the efforts based on guiding principles or virtues less important as a means of creating value. The brands now produced immediately recognizable value and authenticity, which demanded less sacrifice. When I asked about her previously good hair clipper, Dalva answered, "Before, we were the brand, now the brand is here."

The policy of formalization that removed the *camelôs* from the streets was a response to local, national, and international pressure aimed at repressing piracy, along with smuggling and informal markets. The effect achieved was the opposite, however, as the whole process of formalization boosted the trade of fakes in Porto Alegre in several ways. The local press did eventually stop discussing the problem of piracy and informality, and by 2014 the mall's website described the venture as an innovative business model that eliminated "illegality." By this they were referring less to the illegal economic practices that evidently continued to exist and more to the removal of marginalized actors from the streets. Nationally, the shopping mall was considered a successful example of the project known as the "city free of piracy," and it became a model for several other Brazilian cities. Internationally, the USTR's Special 301 report from 2009 praised and recommended the anti-piracy efforts conducted in Porto Alegre. From that year onward, Porto Alegre's *camelódromo* was no longer mentioned, though it had been described as a place where "piracy exists with impunity" in the same report in 2001.

## Conclusion

In this chapter, I described how global and national changes in the politics of value, especially the IP regime, impacted a particular regime of value that had been built within the Paraguay-pedra system—a system that previously demanded personal effort from its participants to create value for unbranded and low-quality commodities that came from Ciudad del Este and were sold at Porto Alegre's *camelódromo*. Sacrifice, skill, honor, and cleanliness were some of the guiding principles that sustained this construction of value. In a highly stigmatized environment, these attributes created legitimacy for the goods and informed local notions of IP and authenticity, which consisted of a binary division between "good" and "bad" things. Such a regime of value worked well for more than two decades and structured the lives of dozens of families. Yet this self-organized system came to an end during the first years of the twenty-first century, when the global enforcement against piracy reached Brazil, and the Brazilian government strongly endorsed it. The blockage of the Brazil–Paraguay border and the formalization of the *camelódromos* nationwide impacted the ways this circuit was structured. By altering the system, the regime of value changed as well. My ethnography demonstrates that this set of policies fostered unintended consequences, which led the traders to commercialize branded counterfeits.

In these concluding notes I draw attention to two main aspects of my findings. The first aspect is structural and refers to the output of the IP regime in Brazil. From a longitudinal ethnographic perspective, it is possible to show that the case I researched is exemplary regarding the failure of the enforcement against piracy, a finding that coincides with some macro perspectives about the IP regime efficiency (Karaganis 7). By following Interpol and USTR's guidelines, national as well as local agents grouped piracy, informality, and smuggling under the same umbrella as organized crime, with the intention of repressing it. This proved a convenient way to deal with an old problem: the removal of so-called Brazilian "marginality" from central areas of the Brazilian cities. The *camelôs* were removed from the streets, and local, national, and global elites expressed their satisfaction with the outcomes of the local policy. What in fact happened was the opposite of what had been planned: the traders replaced the trinkets with luxury counterfeits, which coincided simultaneously with their deep financial indebtedness. These unintended consequences were hidden from the official narrative, which described the case of formalization in Brazil as a success. Such tacit institutional cynicism reveals that the consolidation of top-down power structures was a strong motivation underlying the anti-piracy operations. "Piracy" was a means through which the United States exercised control over Brazilian markets and frontiers, and a means by which national and local elites exercised control over the urban poor.

The second and final aspect I draw attention to in these concluding notes is the way in which the traders resignified this whole process. As outlined above, the formalization policies fostered a desire for brands, working as a formal and informal pedagogical force that, through active repression, increased the desire for fakes. For many years, the four guiding principles had not only created value but had also enabled the *camelôs* to create brands of their own—in Dalva's words, "We were the brand." The traders branded the products through their own physical effort and imagination, including the fantastic stories told about how they hid themselves in the forest to save their commodities, the art of displaying colorful stands, and the purifying rituals that cleansed both the traders and their goods of illegality. Hence the traders themselves were the agents responsible for fostering the value and legitimacy of their goods through their bodies, imagination, social relations, and practices, thereby merging gifts and commodities in the exchange process. The emergence of fake brands in my interlocutors' commercial lives was highly alienating and de-structured this arrangement. The new branded commodities that were sold at the mall were less personalized and lacked the same fundamental system of value. This chapter therefore shows that though the regulatory regime affected the way the traders were organized within a commodity chain, it failed both in its ultimate objectives as well as in producing a normative subjectivity aligned with the neoliberal principles of the contemporary global market and IP. It did, however, bring financialization and debt into the traders' lives.

## Note

1 www.facebook.com/ShoppingPOPCenter. Accessed December 18, 2019.

## Bibliography

Appadurai, Arjun. *The Social Life of Things: Commodities in Cultural Perspective*. Cambridge UP, 1988.

Benjamin, Walter. *The Work of Art in the Age of Its Technological Reproducibility, and Other Writings on Media*. Harvard UP, 2008.

Bestor, Nestor. "Supply-Side Sushi." *American Anthropology*, vol. 103, no. 1, 2001, pp. 76–95.

Bourdieu, Pierre. *O costureiro e sua grife: contribuição para uma teoria da magia*. Zouk, 2004.

Coombe, Rosemary J. *The Cultural Life of Intellectual Properties: Authorship, Appropriation, and the Law*. Duke UP, 1998.

CPI da Pirataria. *Comissão Parlamentar de Inquérito*, 2004,

www2.camara.leg.br/atividade-legislativa/comissoes/comissoes-temporarias/parlamentar-de-inquerito/52-legislatura/cpipirat/relatoriofinal.pdf. Accessed December 18, 2019.

Dent, Alexander S. "Piracy, Circulatory Legitimacy, and Neoliberal Subjectivity in Brazil." *Cultural Anthropology*, vol. 27, no. 1, 2012, pp. 28–49.

Ferguson, James. *The Anti-Politics Machine: "Development," Depoliticization, and Bureaucratic Power in Lesotho*. Cambridge UP, 1990.

Foster, Robert. "Tracking Globalization: Commodities and Value in Motion." *Handbook of Material Culture*, edited by Chris Tilly, Webb Keane, Susanne Küchler, Mike Rowlands, and Patricia Spyer, Sage, 2013, pp. 285–302.

Foster, Robert. "The Work of the New Economy: Consumers, Brands, and Value Creation." *Cultural Anthropology*, vol. 22, no. 4, 2007, pp. 707–731.

Graeber, David. *Toward an Anthropological Theory of Value: The False Coin of Our Own Dreams*. Palgrave, 2001.

Hubert, Henri, and Marcel Mauss. *Sacrifice: Its Nature and Function*. U of Chicago P, 1964.

Karaganis, Joe, editor, *Media Piracy in Emerging Economies*. Social Science Research Council, 2011, http://piracy.ssrc.org/wp-content/uploads/2011/06/MPEE-PDF-1.0.4.pdf. Accessed June 15, 2019.

Marx, Karl, and Friedrich Engels. *Capital*. Wordsworth Editions, 2013.

Oliven, Ruben George. *Urbanização e mudança social no Brasil*. Vozes, 1980.

Otto, Ton, and Rane Willerslev. "Introduction: Value as Theory: Comparison, Cultural Critique, and Guerilla Ethnographic Theory." *HAU: Journal of Ethnographic Theory*, vol 3, no. 1, 2013, pp. 1–20.

Perlman, Janice E. *The Myth of Marginality: Urban Poverty and Politics in Rio de Janeiro*. U of California P, 1979.

Pinheiro-Machado, Rosana. *Counterfeit Itineraries on the Global South: The Human Consequences of Piracy in China and Brazil*. Routledge, 2017.

Trezzi, Humberto. "Inauguração do Camelódromo muda imagem do centro de Porto Alegre." *Zero Hora*, www.clicrbs.com.br/especial/rs/tecnologia/19,0,2399864,Inauguracao-do-Camelodromo-muda-imagem-do-centro-de-Porto-Alegre.html. Accessed February 10, 2009.

Tsing, Anna. "Sorting Out Commodities: How Capitalist Value Is Made Through Gifts." *HAU: Journal of Ethnographic Theory*, vol. 3, no. 1, 2013, pp. 21–43.

Vann, Elizabeth. "Limits of Authenticity in Vietnamese Consumer Markets." *American Anthropologist*, vol. 108, no. 2, 2006, pp. 286–296.

Young, Diana. "The Colours of Things." *Handbook of Material Culture*, edited by Chris Tilly, Webb Keane, Susanne Küchler, Mike Rowlands, and Patricia Spyer, Sage, 2013, pp. 173–185.

# 2

# THE PIRACY PROBLEM

## Indigeneity, Hybridity, and the Racial Politics of IP Enforcement in Guatemala

*Kedron Thomas*

The past three decades have seen unprecedented efforts to standardize and enforce intellectual property (IP) laws on a global scale. As a signatory of multilateral accords including the World Trade Organization's (WTO) Trade-Related Aspects of Intellectual Property Rights (TRIPS) Agreement, implemented in Guatemala in 2000, the Guatemalan government has moved to remake a legal context in which "there was little effective protection for intellectual property" (Godoy 59) into an enforcement regime fully harmonized with international law and enforcement standards. These efforts have included the appointment of a special prosecutor for IP crimes and the execution of sporadic, well-reported raids during which police confiscate illegal compact discs, DVDs, and clothing sold in Guatemala City streets (Larios). Representatives of US-based trade associations regularly comment in Guatemalan media on economic losses associated with the piracy trade (Coronado; Patzán; Prensa Libre, "Guatemala"), hyping the supposedly detrimental effects on the national economy and public moral integrity. Amid ongoing industry-led attempts to consolidate and strengthen IP protections through trade agreements and legislation, newspaper headlines warn that "piracy is on the rise" (Ramírez) and that Guatemala is among the worst piracy offenders in Latin America (Interiano). In this chapter, I critically assess rhetorics and practices of IP promotion and implementation in Guatemala, demonstrating that anti-piracy propaganda and policing perpetuate and reinforce race and class ideologies that are important for the maintenance of entrenched modes of economic and political power in Central America.

Legal frameworks and enforcement efforts that target unauthorized modes of copying and imitation touch down in Guatemala as part of a postcolonial field in which issues of "mimesis and alterity" (Taussig) already structure national debates about what it means to pursue modernization and development. In a country where more than half of the population is indigenous Maya, public discourse among nonindigenous scholars and government officials regarding politics and economic development have long revolved around the so-called "Indian problem," the underlying premise of which is that indigenous culture "represents the antithesis of what they [the national elite] aspire to, namely, a unified, thoroughly modern, Western-based nation-state," as Edward F. Fischer explains. Fischer continues,

> While popular ideologies have waxed and waned over the years, the Guatemalan government has consistently pursued policies that encourage, even force, the Maya to give up their "primitive" culture for more civilized European lifeways in the hope that this will lead to economic integration and growth. (52)

National development in Guatemala has been figured as hinging on the ability of indigenous Guatemalans to assimilate to a hegemonic national culture that is supposedly European in its orientations and aspirations.

Today, reductionist economic logics and parochial conceptions of property, ownership, and authorship that derive from Euro-American traditions and underwrite the continued expansion of IP protections provide Guatemala's elite class with a new framework for problematizing racialized citizens. The national elite evaluates piracy as threatening to the country's social and economic development insofar as piracy is figured as a bad or corrupt form of imitation, one carried out through unauthorized means and in unauthorized ways, outside of and in opposition to official hierarchies and sovereignties. Talk of imitation, threat, and primitiveness come together in national discourses on piracy that nervously anticipate and reflect changing patterns of ethnic identification and social location in a country that is experiencing what Jorge Ramón González Ponciano has characterized as "cosmopolitanism from below" ("The *Shumo* Challenge" 309). Through transnational migration, urbanization, and evolving modes of production and consumption (including IP piracy) that facilitate new forms of access to media and goods, Guatemala's underclasses are actively crafting material lifeworlds and hybridized aesthetics that belie the sumptuary norms that structure a national social order. Below, I draw on long-term field research with indigenous Maya apparel manufacturers who make and sell fashionable clothing that features "pirated" brand names and logos (Thomas), as well as journalism, government reports, and industry propaganda, to describe a set of racial and cultural narratives that circulate in Guatemala about who IP pirates are. Taking inspiration from González Ponciano's analysis of the shifting problematization of Guatemala's underclasses, I interpret emergent discourses on Guatemala's "piracy problem" as a superficially deracialized reformulation of the "Indian problem," a move indicative of how the national elite is attempting to manage cosmopolitanism and multiculturalism while maintaining systems of racialized subordination.

## Indigeneity and IP

In recent years, anthropologists have debated the benefits and drawbacks of an expanding IP regime, weighing the promises of rights-based protections for forms of property that matter to indigenous people and other marginalized populations against the incommensurability of IP frameworks with the diverse ontologies, property systems, and ways of life evident among various social groups.[1] Within international development institutions, "culture" and "traditional knowledge" have emerged as keywords, and the WTO and World Intellectual Property Organization (WIPO) have negotiated a set of alternative, *sui generis* property rights systems that purport to take communal forms of ownership and local and indigenous relationships to knowledge and natural resources into account. Insofar as these scholarly discussions and institutional frameworks regarding the property rights of indigenous peoples tend to focus on traditional knowledge, folklore, and the management of biodiversity, they risk reflecting stereotypical assumptions about who indigenous people are and what they do (i.e., they are agriculturalists or ritual specialists) and about their relationship to the world and to technology (i.e., they have knowledge of and access to raw materials that may be converted into modern technologies, but they are not themselves part of the modern world system). That indigenous populations actively participate in transnational movements of goods and ideas, are integrated into national and global economies (often sitting at the bottom of the socioeconomic order), and increasingly live in cities (see Morgan and Gulson) is often overlooked.

Current IP debates also tend to treat indigenous identity as a fixed category, whereas in Guatemala, as in other parts of Latin America, ethnic and racial classificatory schemes have shifted over time and remain somewhat flexible. For example, Guatemalans of indigenous descent may attempt or feel compelled "to pass" as *ladino* (nonindigenous) outside their homes in order to avoid discrimination and violence (Warren 10–11). Conversely, and in keeping with a national ideology that links poverty, rural space, tradition, and indigeneity, on the one hand, and class mobility, urban space, formal institutions, modernity, and nonindigenous identity, on the other (see Fischer and Brown 10–11), people who live in cities or who achieve certain educational or socioeconomic status may be denied their self-ascribed indigenous identity by others because of their social location. Narrowly construing the relationship between indigenous people and IP law in terms of stable identities, perennial lifeways, or collective rights may miss the ways that race and ethnicity are intimately tied to class, geography, and other markers of belonging and affiliation, as well as how identifications may be contested and at stake for people claiming either indigenous or nonindigenous status.

There is also the fact that indigenous people are more and more confronted with IP law not as benefactors of special copyright and patent protections but as producers and consumers of criminalized classes of goods. In scholarly discussions and institutional frameworks regarding populations that participate in piracy and counterfeiting, "cultural difference" tends to be treated as a source of or synonym for ethical underdevelopment or economic irrationality rather than as an opportunity for the reflexive reworking of a universalist rights regime. Legal and business scholars commonly blame "culture" for the proliferation of unauthorized goods and the inevitable failures of IP enforcement efforts, advancing reductionist portraits of problematic "national cultures" of collectivism (Husted) and ranking countries and culture groups hierarchically according to their degree of affiliation with the West and modernity (Green and Smith). These approaches call to mind Dipesh Chakrabarty's critique of the "given, reified categories, opposites paired in a structure of domination and subordination" (27) that underwrite Orientalism.

Business scholars presume that people who violate IP protections—people characterized as deviant, aberrant, and criminal (Albers-Miller)—can be reoriented toward a new culture and ethics if the law is clearly explained to them (Nill and Shultz). In many places, however, the relationship between law and ethics is anything but clear and simple. Rachel Sieder, writing of "the historical legacy of citizen mistrust of the law" in Guatemala, describes the state judiciary as "bereft of legitimacy in the eyes of the majority of the population" (141). Such mistrust is an outgrowth of centuries of violence and discrimination directed toward the indigenous population, including the genocidal violence of the country's long civil war (1960–1996), as well as the lack of accountability related to wartime atrocities and persistent impunity amid rising violent crime rates and public–private sector collusions and corruption. For many Guatemalans, the promotion of anti-piracy laws and the penal logics ensconced therein reflects a rather foreign concept: that crime is crime.

A culturally peculiar criminology, premised on the notion that punitive law prevents crime and improves civic life and governmental and economic efficiencies (see Pasquino), shapes the ideological context in which arguments advanced by international institutions, trade associations, and governments in favor of the expansion of IP protections are often couched in terms of the spread of democracy, progress, and prosperity to nations and peoples that are seen as politically, ethically, and culturally backward (Bettig; Lippert). These civilizational discourses layer onto political-economic relations of extraction and further marginalization. As Carlos Correa notes, at a basic level, IP law ends up positioning countries in the Global North as innovators, owners, and authorized consumers while saddling governments in the Global South with the burden of "protecting" rights-holders from the "pirates" said to thrive in that region (23–24, 154). In Guatemala, these ideological frames of culture and development that are part and parcel of the IP regime are taken up by politically and economically powerful groups in terms of a civilizational divide between an elite class and a racialized underclass, helping to shape a national context, described below, in which indigenous "culture" can be celebrated as an essentialized tradition that contributes to the multicultural character of the nation-state at the same time as the "culture" of poor, working-class, and indigenous Guatemalans (groups that are often conflated in hegemonic national discourses) can be denigrated as a problematic mode of anti-modern citizenship.

## Ethics and Aesthetics in the "Piracy" Trade

Examining IP debates and enforcement efforts in Guatemala can expand interdisciplinary conversations about indigeneity in important directions and contribute to the critical assessment of the political economy and racial politics of IP law. In my research among Kaqchikel Maya men who operate small-scale clothing workshops in the central highlands, I have documented the alternative and vernacular conceptions of property, ownership, and authorship that animate Guatemala's apparel trade and the perspectives of people labeled "pirates" on IP law's implementation. People who make and sell knockoffs—including Abercrombie & Fitch sweatshirts, Levi's jeans, and Lacoste polo shirts—and people who purchase that clothing do not necessarily share the definitions of "original," "copy," "real," and "fake" that are written into IP law. Apparel producers routinely emphasized to me the creativity inherent in their design and manufacturing processes, even if the resulting clothes feature brand names for which the producer does not own the rights. A young manufacturer noted proudly in an interview that his family deals in *imitaciones* (imitations). "We copy it, but we make it better," he said, explaining that they start with popular youth styles they see on websites and in upscale commercial centers and tailor them to the local market, producing garments that suit their clientele in terms of price but also in terms of color palette and overall design. For example, a manufacturer who deals in children's clothing might take a fleece romper design that he sees on the Baby Gap website and substitute sweater knit fabric for the material of the bodice—partly because he can make knit fabric with his machinery, so it is cheaper for him, and partly because this improvisation will be a selling point for him with highland consumers. He might embellish the romper with an embroidered Mickey Mouse figure, a move that would qualify as trademark piracy under national and international law. Manufacturers commonly described the use of trademarked images as evidencing their attention to detail and commitments to quality work. Affixing tags, labels, and logos is about giving one's products a contemporary, fashionable, and professional look and feel as well as realizing some measure of business success in a marketplace dominated by a cadre of popular brands due to corporate marketing, globalized media, and free trade.

Maya workshop owners also have their own ethical debates regarding how, when, and whom to copy. For instance, when an apparel producer mimics a design being produced by a neighboring workshop owner with whom relevant forms of community and perhaps also ethnic belonging are shared, he is expected to make changes that set his garments apart in a meaningful way. A producer might copy the cut and brand of a cotton T-shirt that his neighbor is manufacturing but change the color scheme and also screen print the Nike logo rather than sewing it on. If a producer did not introduce some creative element when copying a neighbor's design, he would be called a *copión*, a copycat. This term was commonly used to disparage garment manufacturers who copied other producers in ways that were considered to be taking advantage of an already open system in which the economic and moral legitimacy of copying and imitation is readily acknowledged. Besides copying exactly what someone else was selling, those labeled *copiones* also sold their products for less than what the other manufacturer was charging. "It is a normal reaction for people to get angry with one another," one producer explained, "especially when you are offering the same product at a lower price to the same buyer. That is when people get really upset." He and many other garment manufacturers interpreted price-based competition—a predictable and rather ordinary business strategy in neoclassical economics—as both unfair, since everyone suffers when prices go down, and morally problematic, evidence of greed, jealousy, and maliciousness directed toward one's neighbors.

In our conversations, apparel producers sometimes reflected on the discourses of piracy circulating in media accounts, comparing the IP regime with norms and values more salient to their trade. One small-scale producer suggested that the *copiones* are just like the *piratas* (pirates) he had read about in the newspaper who were accused of selling CDs and DVDs containing unauthorized content in the streets of Guatemala City. "The people who make the original discs complain because they can't sell them for the price they want," he explained. This producer, who traded in "pirated" brand names himself, interpreted the criminalized problem of piracy in line with the localized ethics of copying. His view was that piracy harms some producers because it undercuts their ability to earn a living when others copy digital material and engage in unethical and immoral price-cutting. This is different from the claims about authorship, ownership, and originality that condition IP law. He did not evaluate the mere act of copying as problematic, nor did he express concern regarding the property rights that content producers might have for their creations. Within a moral economy committed to sharing and a community of practice dedicated to creative production, he and others accepted some forms of copying as appropriate, legitimate, and ethical while simultaneously denouncing business practices that they perceived as motivated by greed and jealousy, such as the kinds of cut-throat competition that detracted from the ability of community members to earn a living and that thus seemed morally and financially threatening to the overall stability of a local industry. These ethical frameworks that guide the design processes and marketing strategies of highland producers parochialize official portraits of business ethics and innovation built into the IP regime and challenge assumptions about progress, improvement, and ordering on which the wider development industry is based. Rather than evidence of backwards "culture," "piracy" is a location from which Maya apparel producers actively work out "various ways of being modern" that are rooted in "concrete local ways of 'being human'" (Eckstein and Schwarz 18) and of building both enterprise and community.

Maya apparel producers craft clothing styles and styles of business in a context in which racial and class status are powerfully marked by what people wear and consume. Maya people are closely associated with traditional styles of dress, and efforts on the part of the national elite to address the "Indian problem" have often centered on clothing and other cultural forms as key sites of intervention. For example, the Guatemalan liberal politics of the late nineteenth to mid-twentieth centuries emphasized a peculiar form of *indigenismo*, understood, in this context, as the cultural, ethnic, and racial assimilation of indigenous people in Guatemala, positing indigenous languages, religious practices, and traditional dress as signs and symptoms of backwardness (see Grandin). In the 1970s and 1980s, at the height of the genocidal war, the donning of traditional dress served as a pretext for the Guatemalan military to designate individuals and often entire villages as communist subversives and target them for extermination. Since the war's official end, the Guatemalan government has struggled to align plans and visions for national development with social movements and international accords that advance the rights of indigenous peoples to their dress, cultures, land, and languages.

Charles Hale has characterized the political effects of indigenous rights movements in Guatemala in terms of "neoliberal multiculturalism," whereby the nation-state guarantees a minimal set of rights for indigenous groups and celebrates cultural diversity exhibited in dress, music, art, and language without addressing the historical injustices, persistent violences, deep socioeconomic inequalities, or structural processes of marginalization that affect indigenous Guatemalans. Today, the *mujer maya* (see Nelson, *A Finger in the Wound*) enveloped in her handwoven blouse and skirt not only symbolizes indigeneity for Maya cultural activists (see Otzoy), but also serves as a basis for Guatemalan nationalism and for the country's international marketing and promotion. Maya women in *traje* adorn the pages of guidebooks and illustrate tourism websites and advertising. The Maya and their textiles are now the primary means by which Guatemala attracts foreign investment and tourism dollars and elaborates a fantastical image of itself as having a ready-to-consume cultural heritage. The state and private enterprise capitalize on culture to create a national brand around indigeneity (cf. Comaroff and Comaroff).

The emergence of the knockoff fashion trade troubles these efforts to relegate Maya people to the domains of "culture" and "tradition," since fashion branding is a decidedly modern sphere of marketing and commerce (see English). The trade results in a hybridized aesthetics, where brand names, logos, and fashionable looks that multinational corporations publicize as markers of whiteness in their appeals to the aspirational desires of Latin American consumer classes come into contact with the types of people—darker skinned, lower class, rural inhabitants or urban poor, with less formal education—that historically have been disparaged as part of the "Indian problem" in Guatemala. When efforts to express taste and discernment and participate in popular trends in line with the modes of distinction promoted by the fashion system fall short—that is, when people creatively adapt clothing designs to localized styles and copy globally marketed trademarks as part of that process—they are labeled "pirates," talked about as threatening the health of the national economy, and blamed for illegally stealing the value and good name of European and North American corporations. International IP laws that seek to control and criminalize "the copy" feed into neocolonial narratives that accuse Maya people of employing mimicry, trickery, and double-talk to conceal their "real" intentions of leveraging indigenous rights claims and special protections to undermine the power, privilege, and authority of nonindigenous Guatemalans and continue to disrupt processes of economic development and national progress (see Nelson, *Reckoning*).

## Old Problem, New Pirates

Though the production and consumption of unauthorized goods in Guatemala is widespread, crossing racial and class lines, the criminalization of piracy converges in everyday conversation and media reports with ideologies of race, ethnicity, culture, and class in ways that make already marginalized populations available for new kinds of blame. Because street vendors hawking pirated goods in the capital city are socially and spatially proximate to street crime (e.g., pickpocketing, mugging, and assault), piracy is lumped into a generalized portrait of deviance and violence as an intractable part of urban life. The fact that street vendors generally belong to an urban underclass and are often indigenous (Offit 69) also fits with stereotyped portraits of delinquency that blame poor, rural people, who many nonindigenous people say become "corrupted" (Camus 55)—that is, drawn into a life of crime—when they move to the capital city. This stereotype and ubiquitous "talk of crime" (Caldeira) in Guatemala have emerged partially out of brutal realities. But rising violent crime rates more accurately reflect the influx of transnational drug gangs into the capital city and widespread conditions of poverty and insecurity that make life precarious for most Guatemalans (O'Neill). The government recently removed many street vendors (and the clients who depend on their cheap goods) from the sidewalks of Zone 1, the capital city's historic center, as part of a larger public–private partnership to convert the area into an upscale entertainment district (Véliz and O'Neill). The street vendors were relocated to an interior space in a multistory building, making product piracy a less conspicuous feature of the capital city's urban landscape.

Sensational media accounts and official government reports help to justify crackdowns on piracy producers and vendors by conflating piracy with organized crime, violence, and even international terrorism, a line of argument promoted by the US government and international industry associations (e.g., Prensa Libre, "Los Zetas"; Treverton et al.). The country's major dailies characterize people who manufacture and sell unauthorized reproductions of copyright- and trademark-protected materials as lawbreakers—"mercenaries of illegality," as one national newspaper called them (Menocal). The national Intellectual Property Registry (RPI, Registro de la Propiedad Intelectual) published a "Report on Counterfeiting" in 2004, shortly after Guatemala's implementation of the TRIPS Agreement. Even while noting that "inequality, lack of job opportunities, and free trade markets" have contributed to the growth of piracy, the report claims that "the same networks of human trafficking that used to make a living from other crimes are now working in compact disc piracy. Delinquency does not begin or end, it just transforms" (11–13, qtd. in Arana Segura 13). The report deems piracy "organized crime," claiming that "a large percentage of the income earned from piracy production ends up financing other lucrative trades, such as the trafficking of drugs and arms, fraud, and money laundering" (22, qtd. in Arana Segura 15).

Such characterizations of piracy belie the fact that crime is not a homogenous category and discourage sophisticated analysis of the factors that underpin the physical insecurity that many Guatemalans currently face (see Benson et al.). "Pirates" do not always or even usually belong to drug gangs, and piracy is a widely accepted practice, indeed a staple, of Guatemala's marketplace. As much as 80 percent of software used by Guatemalan companies is pirated, even though there have been dozens of court cases that have resulted in private businesses being fined (Marroquín). Pirated goods are sold openly on urban streets and in highland market towns. And, as discussed above, the Maya manufacturers with whom I conducted fieldwork do not see themselves as "bad people" engaging in criminal behavior, although most are aware of the anti-piracy rhetoric that echoes through national newspapers. They do not view their activity as something that undermines the health of the economy either. A simple criminology of piracy overlooks the ways that particular populations and behaviors are socially produced as available for criminalization (see Thomas and Galemba).

The racialized dynamics of enforcement efforts are apparent in the discourses of government agencies charged with enforcing IP laws. The 2004 RPI report characterizes piracy and counterfeiting as a "parasitic business that lives on the blood of the legal economy," using biological metaphors and eugenicist language to relegate people who commit IP violations to subhuman status and render them as threats to the healthy "blood"-lines of the proper nation and economy. Government agents, including police, also characterize piracy producers and consumers as routinely engaging in a form of collective violence known as *linchamiento* (lynching). The term refers to acts of vigilante justice carried out against suspected criminals as well as attacks on law enforcement officials who attempt to intervene, and this phenomenon has been ideologically associated with indigenous Guatemalans in the postwar period. The RPI report posits that, "On several occasions, people walking by on the street have attempted to impede the arrest of black-market vendors" (16, qtd. in Arana Segura 14). These accusations are elaborated in an interview conducted by a Guatemalan university student in 2006 with the Chief of the Economic Crimes Division of the National Civil Police's (PNC, Policía Nacional Civil) Criminal Investigation Office in Guatemala City, who said,

> When we carry out our operations, the people who work in the street markets get together and attack the agents of the National Police, the Public Ministry, even the transport units … We need assistance from the PNC's

> Rapid Action unit, the Anti-Riot unit, the public prosecutor's office at the Public Ministry, and most of the time the Criminal Investigation Division of the PNC in order to combat this phenomenon. In the raids that we've carried out, we haven't asked for the military's help, but if we see that this problem is getting worse, I think it will be necessary to have their assistance. (Qtd. in Arana Segura 40–41)

In a national context in which highland Maya communities are stereotyped as bloodthirsty and "backward 'savages'" (Burrell 242) in tabloid media accounts of *linchamientos*, the idea that street vendors and piracy consumers are given to threatening public officials and thwarting formal legal procedures connects an urban underclass with rural backwardness, portraying piracy producers and consumers as utterly and scandalously out of place amid efforts to modernize the national economy and uphold the rule of law. The idea that military intervention "will be necessary" in order to subdue these populations suggests that the security logics that drove and served to justify extreme violence on the part of the state during the war continue to inform law-enforcement approaches and procedures. The biological metaphors and references to stereotyped behaviors, including sensationalized mob violence, which show up in media coverage, government reports, and narratives advanced by officials charged with IP enforcement reveal a context in which long-standing, anti-indigenous sentiment serves to justify anti-piracy laws and their enforcement at the same time that IP laws and logics provide cover for the ongoing criminalization of indigenous and lower-class citizens in an era of neoliberal multiculturalism.

Stories told about the "piracy problem" often involve attempts to racialize and spatialize pirates as rural, indigenous people who bring crime and disorder to Guatemala's urban landscape. These narratives emerge amid concerns among Guatemala's elite that the racial, spatial, and aesthetic categories on which a national social order and its modes of subordination have long rested is being challenged by new kinds of mobility, production, and consumption. González Ponciano critically interrogates these concerns among upper-class Guatemalans who worry that Maya people are attempting to "leave their assigned slot in the local and global hierarchies of whiteness" through rural-urban and South-North labor migration and acts of conspicuous consumption ("The *Shumo* Challenge" 313). González Ponciano notes that terms such as *shumo*, *muco*, and *cholero*, words that do not directly index race as a marker of identity, are nonetheless defined according to racist discourses against indigenous people. These terms are commonly employed by "white/r" (311) upper-class Guatemalans as a means of disparaging darker-skinned, lower-class individuals who display signs and statuses that defy their designated social positions. For instance, nonindigenous elite characterize *shumos* as "primitive" people with "caveman customs" who do not speak grammatically correct Spanish and who exhibit "an incorrigible rebelliousness against the rule of law." *Shumos* are further described as "dirty, abusive, impertinent … and rude" people with bad taste and a penchant for extravagant fashions, body piercings, and rap music (313). Such depictions meld anti-indigenous stereotypes with aesthetic markers that index a transnational style that Guatemala's elite ridicule as "*cholo latino*" (317) and associate with migrant "networks that symbolically revolve around Los Angeles and Chicago" (316)—cities stigmatized in anti-*shumo* discourse as scenes of lower-class Central American, Mexican American, and African American delinquency and gang affiliation. While González Ponciano highlights how underclass youth have been problematized via this discourse—a shift "del problema del indio al problema de la juventud" (from the Indian problem to the youth problem), as he phrases it ("Blancura" 128)—it is notable that *shumos* are associated with piracy in the examples that he proffers. *Shumos* "take what doesn't belong to them, because they have no respect for other people's property, just their own," wrote a commentator in one of Guatemala's major newspapers (qtd. in González Ponciano, "The *Shumo* Challenge" 313). And according to one popular website, the worst offenders of elite sensibilities—dubbed the "Loser Hyper-shumo"—have "more than four pirate CDs bought on Sixth Avenue or at a traffic light" (qtd. in González Ponciano, "The *Shumo* Challenge" 317). As González Ponciano summates, "*Shumo* style is tasteless … because it is a poor imitation, one that is out of place … This poor judgment is not only distasteful but is also threatening" ("The *Shumo* Challenge" 321). Anti-*shumo*/anti-pirate discourse participates in a kind of "color-blind racism" (Bonilla-Silva) that makes racialized populations available for criminalization on the grounds that their social and geographical mobility and hybridized aesthetics are unauthorized, illegal, and dangerous, converging with and registering support for the *mano dura* (iron fist), tough-on-crime politics and policies that have gained widespread electoral support in the postwar era (Thomas 201–202) while still permitting Guatemala's elite to lay claim to cosmopolitan values of racial and cultural diversity and inclusiveness.

Some official reports explicitly justify strong IP protections as a means of maintaining a system of social stratification and allaying the political, cultural, and racial anxieties that piracy provokes, insofar as IP enforcement is presumed to ensure that people consume products befitting of their social class. The 2004 RPI report, for example, explains that trademark piracy—the unauthorized use of brand names and logos—would cease if consumers would commit themselves to buying only "what suits them, in line with their economic means, and with the possibility of demanding quality at that level." The idea is that IP law provides an important mechanism for enforcing sumptuary norms and protecting a symbolic and material order that has been built up over time via collusions between governments and corporations whose modes of branding, pricing, and market segmentation have been naturalized as representing some truth about differently positioned consumer populations. Trademark piracy is symptomatic, the reports states, of the "fetishism" (18–19, qtd. in Arana Segura 15) that surrounds brands, which drives some consumers to behave in irrational and harmful ways, resulting in disorder and confusion in the marketplace and across society (cf. Thomas). In line with anti-*shumo* discourse, this portrait of piracy invokes anti-indigenous stereotypes that also recall early anthropological representations of the cultish behavior of native people coming into contact with Western material wealth, advancing a portrait of Guatemala's racialized underclasses as primitives obsessed with other people's goods.

## Whiteness and Racialized Hybridity

In my research with highland apparel manufacturers, I have attempted to situate the forms of racism that Maya business owners and market vendors routinely experience within a broader, globalized racial formation that advances "white style" as an aesthetic and material regime wrapped up with ways of dressing, speaking, and presenting oneself that conform to the norms and expectations produced and circulated across international institutions, by media, and through marketing messages as signs of "whiteness" (Thomas 115). IP regimes participate in the construction of white style and the policing of its boundaries on national and international scales. The culture industries and wider legal and business communities that support anti-piracy enforcement do not have to acknowledge race as a key diacritic of the branding and promotion of their products or cite the enforcement of racialized social orders as a reason for their efforts. This is because IP law provides an official, legal, and deracialized discourse about the protection of rights, the orderly functioning of the marketplace, and a seemingly self-evident distinction between originals and copies as meaningful justifications for the regulation and criminalization of particular groups of people. Although talk about the problem of piracy does not often involve explicit references to race and the importance of racialized social stratification for the continued success of the fashion, music, or film industries, anti-piracy campaigns are couched in terms of, and come to seem like a common-sense approach to, protecting the property and integrity of people who create from the immoral and illegal actions of populations who copy. Race is masked by crime as the main point of disputation and disturbance. In this way, anti-piracy discourse provides ideological cover for racialized systems of distinction, corporate profiteering, and governance.

González Ponciano argues that upper-class, nonindigenous Guatemalans heavily invest in certain kinds of racial boundary-making projects because they face their own difficulties "in claiming whiteness before both national and global audiences" ("The *Shumo* Challenge" 308). On an international level, Guatemala is caught in the postcolonial bind of continuously having to prove that it belongs on the proverbial list of modern, developed countries. Meanwhile, Guatemala perennially appears on the *actual* "watch list" published by the US Trade Representative, denoting "serious intellectual property deficiencies." In this context, anti-*shumo*/anti-piracy discourse helps to forge an image of "true" Guatemalans as appropriately cosmopolitan, comfortably and unquestionably "white," and utterly distinct from the "dark plebeian" (González Ponciano, "The *Shumo* Challenge" 315) said to participate in organized crime rings and vigilante mobs, who steals what rightfully belongs to others by violating IP laws, thereby impeding progress and degrading the national reputation.

Relationships to globalized whiteness are evident in the IP-related materials that various public agencies and industry organizations have disseminated in recent years. For example, a key venue for RPI's anti-piracy propaganda has been the International Book Fair (FILGUA, Feria Internacional del Libro en Guatemala) held annually in Guatemala City. A booth sponsored by RPI proclaims the importance of "the rights of authors" and, as a means of steering Guatemala's youth away from piracy and towards officially sanctioned channels of creativity and authorship, RPI typically tailors its messaging at FILGUA to children. When I visited the booth in 2017, visitors could pick up a board game titled, "My First Creation, My First Registration," in which players move from space to space in pursuit of patent, copyright, and trademark protections, careful to avoid the leering pirates—characters with eye patches, sabers, and gold teeth (a feature associated in Guatemala with Maya aesthetics as much as eighteenth-century buccaneers) who threaten progress toward both personal and national success. "I'm a Guatemalan author!" reads the final, winning square, a statement that encourages entrepreneurial creativity as well as national pride (not just "an author," but a "Guatemalan author," a label that binds nationality with indications of literacy and professional attainment).

At the booth, RPI representatives also distributed an IP-themed comic book (Gómez de Estrada) featuring two young characters, Dani and Vale. In the comic's opening pages, Vale asks Dani's advice on what sort of gift to buy for a friend—perhaps a CD, movie, or book (the kinds of materials protected under copyright law and frequently pirated). Her question sparks a detailed conversation about copyright protections, with Dani introducing and defining a set of technical legal terms. The characters agree that learning about copyright protections should be "part of the education" that everyone receives in school, and they commit to sharing their own knowledge widely. "And this way, we will help Guatemalan authors and work together to promote cultural industries and contribute to the country's economic development," Vale proclaims. Representing the "children and youth" of Guatemala, both characters in the full-color comic are shaded with light peach skin tones. Vale sports a belted dress with a collar, her dark hair cut to a modest shoulder length, while Dani wears a bright yellow T-shirt, tucked into blue jeans and secured with a belt. Their dress and hairstyles suggest an attempt by the booklet's illustrators to give both characters a clean-cut, wholesome, and—in keeping with the racialized dynamics of IP enforcement described above—decidedly nonindigenous look, one thus befitting their respectful orientation toward creativity, authorship, education, and national and civilizational progress.

At one point, Dani recites a long list of the multilateral accords—the Berne Convention, Paris Convention, Rome Convention, WIPO Performances and Phonograms Treaty, the list goes on—that together comprise international copyright law and to which Guatemala has recently subscribed. "So, we're up to date," Vale confirms. "That's right," Dani beams, "in Guatemala, we have approved and ratified these international treaties and conventions." This booklet, distributed at FILGUA and perhaps the other events that RPI representatives organize and attend at universities, bookstores, and art and cultural centers, targets a national public. Providing confirmation that "we're" on the "progressive path" (Vann 289) toward development and modernity that accession to international IP accords both signals and engenders, the story is reassuring to Guatemalans who have a stake in seeing themselves as part of and party to a legal and economic system associated with decidedly Global North places (Berne, Paris, Rome, the WIPO headquarters in Geneva) and processes. With the WTO, the US Trade Representative, and industry associations watching the "piracy problem" in Guatemala very closely to see what a suspiciously underdeveloped nation-state is doing to protect Global North creativities and authorships, the booklet is also part of the larger attempt by Guatemala's government agencies to provide rather desperate assurances to trading partners that there is no need to worry, since "we're up to date."

While Dani's mentoring successfully steers Vale away from potential acts of piracy, other IP promotion and enforcement efforts in Guatemala have actually resulted in dizzying displays of hybridity, turning anti-pirates into pirates and pirates into anti-pirates, further confounding the social boundaries that these efforts are intended to police and maintain. In 2008, the Fund for the Protection of Intellectual Property (FOMPI, Fomento y Protección de la Propiedad Intelectual), an organization representing the two largest cinema groups in Guatemala, hired a multinational advertising agency to produce a marketing campaign to discourage the trade in unauthorized copies of popular movies. The agency decided to hire salespeople to hawk special "pirated discs" in Guatemala City's street markets. The discs featured cover art and content from top-selling films. According to the advertising agency's winning submission to an international media competition,

> After a few minutes the movie was played, it jammed and our message appeared on the screen: You get, what you pay for. The money you paid for this movie will be used to produce more copies like this one. If you don't want this happening to you again, don't buy pirated movies.

At least 3,000 of these discs were sold to unsuspecting consumers in the capital city. The award submission continues, "The word on the street about our movies has spread and now people are thinking twice before buying a pirated movie. At the end, pirated movies turned out to be the perfect media to go against pirated movies" (Leo Burnett Guatemala, original in English). The near-cinematic looping and doubling of the imitative process involved in this effort—anti-pirates disguised as pirates in order to infiltrate a class said to have itself infiltrated "true" Guatemalan society—reveals elite Guatemalans who work for prestigious, multinational advertising agencies and who control the authorized cinema market as the actual agents of trickery and deception. Their efforts to discourage illegal activities in a country where the standard mechanisms and routines of rule-of-law modernity (policing and the judiciary) are notoriously corrupt and ineffectual ended up transforming anti-piracy advocates into disc-burning and disc-hawking "pirates," while piracy consumers morphed into anti-pirates, insofar as their purchases funded the burning of more discs for the campaign. And whereas extra-judicial modes of justice-seeking, shaming, and sanction pursued by lower-class and indigenous people are scandalized in Guatemala as symptoms of backwardness, FOMPI's orchestration of an extra-legal spectacle intended to shame and punish consumers tempted by "pirated" discs garnered international acclaim. The campaign also and unintentionally played on the realities of piracy participation on the part of law enforcement officials. The many market vendors I interviewed in 2009 told me that, following raids on vendor stalls in the capital city streets, the underpaid police would simply cross the street and fence the seized products for their own gain (cf. Arana Segura 31).

## Conclusion

The globalized IP regime provides an official rubric for criminalizing and moralizing against forms of production and consumption that fall outside of national and international narratives of progress and development. When lower-class Guatemalans are fined or arrested for selling "fake" Nike T-shirts or unauthorized copies of pop music hits and disparaged for wearing or listening to these cultural products, IP law functions to reproduce a "system of consumption-based social distinction and the social structures and norms based on it" (Beebe 814) even as the broader development and modernization framework aims to cultivate consumer desire and orient people toward market participation as a means of fulfillment and a mode of exercising citizenship rights. Indigenous people, who often occupy marginalized socioeconomic positions, are in an especially precarious predicament in relation to these social and institutional dynamics, since they face intersectional race and class discriminations. Maya people have long been compelled by the Guatemalan government and international development industry to "update" their ways of life and conform to recognizable, "modern" styles, but they are denigrated as imposters when they attempt to do so. Elizabeth Povinelli recounts a similar double bind faced by indigenous Australians. State authorities, she notes, recoil from "encounters with difference they consider abhorrent, inhuman, and bestial," but also balk at encounters "with differences they consider too hauntingly similar to themselves to warrant social entitlements—for example, land claims by indigenous people who dress, act, and sound like the suburban neighbors they are" (13).

Anti-piracy campaigns sit at the nexus of transnational projects aimed at establishing democratic rule of law in postwar Guatemala, waves of legal globalization that include the spread of IP rights and the institutionalization of multiculturalist values, ongoing pressures of market liberalization (with its accompanying narratives on human nature and proper market behavior), and durable histories of violence and discrimination affecting the country's indigenous population. The Guatemalan case illustrates how discourses on and efforts to control "cultures of the copy" (see the Introduction to this volume) can serve as ideological justification for the enforcement of national and international social orders characterized by the uneven distribution of property and power along lines of race, ethnicity, and class. As multinational corporations, nation-states, and multilateral agencies set the parameters of what counts as creativity and originality and what does not, the IP regime tends toward the deepening of historically rooted social, cultural, and economic processes that perpetually relegate subordinated groups to the wrong sides of whiteness and modernity.

## Note

1 Rosemary Coombe, for example, has argued that IP mechanisms could be a powerful tool for indigenous peoples struggling against exploitative market forces. Demands for copyright and patent protections for native art forms, ethnic identifiers, and agricultural knowledge have become important "axes of mobilization" in the larger sphere of indigenous organizing (Hayden 38). Other scholars (Aoki; Brown; Hirsch and Strathern) question whether granting indigenous groups rights and protections based on the international IP framework primarily expands the reach of Western institutional and market logics with little demonstrated regard for indigenous concepts of property or ownership and in ways that may actually further disadvantage indigenous peoples in relation to multinational capital and bureaucratic states. Creative projects that stretch back through time and across entire communities do not easily fit into hegemonic IP models. Many anthropologists remain skeptical of WTO and World Intellectual Property Organization (WIPO) initiatives around indigenous IP law since the effectiveness of such frameworks necessarily depends on the translation of local cultural norms into a set of legal rights that can be harmonized with international law, leaving important questions of incommensurability by the wayside (see Kirsch).

## Bibliography

Albers-Miller, Nancy D. "Consumer Misbehavior: Why People Buy Illicit Goods." *Journal of Consumer Marketing*, vol. 16, no. 3, 1999, pp. 273–287.

Aoki, Keith. "Neocolonialism, Anticommons Property, and Biopiracy in the (Not-So-Brave) New World Order of International Intellectual Property Protection." *Indiana Journal of Global Legal Studies*, vol. 6, no. 1, 1998, pp. 11–58.

Arana Segura, Karla Paola. *Situación Actual de la Comercialización de Discos Compactos "Pirata" en el Centro Histórico Capitalino*. Undergraduate thesis. Universidad de San Carlos de Guatemala, 2006.

Beebe, Barton. "Intellectual Property Law and the Sumptuary Code." *Harvard Law Review*, vol. 123, no. 4, 2010, pp. 810–889.

Benson, Peter, Edward F. Fischer, and Kedron Thomas. "Resocializing Suffering: Neoliberalism, Accusation, and the Sociopolitical Context of Guatemala's New Violence." *Latin American Perspectives*, vol. 35, no. 5, 2008, pp. 38–58.

Bettig, Ronald V. *Copyrighting Culture: The Political Economy of Intellectual Property*. Westview Press, 1996.

Bonilla-Silva, Eduardo. *Racism Without Racists: Color-Blind Racism and the Persistence of Racial Inequality in America*. Rowman & Littlefield, 2003.

Brown, Michael F. "Can Culture Be Copyrighted?" *Current Anthropology*, vol. 39, no. 2, 1998, pp. 193–222.

Burrell, Jennifer. "After Lynching." *War By Other Means: Aftermath in Post-Genocide Guatemala*, edited by Carlotta McAllister and Diane M. Nelson, Duke UP, 2013, pp. 214–260.

Caldeira, Teresa. *City of Walls: Crime, Segregation, and Citizenship in São Paulo*. U of California P, 2001.

Camus, Manuela. "Primero de Julio: Urban Experiences of Class Decline and Violence." *Securing the City: Neoliberalism, Space, and Insecurity in Postwar Guatemala*, edited by Kevin Lewis O'Neill and Kedron Thomas, Duke UP, 2011, pp. 49–66.

Chakrabarty, Dipesh. *Provincializing Europe: Postcolonial Thought and Historical Difference*. Princeton UP, 2000.

Comaroff, John L., and Jean Comaroff. *Ethnicity, Inc.* U of Chicago P, 2009.

Coombe, Rosemary J. *The Cultural Life of Intellectual Properties: Authorship, Appropriation, and the Law*. Duke UP, 1998.

Coronado, Eddy. "Empresarios, preocupados por piratería." *Prensa Libre*, June 12, 2013.

Correa, Carlos M. *Intellectual Property Rights, the WTO and Developing Countries: The TRIPS Agreement and Policy Options*. Zed Books, 2000.

Eckstein, Lars, and Anja Schwarz, editors. *Postcolonial Piracy: Media Distribution and Cultural Production in the Global South*. Bloomsburg, 2014.

English, Bonnie. *A Cultural History of Fashion in the 20th and 21st Centuries: From Catwalk to Sidewalk*. Bloomsburg, 2013.

Fischer, Edward F. "Induced Culture Change as a Strategy for Socioeconomic Development: The Pan-Maya Movement in Guatemala." *Maya Cultural Activism in Guatemala*, edited by Edward F. Fischer and R. McKenna Brown, U of Texas P, 1996, pp. 51–73.

Fischer, Edward F., and R. McKenna Brown, editors. *Maya Cultural Activism in Guatemala*. U of Texas P, 1996.

Godoy, Angelina Snodgrass. *Of Medicines and Markets: Intellectual Property and Human Rights in the Free Trade Era*. Stanford UP, 2013.

Gómez de Estrada, Genera. *Dani y Vale: El Derecho de Autor y los Derechos Conexos*. Ministerio de Economía, 2016.

González Ponciano, Jorge Ramón. "Blancura, cosmopolitismo, y representación en Guatemala." *Estudios de Cultura Maya*, vol. 27, 2006, pp. 125–147.

González Ponciano, Jorge Ramón. "The Shumo Challenge: White Class Privilege and the Post-Race, Post-Genocide Alliances of Cosmopolitanism from Below." *War by Other Means: Aftermath in Post-Genocide Guatemala*, edited by Carlotta McAllister and Diane M. Nelson, Duke UP, 2013, pp. 307–329.

Grandin, Greg. *The Blood of Guatemala: A History of Race and Nation*. Duke UP, 2000.

Green, Robert, and Tasman Smith. "Executive Insights: Countering Brand Counterfeiters." *Journal of International Marketing*, vol. 10, 2002, pp. 89–106.

Hale, Charles R. *Más Que un Indio: Racial Ambivalence and Neoliberal Multiculturalism in Guatemala*. School for American Research, 2007.
Hayden, Cori. *When Nature Goes Public: The Making and Unmaking of Bio-Prospecting in Mexico*. Princeton UP, 2003.
Hirsch, Eric, and Marilyn Strathern, editors. *Transactions and Creations: Property Debates and the Stimulus of Melanesia*. Berghahn Books, 2004.
Husted, Bryan W. "The Impact of National Culture on Software Piracy." *Journal of Business Ethics*, vol. 26, no. 3, 2000, pp. 197–211.
Interiano, Elder. "Guatemala y Costa Rica, con más piratería en Centroamérica." *Crónica*, May 3, 2016.
Kirsch, Stuart. "Property Limits: Debates on the Body, Nature, and Culture." *Transactions and Creations: Property Debates and the Stimulus of Melanesia*, edited by Eric Hirsch and Marilyn Strathern, Berghahn Books, 2004, pp. 21–39.
Larios, Roxana. "Pantalones de lona lideran la piratería." *Siglo 21*, January 17, 2011.
Leo Burnett Guatemala. "Piracy." *Ad Forum*, 2009, www.adforum.com/creative-work/ad/player/34448534/piracy/fompic-a-cinemas. Accessed March 5, 2018.
Lippert, Owen. *Competitive Strategies for the Protection of Intellectual Property*. Fraser Institute, 1999.
Marroquín, Jennifer. "Leve baja en piratería." *Siglo 21*, May 11, 2010.
Menocal, Carlos. "Guatemala es paraíso de la falsificación." *Prensa Libre*, August 7, 2005.
Morgan, George, and Kalervo Gulson. "Indigenous People and Urbanization." *Environment and Planning A.*, vol. 42, no. 2, 2010, pp. 265–267.
Nelson, Diane M. *A Finger in the Wound: Body Politics in Quincentennial Guatemala*. U of California P, 1999.
Nelson, Diane M. *Reckoning: The Ends of War in Guatemala*. Duke UP, 2009.
Nill, Alexander, and Clifford Shultz. "The Scourge of Global Counterfeiting." *Business Horizons*, vol. 39, no. 6, 1996, pp. 37–42.
Offit, Thomas. "Cacique for a Neoliberal Age: A Maya Retail Empire in the Streets of Guatemala City." *Securing the City: Neoliberalism, Space, and Insecurity in Postwar Guatemala*, edited by Kevin Lewis O'Neill and Kedron Thomas, Duke UP, 2011, pp. 67–82.
O'Neill, Kevin Lewis. *Secure the Soul: Christian Piety and Gang Prevention in Guatemala*. U of California P, 2015.
Otzoy, Irma. "Maya Clothing and Identity." *Maya Cultural Activism in Guatemala*, edited by Edward F. Fischer and R. McKenna Brown, U of Texas P, 1996, pp. 141–155.
Pasquino, Pasquale. "Criminology: The Birth of a Special Knowledge." *The Foucault Effect: Studies in Governmentality*, edited by Graham Burchell, Colin Gordon, and Peter Miller, U of Chicago P, 1991, pp. 235–250.
Patzán, José Manuel. "Piratería causa graves pérdidas." *Prensa Libre*, December 27, 2014.
Povinelli, Elizabeth A. *The Cunning of Recognition: Indigenous Alterities and the Making of Australian Multiculturalism*. Duke UP, 2002.
*Prensa Libre*. "Guatemala deja de percibir US$48 miliones anuales por piratería." April 26, 2011.
*Prensa Libre*. "Los Zetas dedicados a piratería intelectual en México y Centroamérica." January 13, 2011.
Ramírez, Guillermo Isaí. "Aumenta piratería en el país." *Prensa Libre*, December 10, 2015.
Sieder, Rachel. "Renegotiating 'Law and Order': Judicial Reform and Citizen Responses in Post-War Guatemala." *Democratization*, vol. 10, no. 4, 2003, pp. 137–160.
Taussig, Michael. *Mimesis and Alterity: A Particular History of the Senses*. Routledge, 1993.

Thomas, Kedron. *Regulating Style: Intellectual Property Law and the Business of Fashion in Guatemala*. U of California P, 2016.

Thomas, Kedron, and Rebecca B. Galemba. "Illegal Anthropology: An Introduction." *PoLAR: Political and Legal Anthropology Review*, vol. 36, no. 2, 2013, pp. 211–215.

Treverton, Gregory, Carl Matthies, Karla Cunningham, Jeremiah Goulka, Greg Ridgeway, and Anny Wong. *Film Piracy, Organized Crime, and Terrorism*. RAND Corporation, 2009.

United States Trade Representative (USTR). *Special 301 Report*, 2017, ustr.gov/sites/default/files/301/2017%20Special%20301%20Report%20FINAL.PDF. Accessed March 5, 2018.

Vann, Elizabeth F. "The Limits of Authenticity in Vietnamese Consumer Markets." *American Anthropologist*, vol. 108, no. 2, 2006, pp. 286–296.

Véliz, Rodrigo J., and Kevin Lewis O'Neill. "Privatization of Public Space: The Displacement of Street Vendors in Guatemala City." *Securing the City: Neoliberalism, Space, and Insecurity in Postwar Guatemala*, edited by Kevin Lewis O'Neill and Kedron Thomas, Duke UP, 2011, pp. 83–101.

Warren, Kay B. *Indigenous Movements and Their Critics: Pan-Maya Activism in Guatemala*. Princeton UP, 1998.

# 3

# PIRACY AND/AS LEGITIMATE BUSINESS

*Phillip Penix-Tadsen*

While piracy is frequently characterized as a criminal practice operating contrary to the interests of so-called legitimate business, the relationship between the two is significantly more complex. In the context of digital media, "piracy" is a term often used to describe the unlicensed reproduction and sale of intellectual property (IP), but this basic definition fails to encompass the complexity of the various practices included within this umbrella term. Indeed, the relationship between piracy and legitimate business is manifold and multilateral—the software industry has nurtured piracy in spite of itself, while on the other hand, software modifiers have benefitted the industry enormously despite being dismissed as amateurs, hackers, or pirates. Although the relationship between piracy and legitimate business is sometimes considered parasitic, it is more accurately characterized as symbiotic, mutually benefitting the major players of the software industry and local programming communities alike.

Using examples related to video game software and hardware from throughout Latin America, this chapter explores several theorizations of the relationship between piracy and legitimate business that help to shed light on the paradoxical effects of their interdependent relationship, which can prove beneficial even for the neoliberal media conglomerates that frequently police piracy by taking a protectionist stance toward intellectual property rights (IPRs). Today, video games hold a prominent place among the myriad media technologies being copied, modified and distributed worldwide through both commercial and non-commercial networks, and the cases examined below clearly demonstrate that conventional conceptualizations of piracy are insufficient for understanding how cultural products such as electronic games circulate globally in the twenty-first century. By way of a series of six claims or provocations grounded in theoretical and material examples from Latin America, this chapter shows how legitimate business benefits from piracy, and how piracy can be a legitimate business.

## 1. Access to Digital Technology Is a Basic Requirement for Participation in Twenty-First-Century Culture, and Piracy Democratizes Access to Global Information Society

The capacity to participate in global economies and information flows is defined in large part by access to technological networks, and therefore networked practices of information sharing are to be expected. Jonathan Paul Marshall et al. have argued that "the construction of 'culture' has always depended on people being able to borrow, steal, exchange or elaborate previously existing stories, tropes, characters, themes, images, styles, pieces of music and so on," and therefore "it should not be surprising that millions of people ('file-sharers' or 'pirates') act as if their right to participate in 'cultural conversations' overrides the restrictive 'legal rights' of corporate copyright holders or the 'moral rights' of artists" (177). Put another way, participation in contemporary global society means access to the "space of flows" and "timeless time" (Castells 375) of technological and computational networks. And for many cultural producers across the globe today, the creation of their works would be impossible without the use of materials that were originally created and developed by other individuals and entities. In his analysis of video game history in Venezuela, Thomas H. Apperley builds on the work of Néstor García Canclini and Jesús Martín Barbero to argue that

> access to information through media and other cultural channels (such as libraries, museums, etc.) is a right of citizenship because it is crucial for individuals to have access to information in order to make informed decisions, and thus act autonomously and creatively.

Apperley's perspective is particularly useful due to the way it "shifts discussion of media piracy away from one of *absolute criminality* toward its potency to provide access to networks," highlighting the fact that "skills and literacies" must be understood "in a manner that includes access to technologies that allow citizens to *consume, remix*, and *create* content" ("Venezuela" 621, original emphasis). It is these "skills and literacies" that piracy so frequently makes available to segments of the population who might otherwise be excluded from full participation in information society.

The forms of media that have most rapidly gained traction in the twenty-first century have been essentially networked, self-reflexive and interactive in nature, dependent upon recreating, recycling, remixing, and reimagining prior media as part of their development process. Many forms of digital media require the participation of an active navigator and manipulator to unlock their meaning, making such media fundamentally interactive, activated in a different way each time and by each user. Tracing a history of media technologies from four-track tape machines in the 1970s to video formats of the 1980s and 1990s to computer hardware and mobile phones, Lars Eckstein and Anja Schwarz explain that pirated media allow users "not only to consume, but crucially also to produce, share and reproduce media in an infrastructure that is more often than not informal and volatile" (2), and that "cultures of piracy" worldwide "have performed as crucial sites in which various ways of being modern have been negotiated and acted out" (18). Therefore, full participation in network society and contemporary media culture requires a basic level of access to information, media, and the tools used to create and navigate contemporary cultural products.

This is where the democratizing role of piracy comes in: when digital media are duplicated and made available for free or at a reduced price, this expands the potential audience for these media, allowing an ever-greater number of people to access and participate in contemporary network society. In other words, as Lawrence Liang has argued, "informal infrastructure, built through piracy, enables the entry into the information and knowledge economy of a large number of 'entrepreneurs' from developing and underdeveloped countries" (57), almost all of whom would be excluded from participation in these economic developments without piracy. In many areas, piracy is not only an aspect of video game play, but rather a practice that establishes the very possibility for play (Apperley, "Venezuela" 620). In areas beyond the reach of major multinational game corporations, there is simply no choice other than to use pirated software and hardware, leading to a high level of innovation and amateur apprenticeship in the engineering and modification of media technologies.

A prime early example of the democratizing role of piracy in Latin America is the Telematch game console, an upgraded version of Ralph Baer's Magnavox Odyssey console that was developed, manufactured, and marketed by Argentine company Panoramic in the mid-1970s. Housed in its own handy hard-plastic carrying case, the Telematch console included five built-in games (*Submarino, Frontón, Volley, Tenis,* and *Fútbol*), four of which were identical to those on the original Odyssey console. The fifth game, *Fútbol,* was created by Panoramic, who had also included additional buttons on the controller to enable the inclusion of this game, which they saw as essential to the Argentine game market (Frasca). While the Magnavox Odyssey was not officially marketed in Argentina, the Telematch gave the platform unforeseen prominence and sustained popularity among local audiences, allowing otherwise excluded users to access this particular type of digital media technology. Often, "cloned" or pirated consoles are in fact improvements on the originals that provide increased accessibility and usability. This can be seen with the Telematch as well as with the Famicom console, marketed in the English-speaking world as the Nintendo Entertainment System (NES), and upgraded by Argentine hardware developer Electrolab, whose regionally popular Family Game console allowed early-1990s South American gamers to play on cartridges with either a 60-pin Japanese connection or a 72-pin American connection. The innovations of these "pirated" consoles show that they are in fact the products of talented engineers who used their own creative visions to make significant improvements upon the original technologies on which their creations were based.

When the corporations and conglomerates that control major segments of the global media industries crack down on piracy, their focus on the "bottom line" of profitability can blind them to the many benefits of widespread access to media technologies. This has led many such companies to shun regions where piracy is prevalent, creating a catch-22 for local media producers and consumers—as Peruvian game developer and journalist Luis Wong explains, players "don't buy original videogames in stores because they are too expensive," while "companies don't offer better deals because of the piracy" ("Feeling Blue"). In the case of video-game technologies, since the very first arcade cabinets and game consoles hit global markets in the late 1970s and early 1980s, local consumer demand for technologies quickly spurred innovative amateur engineers to produce their own local versions of globally dominant gaming technologies. Thus, as scholarship on gaming in Brazil and Venezuela has demonstrated, piracy is frequently "a direct consequence of the factors that stand in between the consumer and the content" (Portnow et al. 76), constituting a tactical response to global inequalities (Apperley, *Gaming Rhythms* 15) that enables greater participation by those most marginalized within information society. Far from being "global" from the start, contemporary digital culture has spread simultaneously but unevenly in different regions, countries, and areas, requiring grassroots development of technologies in order to offer local users access to networks of global significance.

Other cases from around Latin America demonstrate precisely how pirated software and hardware have expanded access to global media, enabling media consumers to gain the skills and literacies necessary to become media creators. As Humberto Cervera and Jacinto Quesnel note in their research on the history of gaming in Mexico, as early as 1973, Mexican engineer Morris Behar had developed a home gaming console, the NESA-Pong, based on Atari's PONG console, which had been released just a year before (349). In Argentina, where high tariffs on technological products markets push game hardware and software beyond the grasp of the average consumer, the factor defining which game console has been the leader of each successive generation has been precisely the number and distribution of *pirated* games available, leading to the dominance of home platforms including Sony's PlayStation and Microsoft's Xbox 360 (Esnaola Horacek et al. 53). And while the *Street Fighter* and *Tekken* series dominate sales in the binary fighting genre worldwide, Japanese developer SNK's *The King of Fighters* (1994) has maintained a high level of popularity since its original release largely due to its availability on "illegal emulation-enabled arcade machines," expanding access in a way that has helped make fighting games arguably "the national video game genre of Mexico" and contributed to the careers of successful Mexican competitors in worldwide eSports (professional competitive gaming) tournaments, and events such as Evolution Championship (EVO) (Cervera and Quesnel 348). These cases demonstrate once again how access to pirated hardware and software can provide the basic skills and literacy necessary for otherwise marginalized individuals and groups to participate more fully in contemporary information society, even while frequently adding to the bottom lines of multinational gaming corporations.

## 2. Piracy, Copyright, and IP Are Culturally Contingent Concepts

Far from being a universal or objective value, the concept of IP differs from medium to medium and context to context. What clearly represents copyright infringement from one perspective may be the only logical choice from another. This is why Liang argues that piracy creates "a representational problem in the contemporary discourse on law, public goods, and creativity" due to its definition as "*an impure* transgression, tainted by commerce"—unlike hacktivism, social media movements, or net art, piracy "fits neither a narrative of resistance nor normative critique, nor does piracy seem to fit received models of creativity or innovation" (63, original emphasis). Definitions of what constitutes impurity and transgression, of course, differ depending on sociocultural context. What represents piracy for one person may be the only point of access to network society for another.

Different national and regional perspectives can also have a profound impact on legal and popular definitions of piracy. In his essay "Copyright, Piracy and Software," Jon Crowcroft notes that there are four times more "illegal" copies than "legal" copies of operating systems like Microsoft Windows and application packages like Microsoft Office running in China, due in part to the fact that Chinese perspectives on software have been defined by the "business culture" in a country that only recently joined the World Trade Organization (WTO), which has led to the common view that copying software is not infringement (225). An example from the world of Latin American gaming is the above-mentioned Family Game console, an early 1990s Argentine NES clone whose hardware and software cost about half the price of the official Nintendo products—this lower price of entry led players who owned the NES to seek out adapters allowing them to play the "knockoff" Family Games, and made the Family Game so popular at the time that it accounted for an estimated 95 percent of console sales in Argentina (Esnaola Horacek et al. 51). Like other gamers across Latin America, Argentine players have long been accustomed to a lack of official-market game hardware and software, and thus pirated versions of these media products are the norm rather than the exception, meaning that players never think twice before buying an "unofficial" copy of a game or game console. In this and other ways, cultural perspectives can define the way the populations of entire countries or regions look at questions of IP.

While all Latin American countries are members of the WTO, cultural differences in perspective still produce significant differences in the interpretation and enforcement of copyright laws across different countries in the region. For example, in *Copyfight: The Global Politics of Digital Copyright Reform*, Blayne Haggart explains that Mexico's path toward implementation of international IP standards via the country's Ley Federal del Derecho del Autor in 1997 demonstrates a clear difference in perspective regarding piracy vis-à-vis the dominant view promoted by the United States. Haggart cites the ways that the implementation of multinational Internet treaties can be complicated not only by domestic policies and political resistance (201), but also by Mexico's contradictory official self-image, through which the government promotes itself as both "a cultural superpower that benefits from strong international copyright protection," and also a country whose "developing-country status" provides an incentive not to enforce those strong laws too enthusiastically (224). Indeed, while sales of pirated software in Latin America sometimes take place on sidewalk stands run by vendors who see themselves required to pack up and run whenever the authorities draw near, in other locales the sale of pirated media is openly accepted. In marketplaces like Lima, Peru's Polvos Azules, unlicensed games, movies, and television series are sold by organized vendors in well-lit booths where users can sample games before purchasing, while other merchants located nearby focus on repairing consoles and modifying their firmware (Wong, "Feeling Blue"). This explains why in many countries in Latin America and elsewhere, in rural and urban settings alike, it is more common to find pirated copies of digital media than it is to find originals.

From China to Argentina, Peru and Mexico, and indeed the world over, views and laws related to piracy, copyright, and IP are profoundly impacted by cultural perspectives that vary widely from context to context. Not only do these differences affect legislation related to these concepts, but perhaps more importantly, they define what practices are acceptable and most suitable for generating day-to-day access to informational technologies and therefore to global network society. While there are plenty of good reasons for owners of IP, copyrights, and patents to protect their claims, there is no shortage of evidence of the benefits and logic for expanding access to these same products, in correspondence with the norms of the cultural contexts in which they circulate.

## 3. Definitions of Software Piracy Are Often Vague, Overly Inclusive, and Fail to Distinguish It from Other Software Development Conventions and Practices

Although legislators and the general public may produce judgments about the potential pros and cons of piracy, the definitions they use to define these practices are frequently imprecise and wrought with contradictions. Copying may be allowed in certain circumstances, result from user confusion or access difficulties, or "be culturally acceptable even if it is infringement," and even while some individuals make a living selling copies of others' IP, evidence shows that on a global level, "downright piracy"—defined as "the act of selling unauthorized copies for profit, as opposed to individual copying"—remains relatively rare (Crowcroft 209–210). While this may seem surprising given the dominance of unlicensed software in some regions, for example, this frequently depends less upon black market sales and more on the free sharing of software among online and offline user communities. Indeed, many practices that are frequently grouped with piracy are in fact accepted conventions of computer programming that benefit software development, especially in locales lacking significant higher educational and/or industrial infrastructure for software development. These include practices like software modification, reverse engineering, file sharing and peer-to-peer (P2P) networks, black market and gray market software sales, software reuse and redesign, freeware/open-source software (F/OSS), copyleft, hacktivism, and electronic civil disobedience. Such practices are fundamental to the operations of computer engineers and software programmers worldwide, adding to the skills and literacies that will enable them to establish creative practices with the potential to impact global digital culture.

Tools such as these are enabling independent producers to create new forms of open-access and participatory media. Gabriela E. Coleman's research traces the work of grassroots Independent Media Center (IMC) activists who "make and disseminate locally generated media using various web applications and tools" such as those mentioned above, with key examples including the Direct Action Network and the 1999 Seattle protests against the WTO, as well as the Mexican organizations Ya Basta! and the Zapatista National Liberation Army (193). The practices of independent media organizations such as these are helping to redefine the ways we understand authorship, ownership and IP. In *Piracy: The Intellectual Property Wars from Gutenberg to Gates*, Adrian Johns argues that the push for open-source software, which can be edited and manipulated by users worldwide, corresponds to a potential "reformation of creative rights, responsibilities and privileges" in response to "a crisis in intellectual property" (517). According to Johns, such a reformed view "could rest on quite different distinctions from that between literary and mechanical fields which has obtained for centuries as fundamental to what we call intellectual property," and "could embrace a more radical form of reticulation, recognizing multiple categories—genetic, digital, algorithmic, inscribed, and more—rather than a binomial pair" (517).

Throughout Latin America, communities of *modders*, or software and game modifiers, are putting these theories into practice by using open-source game software to create their own unique versions of globally popular games. A paradigmatic example is *MVP Caribe*, a full-conversion mod of the EA Sports title *MVP Baseball 2005* produced by Venezuelan, Dominican, and Mexican modders who swapped out the US-based major league team names, rosters, and uniforms for those of 28 teams from the Caribbean leagues, as well as creating new simulations of 30 regional stadiums and custom in-game commentary. Video-game mods like this are examples of the types of products being developed by today's *prosumer* audiences using technological platforms created by others, further testimony to the importance of technological access to full participation in contemporary network society.

Given the uniqueness of interactive digital media in particular, there is a need to differentiate between practices related to software—whose existence depends upon a capacity to build upon and network with other forms of media—and earlier types of media, along with their related ways of conceptualizing authorship and property rights. If piracy cannot be effectively distinguished from other acts and processes that are essential to software development, we need definitions that are more precise and conceptually sound, and that can allow us to see creative production in a way that accounts for the unique qualities of the contemporary media landscape.

## 4. IP Law Is Founded on Antiquated Concepts That Are Insufficient for Dealing with Interactive Digital Media

The definition and legal status of IP in the United States and much of the world stems from a melding of the scientific patent system and literary concepts of authorship, both of which are insufficient for approaching multimedia products produced by groups rather than individuals, such as most computer software. The software industry has defined its official stance on piracy by concentrating on policing and minimizing unauthorized use of software—for example, by supporting legislation such as the Anti-Counterfeiting Trade Agreement (ACTA) of 2011—but at the same time the industry ultimately reaps enormous benefits from the extra-official practices of software modification, duplication, and piracy, as further outlined below. For a number of significant reasons, our concepts of IP are out-of-date and incapable of dealing with the current landscape of digital media.

To begin with, digital software, applications, websites, and online communities frequently overlap with and borrow from one another in terms of operations, interfaces, aesthetics, functions, and protocols that cannot be attributed to any single author. To put it another way, digital media is made up of pieces and parts of other digital media, all of which corresponds to a lengthy tradition of practices that are collective in nature. This is why concepts of infringement applicable to other works may not be transferrable to digital media. The distinctions are multiple and produce diverse effects, as Crowcroft explains:

> Most of these differences in characteristics are quantitative, and can be captured in the idea that software has transient value, and is always evolving to improve based on past use, and to meet new needs of old and new users. This impermanence means software is almost always a "work-in-progress," rather than a finished product. The process of that progress may be more important (in terms of creativity, invested effort and value, worth protecting) than any particular "snapshot" of the software at any particular moment. Against this background, novel approaches to ownership and enforcement have emerged, such as open source, as well as copyleft. These have been accompanied by novel business models for recovering costs and making money from the generation of software goods and services. (209)

Recent critiques have argued that even the types of "novel approaches" mentioned by Crowcroft—such as open-source software—are aligned with the interests of neoliberal capitalism in spite of their promise to free knowledge from economic and political concerns. (Tkacz) And although US and global jurisprudence have begun to take steps toward greater protections for works that add or modify content of the original works on which they are based, progress has been slow and uneven overall. Therefore, it is essential that IP legislation be reformulated and updated to account for the fundamental differences in the creative process and industry standards relevant to the production of computer software and digital media.

There are many good reasons to allow for the reuse and free circulation of information in the realm of software engineering, motivations that simply do not exist in the same way for other forms of intellectual and creative production. For example, there is a general consensus in the world of software development that says that the algorithmic core of software, like a mathematical expression, is not the type of intellectual creation that can or should be protected in the conventional manner, since copyrights

> will not protect the core innovation (an algorithm) if it is of such widespread use, and yet there are so many potentially useful algorithms, that the entire creation of useful software would be hopelessly deadlocked if the core building blocks were tied up in such protection. (Crowcroft 218)

This has led to a generally positive view of reuse within the software-development community, since newly developed software almost always builds upon software developed in the past.

Likewise, using others' work to enhance one's own is an essential and productive element of software development, one that cannot and should not be avoided, but rather embraced in a way that recognizes its unique value. Many conventional ways of understanding "borrowing," "sampling," or even "plagiarizing" others' work simply do not apply to the practices of software development. For example, reverse engineering is extremely common in the software world, meaning that a motivated and knowledgeable software programmer could easily find a way to circumvent IP legislation without breaking the law. For Crowcroft, academic definitions of plagiarism offer a useful analogy, since a "clear distinction is made between quotation of work with accreditation, and unattributed use of material," and also because innovation in software production "would proceed more rapidly if one could refine and extend other works (with attribution, and without restriction)" (225–226).

Video-game development would not exist in Latin America if stricter IP and copyright laws had been more restrictive and rigorously enforced throughout the region, especially in the 1980s and 1990s, since pirates, hackers, and modders were responsible for both the development of some of the region's earliest games and the establishment of a body of work and collective experience that laid the groundwork for today's booming regional game industries. In Peru, where the first copyright law was passed in 1995 and has since been only loosely enforced, the most frequently cited game-industry pioneers are the collective known as Twin Eagles Group, or TEG. A loosely associated group of young computing and gaming enthusiasts, TEG began "cracking" games through reverse engineering, then copying, modifying and distributing them to local players, at times through "copy parties" where participants brought their own five-inch floppy disks to copy the group's most recently hacked and modded games (Marisca 22). Many of TEG's games were local adaptations of international titles, including *Fútbol Peruano 97*, a mod of Konami's *International Superstar Soccer; Samba de oruga*, a semi-pornographic *Tetris* mod that the group released as a fundraising effort; and *Gunbee F-99*, a vertical shooter that was an exact copy of a Super Nintendo title to which TEG had added a final, Peruvian-themed level in their port to the Commodore Amiga. The latter game became the first ever to be exported from Peru for sale on US and European markets, when German publisher APC & TCP picked it up in 1998 (Wong, "Mr Byte"). As the respective academic and journalistic work of Eduardo Marisca and Luis Wong shows, it was TEG's free-wheeling approach to disassembling, appropriating, and repurposing the already-existing products of the global game industry that laid the groundwork for the eventual development of a professionalized and sustainable game industry in Peru.

In the case of software and electronic media, the foundational concepts underlying IP legislation can sometimes serve to stymy rather than enhance creative production, due to the reasons cited above. If groups of amateur hackers, modders, and pioneers like TEG had been held back by overly restrictive legislation and overzealous enforcement of IP protections, they could not have gained the shared experience in computer programming and software development that they gained when cracking, copying, and redesigning games that had originally been published by others. This is why, if we wish to serve the interests of those who produce and use computer software and electronic media, we should think of IP in a way that allows for works in progress, reusability, and reverse engineering to flourish as productive practices, seeking definitions that enhance, rather than restrict, creativity.

## 5. The Software Industry Nurtures Piracy

We usually think of the software industry fighting piracy through efforts such as the legislation mentioned above, aimed at restricting distribution and access to their proprietary goods. However, these same efforts can just as often promote piracy, for reasons that are manifold. As I have outlined in my work on video games in Latin America (Penix-Tadsen 48–51), the causes and motivations for software modification, copying, and piracy include high consumer costs for entertainment technologies due to importation taxes that frequently drive the prices of official-market software beyond the reach of the average consumer, more widespread availability of pirated software and hardware, and a historical lack of official presence in the Latin American market for many major game software and hardware developers like Sony, Microsoft, and Nintendo.

In these ways, the overapplication of protectionist policies actually serves to undermine companies' efforts to control piracy, producing an adverse effect that leads to the propagation and expansion of piracy-related practices. When corporations are so protective of their intellectual assets as to prevent them from even being made officially available to many regions and markets throughout the world, they create a situation that leaves little alternative for consumers who wish to use the technologies: it's pirated goods, or nothing.

Piracy is the standard rather than the exception in many parts of the world. In Argentina, for example, Sony's PlayStation brand lacked an official presence until relatively recently, meaning that Argentine players had to either play pirated consoles and games or go without. They of course chose the former, and the relative ease of copying the PlayStation's CD-ROM-based game discs helped make the console one of the most popular in the country's history. Likewise, the rate at which a game was pirated could affect its popularity, for example making a popular 32-bit soccer game released in 1998 available more cheaply than outdated 16- and even 8-bit games (Esnaola Horacek et al. 52). This helped consolidate the PlayStation as the market leader in Argentina, likely contributing to the eventual success of the brand upon Sony's full entry into the market with the PlayStation 4, which was released in the Latin American region in 2014. So while a protectionist stance toward policing IP may be the norm for the game and software industries' major players, exclusionary business practices can create a void, one that is often quickly filled with pirated goods. In this way, even in spite of itself, the software industry nurtures piracy.

## 6. The Software Industry Benefits from Piracy

As a final provocation regarding the relationship between piracy and so-called legitimate business, it is important to recognize that, contrary to conventional wisdom, the software industry benefits handsomely from piracy. Far from putting publishers out of business, in fact, piracy can ultimately fatten their bottom lines. Though this may come as a surprise or seem difficult to comprehend, the software industry and other owners of IP benefit in myriad ways from piracy and its related practices.

Among the many ways piracy benefits the software industry, there is the ever-increasing value of user-produced content, which often adds to the prolonged shelf life of games that might otherwise be forgotten or set aside. Likewise, software modification can contribute to important processes like debugging, improvement, and product-testing, as in the case of technology giant IBM, which uses F/OSS "as a labor- and resource-saving measure" by hiring "a cadre of F/OSS developers to work in-house on F/OSS software" in "a hybrid between volunteer self-directed labor and paid, directed forms of labor that significantly speed the pace of development for some F/OSS projects" (Coleman 192). And amateur programming communities frequently serve as a stand-in for the nurturing support of higher-education programs in computer programming, governmental sponsorship, and major national software industries in regions where these entities are not present. Additionally, as noted in the above-mentioned anecdotes related to the Sony PlayStation's presence in Argentina, piracy can build brand loyalty among future consumers, who frequently become customers of the very "legitimate" businesses whose pirated properties they had played for years.

And there are even more surprising and impactful ways that piracy can benefit the technological industries by pushing forth innovation—without piracy, some of our most frequently used technologies as we know them simply would not exist. As Marshall et al. note, Apple chief executive officer Steve Jobs was inspired to design the iPod hardware and iTunes software due to the popularity of Napster, the peer-to-peer network that was eventually disbanded due to piracy and violation of IPRs: Jobs' "groundbreaking content delivery device coupled with streaming music and TV subscription services created a new 'legitimate' informational order," one whose motivation "arose from the continual 'illegitimate' expansion of social and technological frontiers" (180–181). This is what leads Marshall et al. to rightly conclude that "the 'incidental' or 'unintentional' pirate is an inventor, innovator, inspirer and implementer of new techno-social platforms and circuits of exchange, while the industry largely fights rearguard actions" (199). Indeed, it is essential to recognize the ways piracy can drive technological innovation when the industry's efforts to control IP run counter to its own interests.

In their research on game history in Mexico, Cervera and Quesnel sum this point up succinctly, explaining that in their country, "piracy often works as a marketing device for companies, even though it does not help the market grow" in the short term, because it makes products available to a segment of the population that otherwise would not buy them, leading to "a deep sense of brand loyalty" that is likely to make these consumers into "legitimate customers for their brand" (351). These benefits, along with the others mentioned above, make it clear that piracy is not driving the software industry bankrupt, but rather it is preparing the ground for an ever-expanding market of consumers for the products of that very industry. Undoubtedly, then, piracy benefits the software industry as well as owners of IP in other spheres.

In conclusion, it is evident that piracy and legitimate business are inseparable, because piracy so frequently operates *as* and *to the benefit of* legitimate business, and vice versa. Corporate and governmental entities tend to pursue a protectionist approach to IP and copyright enforcement, driven by a belief that such persecution will eliminate unlicensed usage and add to their bottom lines. But their faith is misplaced, and their interests as well as the interests of cultural producers worldwide would be better served if they focused on loosening, rather than tightening, control over media products. By examining a variety of cases from the sphere of Latin American gaming, this chapter has outlined the reasons it is essential to advance our understanding of piracy in a way that leaves all its complexity and symbiosis intact. Understanding the relationship between piracy and legitimate business means recognizing that access to information is a basic requirement for participation in twenty-first-century culture, and that piracy democratizes access to global information society. It means taking into account that piracy, copyright, and IP are culturally contingent concepts, and recognizing when definitions of software piracy are overly vague or inclusive, or fail to comprehend its role in computer programming and software development. We must expand our view of IP because it has been overly reliant upon antiquated concepts that are insufficient for dealing with interactive digital media. And finally, to understand how piracy relates to legitimate industry, we must recognize that the software industry nurtures piracy through its own policies and practices, while the practices of so-called pirates benefit the software industry in myriad ways. The work of game developers from throughout Latin America examined in this chapter testifies to the deep-seated symbiosis that can bring together the interests of software pirates and industry giants, helping point the way to a more realistic and nuanced view of their complex and mutually beneficial relationship.

## Bibliography


Apperley, Thomas H. *Gaming Rhythms: Play and Counterplay from the Situated to the Global*. Institute of Network Cultures, 2009.

Apperley, Thomas H. "Venezuela." *Video Games Around the World*, edited by Mark J.P. Wolf, MIT Press, 2015, pp. 613–628.

Castells, Manuel. *The Rise of the Network Society*. Blackwell, 1996.

Cervera, Humberto, and Jacinto Quesnel. "Mexico." *Video Games Around the World*, edited by Mark J.P. Wolf, MIT Press, 2015. 345–357.

Coleman, E. Gabriela. *Coding Freedom: The Ethics and Aesthetics of Hacking*. Princeton UP, 2013.

Crowcroft, Jon. "Copyright, Piracy and Software." *Copyright and Piracy: An Interdisciplinary Critique*, edited by Lionel Bently, Jennifer Davis, and Jane C. Ginsburg, Cambridge UP, 2010, pp. 209–229.

Eckstein, Lars, and Anja Schwarz. *Postcolonial Piracy: Media Distribution and Cultural Production in the Global South*. Bloomsbury, 2014.

Esnaola Horacek, Graciela Alicia, Alejandro Ipaguirre, Guillermo Averbuj, and Maía LujánOulton. "Argentina." *Video Games Around the World*, edited by Mark J. P. Wolf, MIT Press, 2015, pp. 35–55.

Frasca, Gonzalo. "La primera consola de videojuegos cumple 40 años." *CNN en español*, September 1, 2012, http://cnnespanol.cnn.com/2012/09/01/la-primera-consola-de-videojuegos-cumple-40-anos. Accessed April 15, 2018.

Good, Owen. "Modders Keep MVP Baseball 2005 Alive with the World Baseball Classic." *Kotaku*, March 10, 2013, http://kotaku.com/5989832/modders-keep-mvp-baseball-2005-alive-with-the-world-baseball-classic. Accessed July 7, 2015.

Haggart, Blayne. *Copyfight: The Global Politics of Digital Copyright Reform*. U of Toronto P, 2014.

Johns, Adrian. *Piracy: The Intellectual Property Wars from Gutenberg to Gates*. U of Chicago P, 2009.

Liang, Lawrence. "Piracy, Creativity, and Infrastructure: Rethinking Access to Culture." *The Global Flow of Information: Legal, Social, and Cultural Perspectives*, edited by Ramesh Subramanian and Eddan Katz, New York UP, 2011, pp. 54–89.

Marisca, Eduardo. "Buscando un gamer: Reconstruyendo la historia del videojuego peruano." *Pozo de letras*, vol. 11, no. 11, 2013, pp. 17–30.

Marshall, Jonathan Paul, James Goodman, Didar Zowghi, and Francesca da Rimini. *Disorder and the Disinformation Society: The Social Dynamics of Information, Networks and Software*. Routledge, 2015.

Penix-Tadsen, Phillip. *Cultural Code: Video Games and Latin America*. MIT Press, 2016.

Portnow, James, Arthur Protasio, and Kate Donaldson. "Brazil: Tomorrow's Market." *Gaming Globally: Production, Play and Place*, edited by Nina B. Huntemann and Ben Aslinger. Palgrave Macmillan, 2013, pp. 75–78.

Tkacz, Nathaniel. "From Open Source to Open Government: A Critique of Open Politics." *Ephemera*, vol. 12, no. 4, 2012, p. 386.

Wong, Luis. "Feeling Blue." *Kill Screen*, May 8, 2011, https://killscreen.com/articles/feeling-blue. Accessed April 15, 2018,

Wong, Luis. "Mr Byte: The 'Gang' Leader of Gaming in Peru." *Polygon*, February 10, 2014, www.polygon.com/features/2014/2/10/5373586/mr-byte-indie-king-of-peru. Accessed July 14, 2014.

# 4

# PIRACY AS MEDIA PRACTICE

## The Informal Market of Music and Videos in Peru

*Santiago Alfaro Rotondo*

In Peru, as in other emergent economics, digital technologies expanded the market for physical piracy of music and films. At the beginning of the twenty-first century, information storage technologies such as the CD, VCD, DVD, and Blu-ray began spreading throughout markets, streets, and homes containing a variety of national and international content. The most popular genres are Hollywood films, Korean telenovelas, Indian musicals, animated films, videoclips of Peruvian cumbia or Andean music, and videos of comedians and traditional fiestas, among others. Their commercial success has made optical discs the second most popular item in Peruvians' consumption and cultural services baskets (INEI, "Encuesta Nacional"). Physical piracy, which involves objects rather than electronic downloading, is a central phenomenon in Peruvian cultural markets and public life.

This chapter analyzes the technological evolution of optical discs and the economic and cultural practices of physical piracy in Peru in order to understand their nature and impacts. Usually piracy is categorized and seen from the viewpoint of two intellectual property (IP) regimes: copyright and author's rights. Though each has its own particularities, both are systems that regulate artistic creativity and ensure the rights of authors and publishers of creative works, providing them with economic rewards and enticing them to continue creating.

When considered from this perspective, piracy is understood only in terms of its illegality, or as a practice based on the unauthorized reproduction, distribution, and sale of works protected by the author's rights or copyright. Within this framework, piracy is presumed to have negative consequences for both authors and society as a whole. The reasoning goes like this: piracy reduces the stimulus for the development of creativity and access to culture. For this reason, within legal frameworks, business circles, and judicial cases, piracy is often labeled a "crime of stealing," a "scourge," or a "loss," whereby some "informal" or "illegal" agents take away what rightfully belongs to other formal or legal agents.

Since the arrival of the aforementioned digital technologies, scholars and commentators have been critically reflecting on the IP regime and its understanding of piracy. As Manuel Castells and Gustavo Cardoso write, "Most of the literature has, until now, carried the mark of its origin in the law schools of the most prominent universities of the Western world" (827–828). This has led to a focus on the legal, criminal, and economic consequences of the exchange of digital content in the Global North.

The study of physical piracy in the countries of the Global South has received much less attention in the critical literature. However, there is a group of researchers who have approached piracy from an alternative viewpoint, identifying it as a set of practices located within specific sociocultural contexts and informal economies (Barrot; Castells and Cardoso; Eckstein and Schwarz; Iwabuchi; Karaganis; Kuotsu; Larkin; Lemos; Lobato; Lobato and Thomas; Mattelart, "Audiovisual Piracy," "The Changing Geographies"; Neves and Sarkar; Wang). These researchers use multidisciplinary approaches to analyze the social, cultural, economic, and political relations established through and around piracy, and they seek to avoid simply reproducing the principles and assumptions of the IP regime without checking them against reality. These studies also provide an account of the multiple relationships between formal and informal economies. Using this research as a point of departure, in what follows I will analyze music and visual piracy as a media practice. Here, practice should not be understood as a natural occurrence but rather "as a frame of reference to interrogate a complex reality" (Hobart). This approach allows us to consider the cultural interactions of piracy and media systems outside strict dichotomic categories of formality–informality or legality–illegality and without the constraints of assuming prescribed behavior, both of which are typical of studies influenced by IP regimes.

The chapter is divided into four parts. The first covers the evolution of the technologies that have accompanied the development of physical piracy in Peru. This account deals with the processes of market insertion of each one of the optical technologies involved and the corresponding expansion of piracy between 1999 and 2019. I posit that optical discs did not create but rather widened piracy markets, whose commercial life cycles are in decline due to increasing Internet access among Peruvians.

The second part focuses on the reach of piracy within cultural markets, based on the practices of both producers and consumers. I propose that piracy diversified the available supply of musical and audiovisual works and has served the needs of popular sectors, including those located in rural areas, i.e., those with the lowest levels of education and income. Optical discs have had a significant role in the development of a local and global "public culture" (Appadurai and Breckenridge) and "mediascapes" (Appadurai) in Peru.

The third part explores the economic dimension of piracy through the practices of its main agents. The practices identified destabilize descriptions of piracy as a homogenous economic sector, separate from the interests of creators and formal markets and limited to the reproduction and distribution of works protected by copyright. The fourth and final part of the chapter contrasts the previous three with the main arguments used to defend the IP regime.

The following analysis is based on piracy fieldwork done in 12 different Peruvian cities (Arequipa, Chiclayo, Cusco, Huamanga, Huancayo, Lima, Moyobamba, Iquitos, Trujillo, Puno, Piura, and Tacna), the studies I have conducted on Peruvian cultural industries since 2002, and the results of fieldwork conducted during the first semester of 2019. In this last period, I visited four piracy markets and interviewed 20 agents involved in this commerce, including authors, musicians, retailers, media businessmen, and public officers. In addition to this ethnographic material, I have also collected and organized some statistical information.

## The Technological Evolution: From CDs and DVDs to Netflix and YouTube

In 2000, due to the fall of the government of Alberto Fujimori (1990–2000), Peru received the new millennium with a political transition. At the same time, it also underwent a technological one. Up until that moment, the dominant formats in sound and audiovisual markets were the cassette (tape) and the Video Home System (VHS). Both had modified the relationship between producers and consumers by giving the latter more control over the content of media. They also diversified the profile of the agents involved in their commerce by reducing the entry barriers to market, due to their low cost. The tape had expanded during the 1980s, almost two decades after having been developed by Philips. The VHS, invented by Panasonic in 1976, entered Peruvian homes during the 1990s.

This new technological transition involving a change in formats, something common throughout the history of cultural industries, arrived with the increase in the importation of Compact Discs (CD) and Video Compact Discs (VCD); technologies created in 1982 by Sony and Philips, and in 1993 Sony, Philips, Matsushita, and JCV, respectively (Long and Schenk 551). The CD already had a presence in Peruvian markets since the 1990s. However, it mainly served a formal demand. It was only in 2000, with the massification of the importation of blank CDs, destined mostly to copying and piracy, that their presence tripled in relation to 1999. Only three years later, in 2003, the volume of imports became 40 times bigger than in 1999, going from 2.3 million units to 82 million (INDECOPI 14).

The VCD, on the other hand, arrived in Peru with an increase in imports from China, after this format was displaced in Chinese homes by the arrival of the DVD (Hancock et al.). Towards 2007, the Digital Versatile Disc (DVD), invented in 1995, begun to question the hegemony of VCD and soon thereafter, to take its place. In 2012 a new technology arrived in Peru: the Blu-ray disc, designed by

Sony, Philips and other companies in 2006. However, with a higher cost and no big technological advantages, the Blu-ray disc failed to displace the DVD and the latter reigns supreme in Peruvian piracy markets. The major threat to its dominance is now the sale of USB sticks with an average of 1,500 songs or hundreds of films, evidenced by the recent decline of optical discs and the new hegemony of download services on the Internet.

Throughout its trajectory, manifested in the transition from the CD to the USB, the piracy market was not created but rather just strengthened. Previously, the unauthorized reproduction of works in tape or VHS format had channeled most of the music and audiovisual demand, each with their own specificities. The tape was a channel for the circulation of all kinds of music genres, consumed by people belonging to the full spectrum of socioeconomic levels. It allowed many of these genres, not serviced by the formal music labels, to be known and marketed. Such was the case of New Age music or punk rock. In this sense, tape piracy did not simply substitute for another form of cultural offer but created its own, as it also happened in India, where it produced a "revolution" by widening the market for regional and local musical genres (Manuel).

The reach of VHS, on the other hand, was more restricted. It had wide home use to tape TV programs. Also, as analyzed by Tom O'Regan for the Australian case, the VHS had a "foundational" role for audiovisual distribution, both legal and illegal. However, in Peru its major impact was in the formal market. It did make easier the piracy of Hollywood productions but never at the levels seen after 2000. That is why the market for film rentals had a chance to develop, as happened with Blockbuster, a company that operated in Peru from 1995 to 2007.

The CD, VCD, and DVD increased piracy until they dominated all sound and audiovisual markets. There are not many official statistics and the few existing are not very consistent, as befits an informal market. However, according to the Superintendencia Nacional Tributaria (SUNAT, National Tax Bureau), the growth of imports peaked in 2004, reaching 140 million blank CD units and 11 million DVDs. By comparison, only 8.7 million CDs and 180 thousand DVDs were imported in 2000 (*La República*, "Importación"). In 1997, the commercial and unauthorized circulation of phonographic works was 80 percent of the market. Between 2005 and 2009 it reached a 98 percent share, placing Peru at almost the same level as Paraguay, the country with the highest level of piracy in Latin America (IIPA; INDECOPI).

According to the piracy sellers I consulted, the growth cycle begun its crisis in 2018. Several of them coincided that in 2019 they were selling about 30 percent of what they sold in the good years such as 2009. "This is dying," said one of them. In the most important Lima market, El Hueco, a number of stalls formerly devoted to selling pirate DVDs, now offer clothing or portable radios. The rental costs have also decreased, with one seller telling me that "they were as high as 1,000 dollars a month, now they are around 100 dollars." Moreover, while many of the sellers continue to deal in piracy, they no longer sell optical discs but offer download services from the Internet or USB sticks.

In the film-specialized commerce, the sales of Hollywood movies are showing the highest decrease. In the basement of the Polvos Azules market (located in Lima's historic center), some businesses have closed, although not to the same extent as in El Hueco. A retail seller in the Magdalena market corroborated this tendency. In his view, Netflix is the culprit. His clients have diminished since that streaming platform became popular. This is, however, not the case with sellers of auteur films in the famous aisle 18, in Polvos Azules. They also have seen a decrease in sales but not bigger than 20 percent. "I sell a different type of cinema. Netflix does not have Renoir, Ford, Kaurismaki. They don't have LGTBI or silent films either," he stated.

In the music market, YouTube is the platform most cited as competing with optical discs, both by piracy sellers and by formal businesspersons. According to Dolly Pereyra, former manager of Apurímac Productions, a small company producing legal CDs and videos of Andean music, "YouTube killed us." Her microbusiness shut down in 2018. "It hurt a lot to abandon music. I have recorded great artists such as Los campesinos," she said, reminiscing that she had started in the phonographic industry in 1998 "during the boom of the cassette [tape]," after having sold sweets and chocolates in the streets. She could compete with piracy, but not with digital streaming.

The access economy, as Jeremy Rifkin called it, has been felt in the business of optical discs and physical piracy. The availability of content via streaming, downloads, and social networks has revolutionized music commerce and has caused a new technological transition, as the VCD and DVD did before. The effects of this process were felt in Peru almost 20 years after they took place in Global North markets, when Naspster debuted, causing the first great dip in CD sales in 2002.

The cause of this transition resides in broader access to the Internet, as seen especially in the period between 2015 and 2018. During this time, the percentage of the Peruvian population that used the Web grew from 40.9 percent to 52.5 percent, i.e., a 11.6 percent, a percentage that was bigger than the growth of the accumulated previous six years. The main reason for this statistical jump is the increase of the degree of penetration of cell phones, itself generated by the vast expansion of sales of smart phones and the decrease in the cost of data plans. If in 2016, 56 percent of those who used the Internet did so using their cell phones, that number grew in 2018 to reach 80.2 percent (INEI, *Las Tecnologías*). Thus, it is more precisely the cell phone that is killing the DVD.

## Cultural Practices: As Global as Local

Despite the evidence that the circulation of content through the Internet has an impact on the levels of consumption of cultural goods, it is impossible to make predictions about the future of physical media. If history has shown us anything, it is that newer and older technologies tend to coexist. The lessons of the past, moreover, show that the consequences produced by technologies are complex and ambivalent. They resist simplifications and forms of technological determinism.

That is why approaching piracy only as a legal problem prevents us from understanding its true meanings and dimensions, one of which is cultural. The boom of optical units, through the twenty-year evolution just described, has had important implications for the media systems of music and audiovisual production. The main one is the diversification of the offer of sonic and audiovisual content. In 2000, neither the markets nor the homes of Peru had as many consumption options as they do today. The variety of content now covers a wide spectrum, with a global and local mainstream and subaltern reach.

Within this plurality, the relative weight of the taste and consumption patterns of popular sectors is high. Optical discs have satisfied the demand, for example of the segments coming from rural contexts, with less education and lower incomes. In the urban contexts, the number of Peruvians who accessed films through optical devices was slightly higher than those who did so through movie theaters and the Internet (Figure 4.1). However, when the comparison is done in the rural context, the differences grow exponentially: the consumption of films through optical devices is higher at 23 percent and 18.2 percent, respectively, than access to content through movie theaters and the Internet (INEI, "Encuesta Nationale").

The same situation obtains when consumption is measured by educational level and income. The proportion of Peruvians who declare having consumed films through optical devices, as compared to the other two modes of access, is much higher among those who have no formal education or just primary or secondary

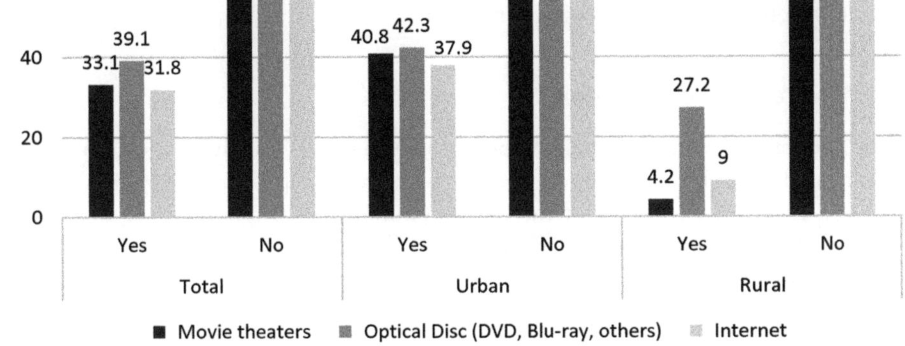


**FIGURE 4.1** Peru: percentages of access to films according to mode of access and geographical distribution, 2017

Source: Prepared by the author, based on data from INEI ("Encuesta National").

schooling, as it also is among those in the lower socioeconomic strata. In the latter case, for example, the percentage of people from the lower income segment who consumed films in 2017 through DVD or other optical discs is 23 percent higher than those who did so by going to a movie theater (INEI, "Encuesta Nationale").

Hollywood films are highest among the public's preferences and their presence is very evident, but given their circulation in the shadows of informal commerce it is difficult to pinpoint their numbers exactly. They can be found in all cities. Neither do we have statistics for the preferred genres, but those most seen in Peruvian movie theaters may be an indication: between 1998 and 2016, 92.6 percent of spectators attended films in English, almost all of them American (Tamayo and Natalie 104). According to a study by the Grupo Peixe, moviegoers prefer actions films (33 percent), science-fiction (26 percent), comedies (18 percent) or children's films (12 percent) (*La República*, "Los Peruanos").

Although in DVD pirate markets the numbers are not necessarily the same, at least from an ethnographic perspective, I have corroborated the preference for action films. In all my visits to markets, performed during the last 17 years, sellers and consumers have always highlighted the sales of this type of Hollywood film, even in rural areas. To give just one example: in a survey taken at the home of the president of the indigenous community of San Antonio, in the Amazonia region of Loreto, of the 51 DVDs checked, around 52 percent were Hollywood films such as *Transformers* or *Green Zone*.

In addition to Hollywood films, piracy markets often showcase another dominant type of international content: children's films. *Peppa Pig, Masha and the Bear, Tom and Jerry*, and *SpongeBob* are very common titles in the pirate markets. Every DVD stall always has a children's section. Children-oriented TV productions circulate widely through piracy networks in video format. Obviously, the same happens with similarly oriented Hollywood films, such as *Mohana, Frozen*, or *Zootopia*. There is also a sizable supply of children's songs, used during the celebration of birthdays and in everyday life.

## *"Subaltern" Globalization*

Important too within the international offer, along with Hollywood films and animated series for children, are Korean music and soap operas, as well as Bollywood films, two products of the Asian cultural industries leading the new subaltern flows of globalization (Thussu 21).

Korean soap operas begun their popularity in Peru with the broadcasting of "Un deseo en las estrellas" by a public television station in 2002, as a result of an agreement sponsored by the Korean government (Lock). Almost at the same time, Korean-pop or K-pop begun to be consumed through *peer-to-peer* (P2P) systems. According to its fans, in 2014 "Villa K-pop," the first community of Microsoft Social Network (MSN) devoted to the genre, was created. The rest of the so-called Korean wave were next: the fan clubs, the stores specialized in K-pop merchandising, the concerts, the practice of K-pop choreographies in public spaces, the Korean food restaurants, and the fanchants (fans meeting to sing). Today, Korean culture produces youth communities all across Peru.

Optical discs have had a leading role in this process. They accompanied and complemented the soap-opera offer and created a market for K-pop, a genre that is not covered by radio or television. Even the most fanatical consumers, willing to spend their savings in products imported from Korea, buy piracy goods, due to their more affordable prices. During an interview in 2017, a 20-year-old woman explained it thus: "Buying original albums you spend more money. As they are very expensive and one loves more than one group, you can't buy only originals."[1]

In the case of Bollywood, optical discs resulted in the formation of a second generation of publics interested in their consumption. The first generation emerged during the 1970s and 1980s by attending movie theaters. The newer publics, unlike the previous ones, developed a participatory culture (Jenkins et al.). This is the reason why along with the purchase of Bollywood songs and films came the creation of virtual (first on MSN, then on Facebook) and presence-based communities (fan clubs, dancing associations). Petra Hirzer, around 2014, calculated that in Peru there were approximately a hundred very well-known associations in cities such as Lima, Arequipa, and Trujillo. These associations were formed by young people between the ages of 15 and 25 and were devoted to their own way of interpreting Bollywood culture (Hirzer).

Optical discs gave all of these publics an opportunity to repeatedly watch the films and the choreographies, going beyond "addictive consumption" (Stigler and Becker) and into a form of consumption based on active performance. In one study on the performance of Bollywood among Lima-based youth, Carlos Ponce found the repetition of a behavioral pattern: mimesis. Its practitioners tend to collect albums (around 30) and watch them repeatedly at home, imitating the actors and dancers. It is the case of Rita, the administrator of the group "Show Indian Dance," who tells how her love for the genre began: "I began watching the films first, which I loved … I danced at home. A dance here, another one there [she laughs] … I would see the film and start dancing right there" (Ponce 162).

According to Arjun Appadurai, "The central problem of global interactions today is the tension between cultural homogenization and heterogenization," which demands to be thought beyond the terms of center-periphery opposition in order to be understood, rather, as part of the configuration of "imagined worlds" or *scapes*, defined by their irregularity and fluidity (Appadurai 46). From this perspective, optical discs can be seen as "zones of cultural debate" defined by mutual cannibalizations between national and transnational processes (Appadurai and Breckenridge 5).

## *The Expansion of Local Markets: From the People ... to the People*

Optical media piracy has also been a channel for local cultural production by decentering the abilities to create and consume sounds and images. Through the DVD and the CD, subaltern individuals and communities have been able to represent themselves and access multiple forms of self-representation through cinema and music, along with comedy videos and traditional celebrations.

Alberto Alarcón Torres, "El Ñato de Paucaray," is a good example. He was born in Santiago de Paucaray, in the Sucre province in Ayacucho. At the age of 10 he migrated to Lima. After recording with several musicians and helping them as musical director of Discos Puquio, he decided to become a "producer." During the 1990s he recorded and sold tapes in the streets of Historic Downtown in Lima. In 2003, in the midst of the boom of the VCD, "I arrived to my own conclusion and saw that in order to be a great producer, I needed to make videos." That is why he created the production company "Del pueblo ... para el pueblo" (From the People ... to the People).

In order to start his business, he hired two cousins with filming and editing expertise and proposed Naranjita de Sucre—at the time the best-known "harp and violin" artist, a musical genre in rural Ayacucho communities—to do a production for her. The results were explosive: "Everybody wanted to listen and see. In two years, I sold something like 50,000 albums." As in the case of any successful product, Naranjita de Sucre's productions circulated widely through piracy networks. The process expanded the popularity of the 'harp and violin' genre, a traditional form circumscribed until then to its historic area of influence in the Andean Center and South of the country.

The same has happened with many *fiestas*, dance dramas and traditional rituals. The boom of optical discs has expanded their recording and diffusion. In some cases, the recordings are paid for by the organizers of the activities, so-called *mayordomos*. They document the event and then circulate the video among attendees. This practice is standard even among Peruvians residing abroad. In their places of residence, the videos are copied among relatives and neighbors, "even though often the first screening is organized in the home of the celebration's sponsor" (Berg 374). The families around the TV set watch the video, talk about the *fiesta*, and identify the people they see. These videos have a long life "thanks to the interest of United States-based Peruvian migrants in reproducing their relationship with their places of origin" (Berg 375).

## Economic Practices: Beyond Reproduction

Regardless of the contents, how are pirated discs made? From the point of view of the IP regime, piracy encompasses three types of practices: reproduction, distribution, and sale of works not authorized by the authors. The case of the Peruvian market shows that this is a reductionist approach to the phenomenon for two reasons. The first is that it does not recognize the existence of production activities. Nor does it take into account the interactions that authors, composers, artists, and businesspersons in the formal market may have with piracy. The latter is perceived as an activity that "steals" the creation of others to put it in the hands of consumers. As in any business, however, between creation and consumption there lies a value chain in which piracy practices intervene in unexpected ways.

## *The* Matriceros

The most important division of functions among piracy traders is the one separating *matriceros* (matrix makers) from distributors. The former have a role with much more scope than the latter. While distributors only reproduce content and sell optical or USB drives, makers compile sound or audiovisual content. They are the ones who record songs, movies, and/or television programs and organize them under a single title. For example, "The 3 Giants of Hindu Music," "Southern Queens," "Funny Drawings Collection," "The Most Played Music from Ayacucho," "The Best Movies of Sicarios," "Peruvian [movies] of the Moment 2020," or "Danceable Huaynos."

In addition to compiling the contents and recording a matrix (hence their name), *matriceros* hire designers to make the covers of the discs and print them. Then they sell the matrix and the prints to distributors, who bring both parts together and sell them in their stands. Each matrix costs two dollars. The main source of income is in the covers, which are more difficult to reproduce. If distributors wanted to save money on a given product, they would need to photocopy hundreds or thousands. That is why, even though the profit margin by unit is reduced, they prefer to buy them directly from the *matriceros.*

While the illegal nature of the activity might lead one to believe the contrary, the *matriceros* do not do this work anonymously. Rather, they design logos and place them in their compilations, which are known as "collections." Some even put their own names along with the logos. That is the case of David Rojas, from Rojas Productions. However, most of them use impersonal brands such as Fire Productions, The Best, Rey Music Productions, or R-Rolo.

Along with the logo and the title, the covers carry images that represent the contents, such as portraits of the artists, film frames, photos of traditional festivals, or symbols such as women and cars (very common in the aesthetics of reggaeton). The images are downloaded from the Internet. In consultation with the designer, each *matricero* chooses them on a case-by-case basis. The goal is to catch the eye and motivate a purchase. That is why oftentimes, in an effort to show that the content is new, they use future years as timeframes for the compilations: 2020, 2022, 2050, and even 3000.

This futurism is a symptom of the disc-production regime. Currently, in the middle of a period of commercial crisis, the collections are released every two to three weeks. In the past, however, each *matricero* created two or three new products per week. Productivity is high and competition intense. At the same time, the markets are wide and multifaceted. Each collection covers generational, regional, and artistic demands. In that sense, the diversity in which it participates explains the dynamism and the number of titles offered.

Another factor, even more decisive in explaining both the production regime and the very nature of piracy, is the sale of spaces in music collections and comic videos. Authors, national artists, and artistic producers pay for their works to appear on the lists in MP3 or MP4. Those who are lesser known do it to gain visibility. The best known, to put new versions or creations in the market. Rates are different for appearing on the cover, but in general the cost is 30 dollars per song. Recently released songs are called "exclusive" (*primicias*) and are usually featured on the cover. In fact, "exclusive" releases are the main attraction of each collection, or the novelty that catches the eyes and/or the ear.

Katy Jara, a well-known *cumbia sureña* singer and TV presenter, usually hires the services of the *matricero*. According to her, "There are no formal producers here. We are all independent. I invest in piracy because I reach more people. It doesn't generate losses for me, it helps me." Every time she makes and films a new song, she calls one of her contacts to put it into a collection and circulate it through piracy networks. In addition, she records albums to give them away at concerts and places the songs on platforms like Spotify and YouTube, as well as on social networks like Facebook and Instagram. She also registers the works (if they are her own) through the Peruvian Association of Authors and Composers (APDAYC) because "then I charge royalties for their use in media or live shows." In other words, she places her works in every single possible location to reach consumers and make money.

Her case is no exception. During my fieldwork, I found several authors who do the same. They all agree on the fact that piracy is a way of reaching consumers that cannot be avoided. To ignore it is to risk not being "well known." In contrast to the official discourse on IP, they do not see any contradiction in offering their works to pirates. Thanks to piracy, they can reach a wider audience and, later, receive more royalties for their reproduction on radio and, especially, concerts.

## *Film and Piracy: The Exception to the Rule*

The case of cinema is different. Piracy is not functional to the interests of any of the filmmakers of Peru, normally classified as *limeños* (whose work is similar to that of the international mainstream) or regional (born outside the capital, many of them with productions similar to those of Nollywood). All of them constantly criticize piracy, and regional filmmakers in particular. They often denounce practices of pirate merchants such as presenting works in "collections" with modified covers, fake titles, or even alterations in the content. Oscar Gonzales, a filmmaker from Puno (at the border with Bolivia), says that in 2010 his film *Marcados por el destino* (*Marked by Destiny*) was split in two by pirates and converted to VCD: "first part, second part, to make money." When it happened, he saw with "sadness, and also with joy, how people huddled [in the markets] and bought [it]." Sadness, because he did not receive benefits from that success. In fact, although the discs sold very well, the film left him in "bankruptcy" (Bustamante and Luna Victoria 366–367).

One of the few filmmakers who recognized that piracy played in their favor is Daniel Nuñez de Huancayo. His first film, produced by an evangelical company (Adonai Films), was a melodrama called *Madre* (*Mother*) (2009). It tells the story of an abusive son and his mother. It was very successful. It is one of the omnipresent works in piracy markets. The evangelical population stimulated demand. In the churches "an offering was requested to watch the movie," says Nuñez (Bustamante and Luna Victoria 263). It also circulated in Bolivia and Ecuador. In 2014, I found it in the latter along with other local works under the title "Ecuadorian and Peruvian Dramas." Without a doubt, although there are no figures, it must be one of the most viewed films in the history of Peruvian cinema. Although in poor quality, it can be seen complete on YouTube. In July 2019 it had more than 1.3 million reproductions, a figure that is rarely achieved by national works released in movie theaters.

According to "Carmen,"[2] a *matricera*, one of the producers of the work gave it to her "for dissemination." She copied it without expecting much but it was quickly in high demand, so she earned "a lot of money." The director has not publicly acknowledged having been the one who promoted its pirate reproduction but he did accept that when making the sequel, *Madre 2* (*Mother 2*), the fame of the last version made a lot of people want to see her in the screenings organized by Adonai Films (Bustamante and Luna Victoria 265). Whether or not any of those responsible for the work wanted it pirated, the truth is that there is no more evidence of this type of practice, unlike what happens in Ecuador, where filmmakers of the same profile usually leave their matrices in piracy networks and pay for reproductions and cover design (Alvear and León).

In the Lima film circuit there are no indications of interactions with the piracy market either. Creators and producers question it and there is a formal offer of films that competes with unauthorized reproduction. Nevertheless, there are exceptions. There are more than a few documentary filmmakers and directors who have left their films at the Polvos Azules market to have them circulate. Many of them are foreigners and well known, such as Emir Kusturica. His documentary about Maradona is now sold there with the director's signature on the cover. The practice, likewise, is only common among auteur cinema directors, who are concerned about the dissemination of their work. In contrast to massive music, commercial cinema has not chosen to use piracy to spread its works.

## Understanding Piracy

Based on this, how could we characterize music and video piracy? Two features define it: heterogeneity and ambiguity. The first feature characterizes contents, publics, and effects. When it comes to content, heterogeneity is expressed in the wide variety of markets in which it participates: cinema, music, dance, comedy, traditional culture. In addition, piracy is not only an informal distribution system for local expressions. It also channels the demand for transnational content from the three major regions of global cultural geopolitics: the European Union, the United States and Asia, with a clear emphasis on the last two.

Studies have shown that the diffusion of multidirectional flows is a widespread pattern in piracy, which can therefore be qualified not just as a channel for "globalization from below" but also for "globalization from above" (Mattelart, "The Changing Geographies"). In Afghanistan, in addition to serving as a Bollywood movie distribution infrastructure, it also facilitated the expansion of Hollywood dominance. This is what happened at the beginning of the new millennium with the fever generated by *Titanic* in open resistance to the Taliban government's prohibitions (Klinger).

Heterogeneity also includes audiences. According to INEI statistics, those who consume movies through optical devices are distributed in similar proportions within each socioeconomic level. The same is not true among those who consume movies through movie theaters and the Internet (see Table 4.1). In both cases the weight of people belonging to the socioeconomic level A is greater, while that of those classified in level E is lower (INEI, "Encuesta National"). To give a contrast: 42 percent of the people in level E acknowledged having acquired films on optical discs (although this was not asked, presumably they were illegal, since practically all of them are), while only 29.9 percent of the same level indicated having done the same through the Internet.

**TABLE 4.1** Peru: modes of accessing films according to socioeconomic level

| *Socioeconomic level* | *Movie theaters (%)* | *Optical disc (DVD, Blu-ray, others) (%)* | *Internet (%)* |
|---|---|---|---|
| Total | 33.1 | 39.1 | 31.8 |
| A | 55.4 | 38.4 | 46.4 |
| B | 46.8 | 40.6 | 41.6 |
| C | 41.7 | 43.4 | 38.1 |
| D | 37.8 | 43.8 | 36.6 |
| E | 27.6 | 42.9 | 29.9 |
| F | 4.2 | 27.2 | 9.0 |

Source: INEI ("Encuesta Nacional").

Finally, the effects of piracy can be defined as heterogeneous because they are not the same in each of the cultural markets in which it participates. In music, according to the perception of many performers, the pirate record market has contributed to the dissemination of their songs. Among filmmakers, on the other hand, a negative balance prevails because the merchants either alter their works or profit from them without generating greater benefits for their creators. Musicians are less critical because optical discs serve as advertising vehicles for their concert-focused business model. Filmmakers, on the other hand, do not have complementary ways of increasing their incomes.

On the other hand, it is not easy to evaluate the nature and social benefits of piracy. From a conventional IP point of view, piracy is part of an informal and illegal sector of the economy. In practice, borders are more porous. When an author, as happens in music and cinema, voluntarily offers his or her work for reproduction, the status of "unauthorized" is lost. Similarly, there are actors who carry out both formal and informal activities. So-called "productions companies," for example, usually provide music video-recording services to music groups and declare their income with the tax collector. Then they deliver their recordings to the *matriceros* to be reproduced. They are formal and, at the same time, informal; they use legal means for some activities but not for others.

If we evaluate piracy as an economic sector, beyond the behavior of its actors, borders are not clear either. According to the newspaper *El Comercio*, the transnational company LG, listed as the leader in its field, increased its sales of optical unit players (DVD, CD) in 2005 by 42 percent compared to 2004, reaching 9.3 million dollars. Keeping in mind that in the same year the official calculations estimated the level of phonographic piracy at 98 percent, how could we separate the demand for pirated optical discs from the formal and legal trade of the devices that reproduce them? Local piracy, in other words, generated large profits for transnational technology equipment companies.

Something similar happens with regards to the offer of content. Optical discs contributed to developing a demand that has later been exploited by the media from formal economies. Zee Mundo, a pay-TV channel specializing in Bollywood series and films and a subsidiary of Zee Entertaiment Enterprices (one of the largest media groups in India), began operations in Peru in 2017, more than ten years after thousands of young people imitated the choreographies of Shahrukh Khan through pirate DVDs. The same happened with K-pop. Before the first concert of a band of the genre in Lima, held in 2011, thousands of teenagers learned to sing in Korean watching videos on optical discs. Miller et al. call these types of cases "cultures of anticipation". According to them, based on Hollywood's experience, piracy makes films familiar among viewers who had not been previously reached by legal copies. In places where market failures occur due to the absence of movie theaters or high prices, the unauthorized reproduction of content shapes the taste of the most marginalized audiences and develops a demand that can be legally exploited, without the need for investment in advertising.

## *Ambivalence: The Nature and Consequences of Piracy*

The "cultures of anticipation" not only evidence the porous borders between the formal and the informal, the legal and the illegal. They also illustrate the ambivalent effects of piracy. On the one hand, they hinder the development of business based on copyright. On the other, they can make them sustainable, inasmuch as they motivate the public to expand their cultural capital (Bourdieu; Stigler and Becker).

From this point of view, regardless of the fact that it constitutes an informal activity at the economic level and an illegal one in juridical terms, piracy has an impact on the culture and economy of formal markets. Both economies, formal and informal, can share the same universe of consumers and are interdependent. In that sense, piracy would be functional to some formal businesses through a word-of-mouth or network effect: royalties that are not obtained through a certain type of commerce (the sale of music) boost income through others (concerts or consumption in movie theaters). Assessing the consequences of piracy only as "losses" neglects this whole process and the existing evidence.

In music, for example, the Association of Authors and Composers of Peru (Asociación Peruana de Autores y Compositores, APDAYC) registered a growth of 334.1 percent in its royalty collection between 2004 and 2012, going from 3.7 to 16.3 million dollars. In 2017, the number was 20.5 million dollars (Mogollón). Therefore, during the same period when the import of optical discs and piracy had a significant increase, the income of the Peruvian association that manages copyright increased (Figure 4.2).

The growth is so great that it could not be explained only by the improvement of the collection capabilities of the institution. It corresponds to an expansion in

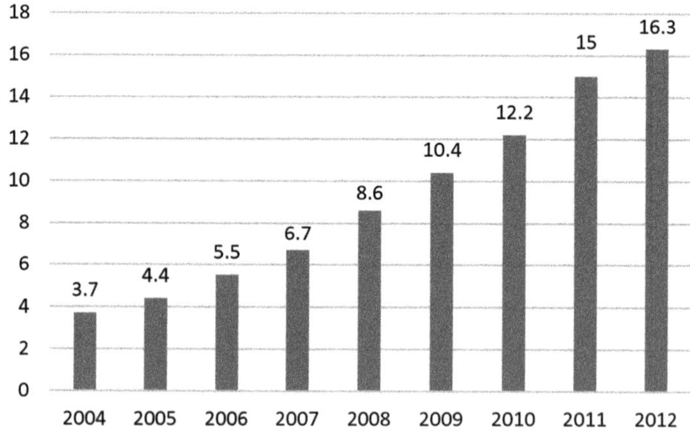


**FIGURE 4.2** Peru: income from APDAYC revenues 2004–2012
Source: Prepared by the author, based on data from APDAYC.

music consumption that accounts for 65.7 percent of total earnings in 2012. The collection of royalties for the exploitation of phonograms decreased but revenues for live music increased. Identifying the specific weight that piracy had in this process goes beyond the scope of this study. However, we should admit that the annual purchase of millions of optical devices cannot be neglected or evaluated as a minus for the music business, as the state and the transnational multimedia conglomerates usually do.

The same can be said in relation to the film market. Between 1998 and 2017, attendance at movie theaters had an increase of almost 600 percent, from 6.8 million to 51.7 million viewers (Tamayo and Nathalie 103). If we take into account the importance that Hollywood has in the consumption of optical discs, piracy could not be separated from this expansion, although there are other factors that explain it, such as the multiplication of shopping centers throughout Peru, which is where the majority of multiplexes screening US films are located. Although not in the same proportion in all market segments, home film consumption and that which takes place in movie theaters are not mutually exclusive: the same consumption habits can develop through both.

Following the same criteria, copyright principles may be called into question. According to one of them, artists only innovate and earn income when they have the right to exploit their works exclusively. From the first copyright norm, the Statute of Anne (1709–1710), IP laws are justified by the ability they would have to foster new creations. However, in markets that are not fully governed by copyright, such as the one analyzed here, every year new productions and artists appear in greater numbers. Piracy has not "destroyed" the music industry or the audiovisual industry, although it has transformed them.

Rather than hindering innovation and revenue for artists or authors, piracy prevents the accumulation of capital by some business models, reduces incentives for the production of high-quality goods (recordings and packaging), expands the informalization of markets, and disperses economic benefits. The latter can contribute to democratizing revenues but also places limits on the size of companies and their expansion, which are important conditions for internationalization.

## Piracy as an Economic Problem

Consequently, the ambivalence of piracy demands that we take into account variables other than those commonly used to identify its effects on employment, GDP, and social benefits. It also demands that we understand its nature and the fight against it from another perspective. As Joe Karaganis indicates, piracy exists where high prices of cultural goods and services combine with low-income consumers and low-cost digital technologies (i). Pricing is key to understanding it. Piracy, in that sense, is an economic problem, rather than a moral or legal one.

Our focus, therefore, should not be on strengthening laws and sanctions or on the dissemination of information on legal products, as none of these strategies have been successful. Rather, we should focus on the economy. In the absence of companies capable of adapting to technological changes to transform their business model and to make the prices of legal products more competitive, the business will continue to be controlled by pirates.

Taking a cue from the Social Science Research Council, I suggest focusing on local companies. Unlike global ones, "they are more likely to leverage the fall in production and distribution costs to expand markets beyond high-income segments of the population" (Karaganis ii).

## Conclusion

For the past 20 years, between 1999 and 2019, optical-device piracy has been one of the main means to produce, distribute, and consume a wide diversity of cultural expressions in Peru. Due to the greater presence of the Internet and increased access to cell phones, this type of piracy has begun to decline, though it is still too early to predict its total disappearance. The ongoing digital divide and limited access to streaming platforms such as Netflix and YouTube could leave an open space in the Peruvian market for piracy.

However, even if optical discs survive the migration to Internet commerce, as has been happening in Mexico (Alvarado), their significance will likely decline. This will not mean the end of piracy but its transformation. As predicted by Vivencio Ballano, nanotechnology and quantum technology could bolster digital media piracy through greater storage capacity, flexibility, anonymity, and access to artificial intelligence to infringe copyright (Ballano 244). We see the beginning of this trend in the Peruvian piracy market, where many merchants have begun selling online-content download services rather than physical discs.

Throughout human history, piracy has always accompanied the development of cultural and creative industries. Its presence will continue to be important, especially in economies as marked by inequality as Peru's, so it is essential that we understand pirate practices if we want to rethink laws and policies and find a balance that benefits both authors and consumers, thereby promoting prosperous and diverse formal markets.

This chapter seeks to contribute to this task by addressing piracy as a media practice and testing the assumptions of the IP regime. The boom of the optical disc market in Peru shows that physical piracy has spurred on the transformation of the music and audiovisual production business rather than dismantling it. Piracy networks have channeled broader access to more diverse content at both the local and global levels. They have also met the demand of popular sectors, including those in rural or poor areas with limited access to education and wealth. In the process, the optical discs have participated in various cultural practices and generated economic activities that challenge conventional understandings of piracy as an illegal and homogeneous system that only serves to work against the interest of creators.

Therefore, any evaluation of piracy is inevitably ambivalent, as the practice has both positive and negative consequences in the formal market. In fact, piracy is so linked to formal markets that it can hardly be described as only an underground or parallel activity. Its presence in the economy produces consumption habits and production activities that erase the boundaries between informal and formal, legal and illegal. Multiple actors, including authors and dominant companies, use piracy to reach consumers and generate income through other channels for the economic exploitation of culture. Its nature, therefore, must be reconsidered.

Piracy is primarily an economic problem linked to pricing. Rather than continuing to invest resources in moralistic campaigns, confiscations, or legal processes that have so far had no impact, the state should support the development of business models that may compete with piracy networks through affordable prices and timely release of new content. In their 2019 survey of more than a thousand people in New Zealand, the company Vocus found that when content is available at a fair price, people choose to pay for it rather than pirating it (Keall). The expansion of the frontiers of formality and legality, then, depends on innovation and the development of business models adjusted to the needs of the public. New conceptions of piracy and its function in culture and the economy will come through social policies and legal frameworks that balance the rights of authors and citizens, not by way of moral education, the criminalization of consumers, or law-enforcement policies.

## Notes

1 These testimonies were gathered as part of the author's research on the consumption of Korean music. The material was presented at the ALAS academic conference in 2017 in Montevideo.
2 The name is fictitious. She did not consent to publish her real name.

## Bibliography


Alvarado, Enrique. "Ni siquiera Netflix puede contra el imperio de la piratería en México." *Vice México*, February 21, 2019.

Alvear, Miguel, and Christian Leon. *Ecuador bajo tierra: Videografías en circulación paralela.* Fundación Cultural Ochoymedio, 2009.

Appadurai, Arjun. *La modernidad desbordada. Dimensiones culturales de la globalización.* Ediciones Trilce/Fondo de Cultura Económica, 2001.

Appadurai, Arjun, and Carol Breckenridge. "Public Modernity in India." *Consuming Modernity: Public Culture in a South Asian World*, edited by Arjun Appadurai and Carol Breckenridge, U of Minnesota P, 1995, pp. 1–22.

Asociación Peruana de Autores y Compositores (APDAYC). *APDAYC: Memoria 2012.* Asociación Peruana de Autores y Compositores, 2013.

Ballano, Vivencio. *Sociological Perspectives on Media Piracy in the Philippines and Vietnam.* Springer, 2016.

Barrot, Pierre. *Nollywood: The Video Phenomenon in Nigeria.* Indiana UP, 2009.

Berg, Ulla. "Videoculturas itinerantes: Visualidad y performance en el espacio diaspórico peruano." *Imaginación visual y cultura en el Perú*, edited by Gisela Cánepa, Fondo Editorial de la Pontificia Universidad Católica del Perú, 2011, pp. 359–382.

Bourdieu, Pierre. *La distinción: bases sociales del gusto*. Taurus, 2012.

Bustamante, Emilio, and Jaime Luna Victoria. *Miradas múltiples: el cine regional peruano*. Universidad de Lima, 2017.

Castells, Manuel, and Gustavo Cardoso. "Piracy Cultures: Editorial Introduction." *International Journal of Communication*, vol. 6, 2012, pp. 826–833.

El Comercio. "El mercado formal de CD's da la pelea." *El Comercio*, April 10, 2012.

Eckstein, Lars, and Anja Schwarz, editors. *Postcolonial Piracy: Media Distribution and Cultural Production in the Global South*. Bloomsbury, 2014.

Hancock, David, David Scott, and Steve Cobett. *Cinema and Home Entertainment in China*. Screen Digest/Nielsen Company, 2007.

Hirzer, Petra. "Peru in Love with SRK." *SRK and Global Bollywood*, edited by Elke Mader, Rajinder Dudrah, and Bernhard Fuchs, Oxford UP, 2015, pp. 182–199.

Hobart, Mark. "What Do We Mean by 'Media Practices'" *Theorising Media and Practice*, edited by John Postill and Brigit Bräuchler, Berghahn, 2010, pp. 55–75.

Instituto de Defensa del Consumidor y la Propiedad Intelectual (INDECOPI). *La industria fonográfica y la piratería en el mercado peruano (1999–2003)*. INDECOPI, 2004.

Instituto Nacional de Estadística e Informática (INEI). "Encuesta Nacional de Programas Estratégicos 2017" [Database]. Unpublished data, 2018.

Instituto Nacional de Estadística e Informática (INEI). *Las Tecnologías de Información y Comunicación en los Hogares: January–March*. Instituto Nacional de Estadística e Informática, 2019.

International Intellectual Property Alliance (IIPA). *Perú: 2010 Special 301 Report on Copyright Protection and Enforcement*, 2010, www.iipa.com/rbc/2010/2010SPEC301PERU.pdf. Accessed April 26, 2019.

Iwabuchi, Koichi, editor. *Feeling Asian Modernities: Transnational Consumption of Japanese TV Dramas*. Screen Digest/Nielsen Company, 2004.

Jenkins, Henry, Sam Ford, and Joshua Green. *Cultura transmedia. La creación de contenido y valor en una cultura en red*. Gedisa, 2015.

Karaganis, Joe, editor. *Piratería de medios en las economías emergentes*. Social Science Research Council, 2012.

Keall, Chris. "Netflix Is Killing Piracy in NZ: Study." *NZ Herald*, February 26, 2019, www.nzherald.co.nz/business/news/article.cfm?c_id=3&objectid=12207351. Accessed May 13, 2019.

Klinger, Barbara. 2010. "Contraband Cinema: Piracy, Titanic, and Central Asia." *Cinema Journal*, vol. 2, no. 49, 2010, pp. 106–124.

Kuotsu, Neikolie. "Architectures of Pirate Film Cultures: Encounters with Korean Wave in 'Northeast' India." *Inter-Asia Cultural Studies*, vol. 14, no. 4, 2013, pp. 579–599.

*La República*. "Importación de los CD y DVD pagará IGV adelantado." November 1, 2005.

*La República*. "Los peruanos son los más cinéfilos de América Latina." August 1, 2019.

Larkin, Brian. "Nigerian Video: The Infrastructure of Piracy." *Politique africaine*, vol. 100, 2005, pp. 146–164.

Lemos, Rolando, and Oana Castro. *O Tecnobrega de Belém do Pará e os modelos de negócio abertos*. Open Business Model, 2007.

Lobato, Ramon. "Creative Industries and Informal Economies: Lessons from Nollywood." *International Journal of Cultural Studies*, vol. 13, 2010, p. 337.

Lobato, Ramon, and Julian Thomas. *The Informal Media Economy*. Polity Press, 2015.

Lock, Fátima. *La adaptación del lenguaje gráfico del manga Hana Yori Dango al lenguaje audiovisual del drama coreano Boys Over Flowers*. Tesis de licenciatura. Pontificia Universidad Catóica del Perú, 2014.

Long, Beng, and Sonja Schenk. *The Digital Filmmaking Handbook*. Cengage Learning, 2006.

Manuel, Peter. "Popular Music as Popular Expression in North India and the Bhojpuri Region, from Cassette Culture to VCD Culture." *South Asian Popular Culture*, vol. 10, no. 3, 2012, pp. 223–236.

Matellart, Tristan. "Audiovisual Piracy, Informal Economy, and Cultural Globalization." *International Journal of Communication*, vol. 6, 2012, pp. 735–750.

Matellart, Tristan. "The Changing Geographies of Pirate Transnational Audiovisual Flows." *International Journal of Communication*, vol. 10, 2016, pp. 3503–3521.

Miller, Toby, Nitin Govil, John McMurria, and Richard Maxwell. *El nuevo Hollywood: del imperialismo cultural a las leyes del marketing*. Gedisa, 2005.

Mogollón, Stanis. *Memoria 2018: Memorias del presidente*. Asociación Peruana de Autores y Compositores, http://www.apdayc.org.pe:81/memoria2018.pdf. Accessed May 22, 2019.

Neves, Joshua, and Bashkar Sarkar. *Asian Video Cultures: In the Penumbra of the Global*. Duke UP, 2017.

O'Regan, Tom. "Remembering Video: Reflections on the First Explosion of Informal Video Markets through the VCR." *TV and New Media*, vol. 13, no. 5, 2012, pp. 383–398.

Ponce, Carlos. *Recepción y Performance de Bollywood en Lima: los casos de "Show Indian Dance" y "Bollywood Perú"*. Tesis de licenciatura. Pontificia Universidad Católica del Perú, 2017.

Rifkin, Jeremy. *La era del acceso: La revolución de la nueva economía*. Paidos, 2000.

Stigler, George, and Gary Becker. "De gustibus non est disputandum." *American Economic Review*, vol. 67, no. 2, 1977, pp. 76–90.

Tamayo, Augusto, and Hendrickx Nathalie. *Financiamiento, distribución y marketing del cine peruano*. Universidad de Lima, 2018.

Thussu, Daya Kisshan. *Media on the Move: Global Flow and Contra-Flow*. Routledge, 2007.

Wang, Shujen. *Framing Piracy: Globalization and Film Distribution in Greater China*. Rowman & Littlefield, 2003.

# 5

# CONTEXT AS CONTENT IN CHILEAN COMMUNITY MEDIA

*Jennifer Ashley*

"I just hope we won't have to give it back," Polo told me when I called to congratulate him. A few minutes earlier he had forwarded me the official notice from the National Council on Television (CNTV) that the community television, Señal 3 La Victoria, had received a license to transmit under the country's new digital television law. "What do you mean 'give it back'?" I asked incredulously, having watched him fight for this right for over a decade. "I don't know if we're going to be able to do it," he replied. He was uncharacteristically subdued. He reminded me that they still needed to secure the funds for a digital antenna and the rest of the technology required for the digital migration, as well as for additional content production.

Despite Polo's explanation, it continued to puzzle me that he greeted the news of the television license with more trepidation than excitement. While the challenge to find the funds for the technical conversion was daunting, it was not very different from the dozens of other infrastructure problems that I had watched them overcome. Station members' careful study of the digital television transition (as it was implemented in other countries as well as the proposals that had circulated in Chile) had prepared them for the very specific economic and technical obstacles they would face. When I returned to La Victoria a few months later, I began to think that Polo's deeper concerns were related to content production. As I heard him repeat to a representative from the National Council on Culture and the Arts, members of Señal 3 work all day in construction jobs and their participation in the station is unpaid. "We're supposed to transmit something like 12 hours a day," Polo told her. "We can't make one program and repeat it all day."

Although the possible ramifications of becoming a legal, licensed operator in Chile were always in the back of station members' minds, their attention all of these years had been placed on the political fight for access to the electromagnetic spectrum. Now that they had received the license, they were focused for the first time on how this transition from analog to digital and "informal" to "formal" might alter their production practices. As Polo commented in an interview with the online newspaper *El Ciudadano*, becoming "legal" in the eyes of the state implied a "change in perspective about what one was and what one is going to be, both in terms of content, and in development" (Menares). During the more than 20 years that Señal 3 had operated, they had regularly transmitted "pirated" material and used unauthorized copies of software to create their content. What role would these "pirate" practices have in this new era?

In this chapter, I explore piracy as a tool for creative production in the context of Chilean community media. My analysis draws from debates around appropriation and the genius in "unoriginal" production as they relate to the history of Chilean community media. Like their national television counterparts, this small station understood production as not only an act of filming original content, but also finding and disseminating interesting content from other producers. That is to say, they had become integral to the community through their reporting on neighborhood events, *and* their use of one cable subscription to transmit locally curated programming (such as soccer games, political documentaries, and the regional network TeleSur) to the entire low-income neighborhood. Drawing on long-term ethnographic research with community television producers in La Victoria, I argue for a theory of cultural production that considers a shift in context as a component of content creation. That is to say, I examine Señal 3's "pirate" practices as an example of how creative production can occur via acts of de- and re-contextualization.

## Chilean Community Television

During Chile's 17-year dictatorship (1973–1990), independent radio and video projects played an important role in opposition efforts by providing news on protest and human rights violations. Following the political transition, Chilean activists argued that the democratization of communications required a continued participation of civil society in the media (Bresnahan, "The Media" 40). In the early 1990s, radio became a particularly active site for this participation with the continuance of projects like Radio Umbral, which bridged the transition from dictatorship to democracy, and the emergence of new projects, such as Radio Tierra (established by the Corporación Feminista La Morada) and Radio Canela de Nos (linked to an environmental nongovernmental organization (NGO)) (Bresnahan, "Community Radio"; Poblete). In 1990, activists formed the National Organization of Popular Radio Stations, and soon after new stations appeared in several left-leaning low-income neighborhoods.

Chile's first community television station was established a few years later in the Población La Victoria, a neighborhood that was founded in 1957 through a land takeover organized by the socialist and communist parties. During the dictatorship, this neighborhood located in the southern periphery of Santiago became a center for resistance to the military regime. Following the return to democracy, residents of La Victoria, including Polo (Luis Lillo) and Cristián Valdivia, organized *pantallazos*, or public screenings of documentaries and other audiovisual material that had been censored during the dictatorship. In the early 1990s, they became associated with a National Network of Popular Video and participated in activities organized by NGOs with funding from Europe to support media democratization in Chile. Through one of these workshops, they accessed an analog television transmitter. Slowly they gained access to additional equipment, and by 1997 they had established a community television station, which would eventually be called "Señal 3 La Victoria."

From 1997–2017, Señal 3 transmitted without any kind of legal authorization. The station was what might be called an "open secret," meaning that the state was aware of its existence but unwilling to formally recognize it or close it down. Although they occasionally have a university student intern floating around the station, members of Señal 3 are, for the most part, self-taught. In different moments, they have received donations from like-minded organizations in Europe, allowing them access to computers and cameras. They have built the studio and control room with leftovers from various other construction projects, and they finance much of their everyday costs by asking for donations in the weekend fruit and vegetable markets, selling antennae, and organizing fish fries. In 2002, Señal 3 accessed a second transmitter through an activity organized by Chilean exiles living in Europe. In order to help develop a network of community television stations, they decided to lend this second transmitter for a period of six months to community organizations throughout the country, often traveling to help install it. Around 2006, when talk began of a digital transition, Señal 3 (along with Canal 3 Pichilemu) led a movement to advocate for the legal recognition of community television stations and their right to access a digital television license as a means of "democratizing" the electromagnetic spectrum (Ashley; Baeza).

After years of debate, the digital television law was finally promulgated in 2014. A few months later, the station received its first visit by a state official: the newly appointed president of the CNTV, Oscar Reyes. A journalist by profession, Reyes had told Polo and Cristián that he felt connected to La Victoria because he had been reporting in the neighborhood in September of 1984 when a stray bullet from Chile's military police killed French priest Andre Jarlán. In 2015 Reyes returned to Señal 3 to announce the first-ever production fund for community television stations. Since that announcement, Señal 3 has received funding from the CNTV once (for a series focusing on local musicians).

In March of 2017, applications opened for community television stations to apply for a digital license. The following January the CNTV announced that Señal 3, along with three other community television stations, would be given a license for 20 years.[1] The state then invited these stations to submit applications for funding to aid in digital migration. Señal 3 was awarded this funding of just over 34 million Chilean pesos to cover the cost of a digital antenna and transmitter.[2] In order to access this funding, however, they were required to submit a deposit for 1 percent of the funding, then 5 percent, and then 10 percent. The state would return a portion of these deposits over the next few years. The enormous amount of effort it took for the station to fundraise in order to secure these deposits left little time or energy for original content development. As Polo said in an interview with *La Raza Cósmica*, "Our first transmission will be bare bones" (Pacheco). The legal context had changed, but the socioeconomic context had not. Apart from the weekly news program and the one series for which they had received funding, station members were unsure of what other content they would be permitted to air once they began digital transmission, or how to reposition themselves as cultural producers in this new context.

## Cultural Production and the "Uncreative"

I link the uncertainty of Señal 3 members around production in this new "formal" era to the debates around the relation between originality and cultural production that have circulated for years in a variety of academic and artistic fields. Lévi-Strauss, for example, signals the importance of appropriation in cultural production in his description of the *bricoleur* as someone who creates by making do with "what is at hand" (17).[3] Although Lévi-Strauss opposes the *bricoleur* with the engineer (who builds from scratch), Derrida critiques this, arguing that, "the engineer is a myth … If one calls *bricolage* the necessity of borrowing one's concepts … it must be said that every discourse is *bricoleur*" (285). In Thomas's ethnography of brand "piracy" in the Guatemalan apparel industry, a similar sentiment is expressed by a young workshop owner/designer when he insists, "There is no original" (9). Instead, he suggests that creative production consists of identifying the elements of something that make it appealing and understanding how they might be recombined successfully. What works in one context may not work in another.

Arguments around the artistry of borrowings and recontextualization in literature, music, and art provide a potential starting point for thinking through Señal 3's relation to cultural production. Marjorie Perloff begins her exploration of the "genius" in appropriation by recounting the negative response by critics to T.S. Elliot's *The Wasteland* soon after its publication in 1922 as a result of its extensive citation. Despite this initial critique, Perloff reminds the reader that this becomes one of the poems for which Elliot is most celebrated (1–3). Perloff then references the extensive intertextual references of poets such as Pound, Zukofsky, Ashberry, Howe, and McCaffrey, before arriving to a discussion of writers (such as Kenneth Goldsmith) who have made a case for writing poetry that is completely "unoriginal" (12). That is to say, creating poems from texts that they did not write. Goldsmith expands on these ideas in *Uncreative Writing*, where he rescues "patchwriting" from its typically pejorative categorization (defining it instead as an art of "weaving together various shards of other people's words into a tonally cohesive whole"), as well as making a case for the art of retyping another's text (2). The genius, according to Goldsmith, "lies in knowing what to include and—more important—what to leave out" (10). Both Perloff and Goldsmith draw attention to how a shift in context—which might be related to time period, material form, or placement among other elements—impacts content in surprising and even moving ways.

In the music world, the practice of sampling and remix has highlighted the tension between the celebration and critique of appropriation.[4] For McLeod and DiCola, the "golden age" of hip-hop (1987–1992) occurred before copyright law was as developed as fully as it is now and artists were more freely experimenting with sampling. As music journalist Jeff Chang suggests, De La Soul

> had an aesthetic of taking everything and the kitchen sink and throwing it in a blender. So, you didn't just have George Clinton, the Meters and the usual funk stuff you would expect on a record. You'd have French language records. You'd have the Turtles. You'd have Led Zeppelin. You'd have Hall and Oates. (Qtd. in McLeod and DiCola 20–21)

For many, the work of artists like De La Soul created a new experience of media production, shifting attention to elements listeners might have missed in the original albums. Like the writers that Goldsmith describes who retype a text and become acutely aware of a hyphen or an unexpected phrase, the ear of the sampler is attuned to a micro segment: a beat, a word, an ambient sound. Attention provides a new context, allowing the same content to take on a different feel.

In recent work on "mashup cultures" (e.g., Sonvilla-Weiss), "remix studies" (e.g., Navas et al.), and alternative media, scholars have explored the politics of aesthetics embedded in these practices. Hamilton, for example, reminds us that Dadaists considered montage "an aesthetic and political principle that sought to undo established, professionalized hierarchies of media production" (160). Similarly, Duncombe points to how the cut-and-paste style of punk zines of the 1980s and 1990s deliberately critiqued professional design, opting instead for an "anti-style" (105). Building on this work, Mowbray argues for what he calls "heterodox-creative logics," emphasizing how aesthetic innovation occurs through these practices of de- and re-contextualization (27–29). That is to say, what works in one context may work in another, but will produce a different effect.

What is particularly useful about these debates in analyzing the case of Señal 3 is the ways in which they bring to the fore the potential for appropriation as a process of democratization. As McLeod and DiCola suggest, sampling can produce a kind of "leveling effect," allowing anyone to create media "even without formal training" (5). In using these practices of intertextuality—citation, patchwriting, sampling, and montage—media makers question monologism, encourage polyvocality, and place in conversation artists and works that would not be normally. In what follows, I explore these ideas within the particular sociohistorical context of Chile's democratic transition.

## Collective Authorship in the Democratization of Chilean Media

Hip-hop's "golden age" of sampling was occurring at the same time in which Chile was working towards a democratic transition. Chilean youth in one low-income neighborhood (who would later form the band *Panteras Negras* named after the Black Panthers in the United States) were listening to *Public Enemy* and experimenting with recording their music over beats from a Run-DMC tape (Jofré). Another group of youth were using the first hand-held video cameras (designed in other countries for home movies) to film protests throughout the country (Liñero 17–20). It was out of this context of questioning authoritarianism (and single authorship) that community television in Chile emerged. The project of community television was, in many ways, an effort to continue the kinds of media projects that had opposed the dictatorship. I draw attention here to two of these projects—the *Honorable Pirates* series and the NO Campaign of the 1988 plebiscite—in order to illustrate the role of appropriation and collective authorship in the process of media democratization in Chile.

In 1986, La Red de Prensa Popular (the Network of Popular Press) distributed the first of three volumes of *El Pirata Honrado* (*The Honorable Pirate*). Edited by the Chilean NGO ECO Comunicaciones, *The Honorable Pirate* series were collections of drawings by artists organized around themes such as gender, youth, human rights, education, and health. With their card stock covers and spiral binding, the aim of these volumes was to support the popular communication efforts leading up to and immediately following the democratic transition. The third volume (printed in 1990) opens with an acknowledgments page in which the editors thank the artists, institutions, and media sources that have "courteously agreed to be pirated." They end their editorial letter by saying: "Our reward is to see this Pirate navigating through all seas and borders, contributing to the democratization of communications and of the country" (3). They follow this with instructions for their use. These begin with the statement (in capital letters): "WITH THIS MATERIAL ANYTHING CAN BE DONE ... The only thing that shouldn't be done is to cut the drawings out so as not to lose the material definitively!" (7) The editors then provide three pages of practical suggestions on how to copy, enlarge, or reduce the drawings in the most economical and effective way, as well as how to adapt the drawings (by changing or adding text, removing details, and/or altering the background to fit the desired context). Following this introduction are 50 pages of drawings classified by theme, but without any reference to the artist or the original context from which they came.[5]

The *Honorable Pirate* project is at once simple in design and complex in its approach to ideas of authorship. By listing the authors at the beginning of the book, the editors acknowledge the artists' individual contribution to the collective work of creating a democratic commons. However, they make the decision to disassociate the artists with their individual pieces of work, and instead generate a work of pastiche. The content is no longer an individual drawing with an indexical relation to a particular artist, but rather a page of drawings related to human rights in which the work of artists such as René Figueroa, Guillo, and Hervi might find themselves side by side (and without signature). The editors' work suggests that by inserting this art into a new context (a popular communication project that encouraged the democratization of communications) they had, in fact, created something new. To draw on Raymond Williams's idea of flow, within this new aesthetic framing, the individual drawing can no longer be interpreted on its own but rather within the context of the page, the volume, the series, and the urgency of the political moment. The invitation by the editors to "use and abuse" these drawings is also a suggestion that content is not stable, but rather changes according to each use and, as such, is no longer the property of one particular artist. The person who adds a new context has also transformed the content.

The importance of privileging a political project over individual authorship was also central to the 1988 television campaign for democracy. In the month leading up to the October 5 vote that would ask Chileans to vote either YES (to continue with the dictatorship) or NO (to return to democratic elections), each side was allowed 15 minutes each night on national television in order to make their case. In a move that took the military government by surprise, the NO campaign managed to bring together an impressive team of publicists, journalists, filmmakers, and actors in an ingenious campaign that hinged on the idea that "happiness was on its way" with the return to democracy. With little time or resources, the directors of the campaign quickly selected and edited from a wealth of material coming from many different sources. Each 15-minute capsule was composed of several short segments such as news reports, interviews, micro documentaries, comedic interludes, and a theme song. As one publicist I interviewed told me, each of these segments "had a first and last name," meaning that for her they were directly linked to the particular work or style of one of the participants in the production of the campaign. However, in the televised campaign, individual creative authorship is rarely acknowledged. For the Chilean public, these individual segments are remembered collectively as "the NO campaign." In other words, as powerful as each of these segments might have been individually, their worth comes through being a part of the NO campaign. Context here is content.

To illustrate, let's take the example of one of the most widely remembered moments in the campaign, which appeared in the first night of the television ads and was repeated frequently throughout the month: the "Doña Yolita" segment. This highly emotive spot created by Pablo Perelman very successfully conveyed the goals of the campaign. However, as the campaign's creative director pointed out to me, it also closely imitated the structure of a typical commercial. In this 30-second segment, an elderly woman, "Doña Yolita," walks into a corner store in a low-income neighborhood. She greets the shopkeeper and asks him for two pieces of bread. As he is wrapping up the bread, she tells him that she would also like to buy tea. He responds, "Two tea bags?" She looks into her empty change purse, looks up, and says, "Just one." The segment ends with a voice saying, "We all have a reason to vote NO." The "Doña Yolita" segment fades out as the campaign song starts to play softly, and an image appears of a hand marking the option NO on a ballot with a vertical line. One of the participants in the campaign, Carlos Flores del Pino, had created this image after a meeting with Jorge Olalla, a creative director at an advertising firm, about another project. Olalla had sketched the idea on a napkin and reported that he was delighted when he watched the campaign later and saw his idea come to life ("Testimonio de Jorge Olalla"). The voiceover weaves together these segments, uniting them with the words, "No more misery." When asked about the NO campaign, nearly everyone in Chile remembers "Doña Yolita." However, only those most closely tied to the television campaign production team are aware that Pablo Perelman was the creator of this segment. Perelman's work itself becomes transformed when inserted into the flow of other segments, united with the campaign song and the image of the hand marking NO. The producers created the NO campaign by sampling the work of several different authors. This first experiment in what democratic television might look like after the dictatorship argued for inclusivity and polyvocality.

These two different examples, one taken from popular communication projects and the other produced by the country's premiere creative class, suggest that practices of sampling, borrowing, and collective authorship are closely tied to the project of media democratization in Chile. Both of these projects appeal to the idea of a democratic commons, a concept for which Señal 3 advocated when they fought for their right to access the electromagnetic spectrum. These projects illustrate that the creative process is not dependent upon originality, nor is it limited to individual authorship. In what follows, I draw on these ideas to explore Señal 3's production in relation to sampling, curating, and context shifting.

## Sampling in the Digital (Television) Era

Even those residents of La Victoria who claim not to be viewers of Señal 3 are likely to watch the community channel at least once during the week-long festival celebrating the anniversary of the founding of the neighborhood. During these days in late October the neighborhood is alive with activity as murals are repainted, soccer tournaments are held, the land takeover is reenacted, common pot meals are organized, a carnival with ingenious (and often highly political) costumes weaves its way through the streets, and a host of local and national musicians take to the stages positioned in various parts of La Victoria. It is perhaps at this time of year that the work of Señal 3 is most similar to what the state had in mind when they decided to award a license to these self-taught media producers. On the days of the large concerts, Señal 3 members set up sound and lights near the main stage and do a live transmission for older neighbors who prefer to watch from home or those who want to check to see who is performing before fighting their way through the crowds in the street. Not all of the week's events are transmitted live, however. Several others are filmed, and then edited back at the station in order to create capsules for transmission on the news program a day or two later.

Whenever station members at Señal 3 sit down to edit, they act as *bricoleurs*, constructing videos with "whatever is on hand." They use pirated software programs and add music that they've managed to download for free. They combine material they filmed on the street with other interviews, videos found on YouTube, and historical footage passed on to them from filmmakers or journalists who spent time in La Victoria during the dictatorship. They are master builders at the editing desk. Sampling, as one music producer describes, "is like Legos. If someone said, 'Here's a bunch of Legos, put them together,' you have something to work with—as opposed to, 'Here's a bunch of plastic, mold it, and then start building it'" (Kid 606 qtd. in McLeod and DiCola 1). While station members are proud of their neighborhood, they do not limit themselves to the creative work produced within it. Instead, they use it as one element among many in their production process.

This same "Lego" approach to construction is the way in which they design their entire programming schedule. It is a combination of live transmissions, programs hosted by neighborhood residents, and material accessed from other sources, including cable programming. When I have interviewed residents of La Victoria (particularly older residents), they make it clear that for them all of this is "Señal 3." La Victoria has always been a neighborhood that has attracted visitors from all over the world because of its political ties, despite being located on the periphery of Santiago (both geographically and symbolically). It does not seem strange to residents that their television station would have traces of this expansive social network in their programming schedule. Señal 3 and La Victoria are works of pastiche. For station members and viewers Señal 3 has a clear neighborhood identity because of—not despite—these production practices. Neighborhood residents, in fact, contribute to these practices by donating in the weekend market so that Señal 3 can pay for the cable subscription that allows media from outside of the neighborhood to find its way into their living rooms.[6]

Although station members ardently defended what Lessig has called "free culture," they were legitimately concerned about their ability to continue to embrace these ideas with the shift to "formality." When the CNTV informed Señal 3 that they had been awarded a license, station members received no other instructions. The 2014 Digital Television Law did not make any references to intellectual property rights

(IPRs), nor was there any related protocol for community television or the other television stations (as was confirmed to me by a representative from the CNTV). When asked in an interview with the online magazine *La Raza Cósmica* to comment on his concerns regarding IPRs, Polo responded,

> If we transmit something from YouTube, are we going to have to pay? Because our television is not commercial, it's community-based. So, if you're not profiting with the spectrum that was given to you, it should be free because we are also not located in [wealthier neighborhoods like] Las Condes, Vitacura, or La Reina, but rather in low-income sectors that do not have access. (Qtd. in Pacheco)

We could argue that Polo's statement echoes the sentiment of former president Michelle Bachelet when she introduced the draft bill to reform Chile's Intellectual Property Law in 2007, asserting that copyright should always be understood from a balanced perspective, "mixing an adequate protection of the rights of the author and those related with legitimate access on the part of the community to artistic and intellectual creations" (qtd. in Mirosevic 70). Following active public debate, the reform to the Intellectual Property Law was finally approved in 2010. Within this reform, the Chilean government established a catalog of exceptions to copyright restrictions (Álvarez 27), as well as a "'seed' for fair use policy" (Álvarez et al. 8). When Polo attempted to clarify what this might mean for community television stations, someone from the CNTV told him, "You are nonprofit. You won't have a problem." However, given that the representatives of CNTV shift with each administration change, the question for Polo was far from settled.

## Curating as Participatory Creation

"So, are you still going to broadcast the soccer games?" I asked Manolo, one of the founding members of Señal 3, when I returned to La Victoria in June of 2018. For me, and for many residents of La Victoria, transmission of cable soccer games was an intrinsic part of the station's identity. "We will as long as we can," he responded. "Maybe we can keep transmitting them analogically. If we have to stop, well, we're going to have to explain to people because they're going to be upset."

Anyone who has ever been in La Victoria on a day in which the rival soccer teams of the Universidad de Chile and Colo-Colo are playing will find that it is essentially possible to listen to the game from the street given that almost every house is tuned to the same channel. Although the fact that soccer games in Chile are aired on the cable channel CDF Premium might prevent many low-income families in other neighborhoods from having access to them, this is not the case in La Victoria where Señal 3 broadcasts them for everyone to see.[7] The extent to which station members see this as part of their responsibility to the neighborhood was made evident to me one summer day in 2009 when Señal 3 was temporarily off the air while they were fundraising to buy the house where the station was located in order to prevent eviction. Walking down the street, I found Ale, one of the station members, setting up a television set in front of the station for some Universidad de Chile fans. Despite being a die-hard Colo-Colo fan, he didn't have the heart to deny his neighbors the right to watch the game. After hooking up the connection in record time, he excused himself to go back to work, and the sound of his truck's characteristic jingle ("Abate Gas, the cheapest in the neighborhood") was soon drowned out by the noise of the soccer game as more neighbors arrived to watch.

Although the mission of Señal 3 has always been to create a station in which residents of La Victoria saw themselves reflected on the screen, this has never meant that their goal was to transmit only material that they themselves had produced. Starting with the initial *pantallazos* in the early 1990s, Polo and Cristián sought out material that they felt represented, for example, the political interests and concerns of residents of La Victoria. During the evenings I have spent in Señal 3, I have frequently seen whoever was in charge of transmitting arrive with material that they had downloaded somewhere or received through a friend and that they thought was worth sharing with the station's public.

According to Chilean Law 20.750 (2014), community television is defined as: "Production by social groups within the coverage zone of the concession." However, community media (in Chile and elsewhere) emerges as a means of providing alternative content (Atton). In 2016, the CNTV did a study on the audiences of community television, including those of La Victoria. The study reports that the audience of La Victoria emphasized that the "programming presents an important cultural component, transmitting documentaries and reports with a high historical content" (CNTV, *La Audiencia* 12). Señal 3, with its very limited staff and resources, has not, up to this point, produced its own full-length documentaries, so the audience members interviewed were, no doubt, referring to the pirated documentaries that station members had gained access to through their social networks. Just as the national networks might decide, for example, to transmit *The Simpsons* or a Turkish soap opera to the Chilean public, so, too, did these community television operators think about "making television" as having a good eye for what might be content of interest for the residents of this low-income neighborhood. In the early days of the station, they would often buy a pirated DVD of a popular movie that was still out in theaters and transmit it on Friday evenings, arguing that the families in the neighborhood did not have the money to go to the movie theater. As they became more technically sophisticated, they began using one cable subscription to "share" with the entire neighborhood not only the soccer games but also programming from the regional network Telesur. This was not a secret to the CNTV. In the study cited above, the authors note, "Some channels emit the programming of pay channels in order to permit their audience access to cultural goods and events of interest that otherwise they would not be able to pay" (CNTV, *La Audiencia* 13). This, for members of Señal 3, was a way of democratizing content.

The appraisal and curating process that goes on in Señal 3 is an element of cultural production. As Stuart Hall was arguing as early as 1973, media acquires meaning not only when producers construct a message, but also when viewers interpret that message. Reception studies have subsequently highlighted the potential for viewer agency and, at times, creative resistance to the messages encoded by producers (e.g., hooks; Jenkins). Platforms such as YouTube have also made it easier for those viewers to act as archivists (by saving media and/or abstracting fragments from that media) and as curators, making decisions about how to categorize media and determining what is worth redistributing (Burgess and Green). When we decide to share content, according to Green and Jenkins, "We are not simply creating meaning based on what the content says; we are also creating meaning through the exchange of that content, which constitutes and reaffirms our interconnections with others in our network" (119–120). Community media for Señal 3 was not just about putting familiar faces on the television screen, but also about strengthening neighborhood ties and identity. By acting as curators of relevant content for the neighborhood, members of Señal 3 were seeking to allow residents of La Victoria, particularly senior citizens who did not have access to the Internet, to participate in broader political conversations and cultural experiences. The content that they selected, in turn, took on new attributes once inserted into the context of community media transmission.

## Conclusion: Context as Content

The relation between context, content, and agency is highlighted in the work of visual artist Nam June Paik. In the 1960s Paik took the television set out of the living room and into the art gallery when he created a series of works that centered on both television's materiality and its symbolic power. One of these was *Magnet TV* (1965) in which the artist placed a horseshoe-shaped electromagnet on top of a television set. If members of the public moved the magnet, they were able to alter the image that appeared on the screen. Paik developed this work during the "network era" in which the individual viewer had no choice but to watch whatever the major television networks programmed at the time that they programmed it. As Goldsmith notes, by inviting the public to spin the magnet and thus alter the image on the television set, Paik "upended television in ways of which both users and producers were unaware, opening up entirely new vocabularies for the medium while deconstructing myths of power, politics, and distribution that were embedded—but hitherto invisible—in the technology" (5). The same object when inserted into a different context—one in which the viewer had the possibility of asserting some degree of agency—allowed for the possibility to create something new.

This idea of context shifting as an act of creation struck me while walking into Señal 3 one evening. Hearing a dog barking, I looked around, and then realized that it was the beginning of a song by Los Prisioneros, a well-known Chilean band from San Miguel (a lower-middle-class neighborhood not too far from La Victoria) that had become famous in the late 1980s, at the end of the dictatorship. Polo was at the control table, transmitting the music video on Señal 3, and drumming his hands on the table to the rhythm of the song. He looked up at me and said, "Listen: this is our theme song." He sang along for emphasis: "Unánse al baile de los que sobran / nadie nos va echar de más / nadie nos quiso ayudar de verdad." ("Join the dance of those leftover / No one is going to miss us / No one really tried to help us.") Despite the neighborhood feel provided by the dog barking, this was a well-traveled song, performed in stadiums across Latin America and played in living rooms across income levels and age groups in Chile. However, the song acquired different meanings as it circulated through these different spaces. It changed as it moved from the band's early performances in local high schools to the cassette in a middle-class teenager's Walkman in 1987. It took on new meaning when publicists inserted it into the second night of the NO campaign, and then again when Polo and Cristián projected the music video on a sheet hung over a clothesline in La Victoria in the early 1990s when they were feeling left behind by the promises made by that same democracy campaign. It took on yet another life when Polo played it that night on Señal 3, a station with a leaky roof, which at that point still did not have legal authorization, and whose participants were fighting for their right to use the airwaves.

It is not coincidental that Señal 3 was born in the context of the democratic transition. In that moment, Polo, Cristián, Manolo, Ale, and the rest of the members of the station were anxious to be producers, and not just spectators, of the democratic process. For them, to be producers did not mean an act of carefully parsing out the exact moments in which they were acting as "authors" rather than "users." Instead, as media producers they occupied a hybrid subject position that paralleled their vision for the democratic process. Television became the material site from which to experiment with ideas of representation and agency. In their fight to have access to the electromagnetic spectrum years later, they were trying to draw attention to the ways in which the task of democratization was incomplete. In some ways, it did not so much matter *what* they transmitted, as much as the fact that they could *decide* what to transmit. The "poetry" of *bricoleurs*, according to Lévi-Strauss, is linked to the "choices [they] make between the limited possibilities," and the ways in which they always include something of themselves in the work they create (21). It was, for that reason that Polo worried that they might have to "give back" the television license. Doing so would mean giving up some of their democratic creative license as well. Whether producing a program on local musicians, inserting a YouTube video into the Friday news program, or broadcasting the soccer games, Señal 3 members were actively engaged in the work of cultural production. None of these elements of content would be the same if aired from elsewhere. The station and its history provided context for this content.

## Notes

1 Reyes inaugurated the four community television stations just before leaving his post when a new administration under President Sebastián Piñera took over.
2 In 2018, this was just under US$50,000.00.
3 De Certeau points to the power dimensions of these acts, signaling how "making do" is a tactic of navigating structures that we do not control.
4 Remixing music began with disco in the 1970s and became increasingly popular within hip-hop (Navas et al.).
5 In June of 2018 when I interviewed Guillo, one of the Chilean artists who appear in the acknowledgments of the book, he smiled when I told him about the project, but didn't remember ever having seen the volumes.
6 The pirating itself echoed other kinds of "Robin Hood" types of practices that had occurred in the neighborhood during the dictatorship, such as when the Frente Patriótico Manuel Rodríguez (an armed movement aligned with the Communist Party) arrived in La Victoria with a stolen chicken truck, an event commemorated in a mural on the walls of the neighborhood.
7 Here Señal 3 members often cite the decision of the Argentine government, under the Kircheners, to "democratize" access to soccer games.

## Bibliography

Alvarez Valenzuela, Daniel. *The Quest for a Normative Balance: The Recent Reforms to Chile's Copyright Law*. Policy Brief, 12, International Centre for Trade and Sustainable Development, December 2011, www.ictsd.org/themes/innovation-and-ip/research/the-quest-for-a-normative-balance-the-recent-reforms-to-chile%E2%80%99s. Accessed July 11, 2019.

Álvarez Valenzuela, Daniel, and Marco CorreaPérez. "La doble dimensión del derecho de autor: El acceso a la cultura y los derechos de autor." *Revista de Derecho Público*, vol. 85, no. 2, December 2016, pp. 11–32.

Ashley, Jennifer. "'Honorable Piracy' and Chile's Digital Transition." *Popular Communication*, vol. 13, no. 1, January 2015, pp. 6–17, doi:10.1080/15405702.2014.978002.

Atton, Chris. "Introduction: Problems and Positions in Alternative and Community Media." *The Routledge Companion to Alternative and Community Media*, edited by Chris Atton, Routledge, 2015, pp. 1–18.

Baeza, Chiara Sáez. "Políticas públicas de comunicación y participación ciudadana: el caso de la televisión digital en Chile." *Signo y Pensamiento*, vol. 32, no. 63, September 2013, pp. 34–51.

Bresnahan, Rosalind. "Community Radio and Social Activism in Chile 1990–2007: Challenges for Grass Roots Voices During the Transition to Democracy." *Journal of Radio Studies*, vol. 14, no. 2, November 2007, pp. 212–233, doi:10.1080/10955040701583320.

Bresnahan, Rosalind. "The Media and the Neoliberal Transition in Chile: Democratic Promise Unfulfilled." *Latin American Perspectives*, vol. 30, no. 6, November 2003, pp. 39–68, doi:10.1177/0095399703256257.

Burgess, Jean, and Joshua Green. *YouTube: Online Video and Participatory Culture*. Polity, 2009.

CNTV. "CNTV abre concurso público para 116 frecuencias de televisión digital en todo el país." Consejo Nacional de Televisión, 2017, www.cntv.cl/cntv-abre-concurso-publico-para-116-frecuencias-de-television-digital-en/cntv/2017-03-10/141202.html. Accessed August 3, 2018.

CNTV. *La Audiencia de La Televisión Comunitaria*. Consejo Nacional de Televisión, 2016, www.cntv.cl/la-audiencia-de-la-television-comunitaria/cntv/2016-07-11/100116.html. Accessed July 11, 2019.

Certeau, Michel de. *The Practice of Everyday Life*. U of California P, 1984.

Chile, Ministry of Transport and Telecommunication. Law No. 20.750, Permitting the Introduction of Digital Television, May 29, 2014. Library of Congress, www.leychile.cl/Navegar?idNorma=1060307&r=1. Accessed December 10, 2019.

Derrida, Jacques. *Writing and Difference*. U of Chicago P, 1978.

Duncombe, Stephen. *Notes from Underground: Zines and the Politics of Alternative Culture*. 1997. 20th anniversary edition. Microcosm, 2017.

Goldsmith, Kenneth. *Uncreative Writing: Managing Language in the Digital Age*. Columbia UP, 2011.

Green, Joshua, and Henry Jenkins. "Spreadable Media: How Audiences Create Value and Meaning in a Networked Economy." *The Handbook of Media Audiences: Nightingale/The Handbook of Media Audiences*, edited by Virginia Nightingale, Wiley-Blackwell, 2011, pp. 109–127.

Hall, Stuart. "Encoding and Decoding in the Media Discourse." *Stencilled Occasional Papers*, vol. 7, 1973.

Hamilton, James. "Visualizing Critique: Montage as a Practice of Alternative Media." *Media History*, vol. 7, no. 2, December 2001, pp. 159–170, doi:10.1080/13688800120092237.

hooks, bell. "The Oppositional Gaze: Black Female Spectator." *The Feminism and Visual Cultural Reader*, edited by Amelia Jones, Routledge, 2003, pp. 94–105.

Jenkins, Henry. *Textual Poachers: Television Fans & Participatory Culture*. Routledge, 1992.

Jofré, Alejandro. "Panteras Negras: la historia se cierra." *PANIKO.cl*, January 2015, https://paniko.cl/panteras-negras-la-historia-se-cierra. Accessed December 10, 2019.

La Red de Prensa Popular. *El pirata honrado: Fondo común de dibujos e ilustraciones*, vol. 3. ECO Comunicaciones, 1990.

Lessig, Lawrence. *Free Culture: How Big Media Uses Technology and the Law to Lock Down Culture and Control Creativity*. Penguin Press, 2004.

Lessig, Lawrence. *Remix: Making Art and Commerce Thrive in the Hybrid Economy*. Penguin Books, 2014.

Lévi-Strauss, Claude. *The Savage Mind*. U of Chicago P, 1966.

Liñero, Germán. *Apuntes para una historia del video en Chile*. Ocho Libros, 2010.

McLeod, Kembrew, and Peter DiCola. *Creative License: The Law and Culture of Digital Sampling*. Duke UP, 2011.

Menares, Felipe. "Señal 3 de La Victoria obtuvo concesión de TV digital: 'El Estado no se había hecho cargo de una realidad que venía hace 20 años.'" *El Ciudadano*, February 1, 2018, www.elciudadano.cl/chile/senal-3-la-victoria-obtuvo-concesion-tv-digital-estado-no-se-habia-hecho-cargo-una-realidad-venia-20-anos/02/01. Accessed August 3, 2018.

Mirosevic Verdugo, Camilo. "Origen y evolución del derecho de autor, con especial referencia al derecho chileno." *Revista de Derecho de La Pontificia Universidad Católica de Valparaíso*, vol. 28, no. 1, May 2007, pp. 35–82.

Mowbray, Mike. "Alternative Logics? Parsing the Literature on Alternative Media." *The Routledge Companion to Alternative and Community Media*, edited by Chris Atton, Routledge, 2015, pp. 21–31.

Navas, Eduardo, Owen Gallagher, and xtine burrough. *The Routledge Companion to Remix Studies*. Routledge, 2015.

Pacheco, Cristián. "Señal 3 La Victoria: 'Nuestra primera transmisión va a ser en pelota.'" *La Raza Cómica*, August 1, 2018, http://razacomica.cl/sitio/2018/08/01/senal-3-la-victoria-nuestra-primera-transmision-va-a-ser-en-pelota. Accessed August 2, 2018.

Perloff, Marjorie. *Unoriginal Genius: Poetry by Other Means in the New Century*. U of Chicago P, 2010.

Poblete, Juan. "Culture, Neo-Liberalism and Citizen Communication: The Case of Radio Tierra in Chile." *Global Media and Communication*, vol. 2, no. 3, December 2006, pp. 315–334.

Sonvilla-Weiss, Stefan, editor. *Mashup Cultures*. Springer, 2010.

"Testimonio de Jorge Olalla." *#30másChile*, Fundación Democracia y Desarrollo, https://30mas.cl/testimonio-jorge-olalla. Accessed October 10, 2018.

Thomas, Kedron. *Regulating Style: Intellectual Property Law and the Business of Fashion in Guatemala*. U of California P, 2016.

Williams, Raymond. *Television: Technology and Cultural Form*. Fontana, 1974.

# 6

# "FEELING PIRATE" AS MEDIA AFFECT IN MEXICAN AMERICAN EXPERIENCE

*Juan Llamas-Rodriguez*

Bellaire Boulevard runs east to west in the Houston southwestern neighborhood known as Sharpstown. During the 20-minute ride between Interstate 69 and State Highway 6, Bellaire offers a tour of the neighborhood's demographic changes and geographical shifts. Down this "river of concrete," as one commentator has called it, its rundown 1980s apartments and refurbished mid-century houses stand as markers of the historical influx and retreat of African Americans, the increasingly higher Latino population, and the recently notable Asian American presence (Lomax). At the intersection of Bellaire and I-69 looms the shopping mall PlazAmericas, formerly known as Sharpstown Center, and the boulevard cuts through the heart of one of Houston's two Chinatowns (Figure 6.1). It comes as no surprise then that Bellaire has been called "a world market of a street" and "a bazaar where Mexicans, Anglos, Salvadorans, African Americans, Hondurans, stoners, Vietnamese, Chinese, Koreans and Thais go to shop and eat" (Lomax).

Further west down this eight-mile slice of Houston suburbia is Super Video Latino, a video store lodged between a hair salon and a taqueria in an ostensibly Latina-oriented strip mall. Although the video store's name alludes to a wide Latin American clientele, its sign implicitly references the Mexican flag, with each of the words in the title in green, white, and red. The store's outside façade is made up of glass panes plastered with posters of various sizes, advertising films, electronics, and different plans for international calling. Also advertised on the glass panes are the other services that the store offers besides video: sale of music equipment, cell-phone airtime, and international calling cards; rental of folding chairs; and a faxing service.

Inside, Super Video Latino's video selection is set up on two shelves running down the center of the store, along with the remaining part of the left wall. The

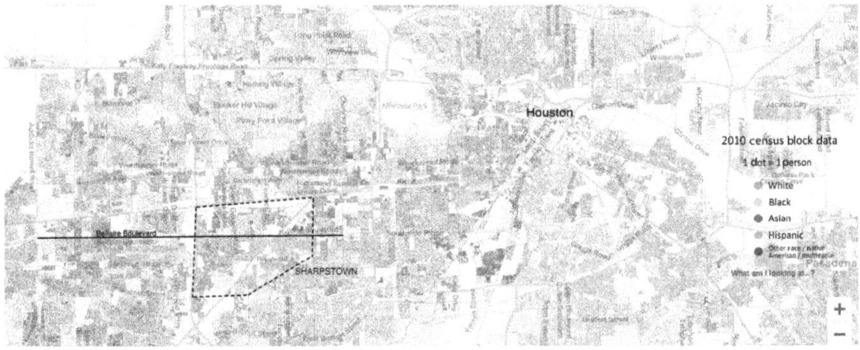


**FIGURE 6.1** Map of Houston demographics, and Sharpstown insert, based on 2010 census data
Source: University of Virginia, Weldon Cooper Center for Public Service.

center shelves include assorted Hollywood films, box sets of telenovelas, and classic Mexican films, while the left wall holds contemporary Latin American cinema, more classic Mexican films, DVDs on sale, and *narcopelículas* (narco movies) in the upper side. Except for two handwritten letter-size sheets of paper indicating which DVDs are on sale, there are no signs classifying the films, so all of these categorizations are my own way of describing the selection (Figure 6.2). That is not to say that these genres are not useful forms of classifying and identifying viewer choices, but rather that these choices present themselves in less standardized, more fluid forms. The DVD boxes indicate that some of these titles used to be rental options now for sale, suggesting that these films have been obtained through a variety of means across a number of years.

The video store's decorative pastiche and eclectic film selection reveal the informal nature characteristic of the ethnic video store. Other scholars have attended to the ethnic video store in regard to aesthetics of video or the construction of diasporic and immigrant identities (Hilderbrand 27–32). In what follows, I theorize these spaces broadly as "piratical" in order to foreground how they blur the markers of distinction prevalent in standard media consumption sites, and how that blurring of boundaries speaks to the mediated constitution of the publics these spaces congregate. In short, this chapter theorizes "feeling pirate" as an affective experience within the minoritarian experience of Mexicans in the United States. Building on scholarship about media piracy and video spectatorship, it pursues this theorization from observations gathered from multiple visits to sites of video consumption targeted towards Mexican immigrants in the southwestern United States. "Feeling pirate" represents a form of worlding wherein the practices of media consumers diffract their own status as members, or nonmembers, of the communities they inhabit.

**FIGURE 6.2** DVD selections of Super Video Latino
Source: Author.

The following theorization of "feeling pirate" owes much to the work of José Esteban Muñoz and his work on "feeling brown." Muñoz argues for whiteness as "a cultural logic which can be understood as an affective code that positions itself as the law" (206). The structural privileges afforded to whiteness also result in a particular form of affective register becoming normative. If this white affect becomes the norm, then minoritarian affects such as that of Latina/os tend to be read as excessive and unruly, or more colloquially as "spicy" or "hot." Muñoz is committed to rethinking the terms of this cultural logic. "Rather than trying to run from this stereotype, Latino as excess," he argues, "it seems much more important to seize it and redirect it in the service of a liberationist politics" (207). One way to redirect this stereotype is to assume a brown affect as primary, rather than secondary to the normative whiteness. Feeling brown retains its autonomy as affect and becomes the ground for a rethinking of minoritarian experience.

"Feeling pirate" similarly redirects the normative affects of piracy towards a more expansive way of conceptualizing minoritarian film consumption. Certain Mexican American groups may feel pirate not only because of consumption practices that are deemed tasteless or illegitimate but also because their social standing remains precarious and constantly under scrutiny for its purported "illegality." Thinking through "feeling pirate" should remind us that categories such as illegality or piracy exist relationally, reinforced by those structures invested in regulating authorized and unauthorized forms of subjectivity and consumption.

Such relationality and constant reinforcement signal the importance of accounting for performativity as intrinsic to the formation of an affective register of the piratical. Performativity, as scholars like Judith Butler remind us, refers to the fact that it is iterative practices, not essentialized nature, which bring forth an identity (iv). Performativity thus allows for a rethinking of the so-called "immigrant experience." At a time when mainstream discourse focuses primarily on legal definitions and state-enforced demarcations of migration, the migrant experience as an affective, mediated condition often remains overlooked.

This chapter theorizes "feeling pirate" by building on existing debates on the suitability of piracy as a catch-all term for illegal, illicit, or otherwise unauthorized media circulation and consumption practices. I argue that calls for doing away with the term and proposed replacements are inadequate since these do not account for the normative force that posits piracy as a biopolitical mode for controlling populations and their (media) consumption practices. Instead, throughout this chapter I propose redirecting the connotations of media piracy in terms similar to Muñoz by analyzing sites of informal media consumption across the city of Houston, in the southwestern United States. Turning to these video-consumption sites, or video stores, as instances where "feeling pirate" emerges should not imply that these places are dedicated to the sale of bootleg or unauthorized copies of media content. In fact, many places do not. However, it is the construction of media space, the social dynamics of exclusion, and the subsequent affective attachments to particular media objects that shape the register of the piratical. Ultimately, I argue that "feeling pirate" evidences structures, dynamics, and affective attachments similar to being an immigrant at a time when citizenship and its legal rights are always precarious. This formulation allows us to understand the day-to-day value and affective force, as well as the liberatory potential, of piratical practices of media consumption.

## "Piracy" Beyond Legal Definitions

The growth of scholarship about media piracy has been accompanied by a terminological crisis. Departing from earlier attempts to nuance and problematize the designation of "piracy," more recent accounts tend to privilege alternative terms to designate bootleg reproductions of commodities. It is not piratical but informal, unauthorized, or illegitimate. Some of these terms hold clear stakes for the scholarly project that deploys them, but doing away with the *term* "piracy" does little to undo the social dynamics that designate certain media practices, and their practitioners, as piratical. Considering a few of the more influential works in this trend illustrates the traps of disavowing the term "piratical" altogether.

First is the influential work of Ramon Lobato and Julian Thomas in their book *The Informal Media Economy*. The aim of this project is to re-energize the concept of informal media economies as a way to wade through contemporary debates in media studies generally, and media economics and media industry studies specifically. The authors shift the focus of these fields from formal economies and industries towards their informal counterparts, centering instead on what has long been their purported "other." In their account, formal and informal economies are two ends of a spectrum wherein most contemporary industrial formations fall (Lobato and Thomas 21). The formal aspects of any formation may influence the informal ones, and vice versa. They also introduce time as a variable for when these different aspects may fluctuate between formality and informality. With great success, Lobato and Thomas press their formal–informal model against key topics in media studies, such as labor, space, and regulation, and from this friction they come up with new questions and further avenues of research. For my project I depart from and extend their definitional premise of informality. At its most basic, informality for Lobato and Thomas has to do with degrees of sanctioning, whether it is governmental or institutional (8). Although they note that informality can be extralegal, nonlegal, or illegal, their examples continuously tend towards the illegal. The authors argue that informality is about *uncertainty*, and that the power of this concept lies in inviting researchers to analyze purportedly stable objects of knowledge from an uncertain point of view (Lobato and Thomas 12). I wish to develop this claim further and fully embrace the implication of informality as conceptual and ontological uncertainty.

In addition to Lobato and Thomas's project, scholars of piracy in the Global South reframe the concept's negative valences by focusing on the ways pirate media practices are creative. First, piracy is creative in that it operates in the absence of state-sponsored models for media development. A notable example of this is Brian Larkin's work on Hausa video networks in Nigeria. Larkin foregrounds how the pirate infrastructures that brought unsanctioned copies of Indian and American films to Nigerians laid the foundation for Nigerian video to circulate and expand to its current size. Importantly, Larkin insists that these two networks of circulation—of pirate copies and Nigerian original productions—are inseparable. Nigerian video would not have been able to emerge without the preexisting pirate networks and, despite the aforementioned attempts at formalizing this proto-industry, it continues to exist because of pirate practices. The piratical genealogy of Nigerian video further also bestows a certain legacy on the latter's aesthetics of distorted images and degraded sounds. Likewise, Ravi Sundaram uses the piratical as an overarching trope for those practices that are not captured within the aims of late neoliberal modernity (14). Practices such as electronics repair or homebrew solutions count as piratical when official state-sanctioned businesses do not stand to profit from manufactured obsolescence. Piracy, then, is creative in that it brings about infrastructures and social relations where state or traditional business enterprises are receding or absent.

Beyond this, piracy is also creative in its iterative, continuous dimensions. Both Larkin and Sundaram emphasize this in their respective studies. For Larkin, pirate infrastructures engender "repair as a cultural mode of existence for technology"

(235). Absent any official controls over technological maintenance, pirate methods fill in the gaps and sustain the networks of production and distribution. Sundaram similarly argues that Indian cities exist within a "rhythm of technological irregularity" that requires "the ingenious search for solutions" (2). Piracy remains outside the nation-state's purview in these accounts; this state of exclusion grants the piratical its potential for transformation.

"Feeling pirate" retains the critical focus on piracy as a relational process emergent from institutions, media, and social practices, among other social agents. Retaining the term "pirate" despite these definitional struggles has clear political stakes. In his work, despite advocating for "feeling brown" as an aperture towards liberationist politics, Muñoz remains aware of the power and influence of normative whiteness. For him, rethinking the affective performativity of ethnicity becomes a maneuver "akin to what [he has] described elsewhere as a disidentification with toxic characterizations and stereotypes of U.S. Latinos." Crucially, a disidentification is neither an identification nor a counteridentification, but rather "it is a working on, with, and against a form at a simultaneous moment" (Muñoz 207). Similar power dynamics occur within both the scholarly study of piracy and within the everyday policing of legality. Keeping the fraught connotations of piracy within "feeling pirate" acknowledges the normative pull of this categorization while also continuously staging the ambiguity of its referents. In short, this affective register foregrounds *indeterminacy* as an operating logic within both ethnic video consumption and immigrant everyday experience.

By reframing piracy as creative indeterminacy, this chapter proposes another creative component of the piratical. It argues that the spaces of the piratical possess distinct affects emergent from their extra-official status, infrastructural design, and social dynamics. In what follows, I illustrate the potential of informal spaces to engender the experience of "feeling pirate" by undertaking situated explorations of video stores in the southwest United States and comparing these to the imaginary of piratical spaces in Mexico. Understanding the spatial logics of these locales as piratical because of their affective potential, rather than their legal standing, enables a rediscovery of the transnational linkages that shape everyday sensations for communities perpetually on the brink of feeling left out.

## The Spaces of the Piratical

Ethnic video stores have long been an index of media's plurality within urban contexts. For instance, a 1991 article in the *Chicago Tribune* titled "Video Stores as Diverse as the City" surveyed the video store options in the city, and concluded by marveling at how "[the city's] enormous diversity of ethnic groups is reflected not only in [its] restaurants and neighborhoods but in video as well" (Sulski). Super Video Latino and other video stores considered here fall within this lineage of video stores giving shape to ethnic experiences by virtue of their connections to traditions from elsewhere.

Across the city from Super Video Latino, over at the predominantly African American and Latino community of Northside, MexVideo is a 14 x 6 ft. space outside of a Fiesta supermarket, a chain of stores aimed at the Hispanic communities in Texas (Figure 6.3). Along with several other businesses, predominantly food stands, the video store lines the front entrance to Fiesta, luring in customers before or after they do their grocery shopping. MexVideo's size only allows for two small counters and a set of shelves inside the space, although some portable shelves spill out on to the sidewalk. The cashier is on a small counter on the left, and next to it stand the shelves containing *narcopelículas*. In addition to its selection of DVDs, which is similar in variety to but smaller in quantity than that of Super Video Latino, MexVideo also sells CDs, handbags, and perfumes. MexVideo's connection to the supermarket chain Fiesta further emphasizes the connections of video consumption within everyday life. The purpose of this establishment is to offer entertainment options to consumers exiting the grocery store. Far from the regulatory institutions of media industries, and especially away from the digital enclosures facilitated by Internet video consumption, MexVideo offers a variety of video options absent the question of where these videos came from. In other words, the logic of picking up a DVD from the video stand outside the supermarket emphasizes the indeterminacy of these videos' provenance. For the

**FIGURE 6.3** MexVideo is a video stand outside a Fiesta supermarket
Source: Author.

consumers, this habitual form of media consumption falls in line with other everyday practices. Choosing a movie from the shelves on the sidewalk is not unlike choosing an avocado from the pile in the fruit and vegetable section.

In their design and decor, these video consumption sites in the southwestern United States recall similar markets for bootleg goods across Latin America. Consider, for instance, the "piratical space" of the neighborhood of Tepito in Mexico City. The neighborhood is world-renowned for being the site where all sorts of pirated consumer goods can be found within a six-block radius. In its outdoor market stalls, Tepito provides access to goods and services, including media, for those who are economically and politically excluded from other sectors of the city. Historically, this place also represents the contentious battleground between local police forces and underprivileged sectors of the city's population. The threat of raids and rumors of police extortion are rampant, leaving those who live and work within this community in a constant state of precarity and insecurity (Cross 125). Tepito is therefore always already a precarious place, alternatively hampered by state repression and sustained by creative resilience. At the same time, it is also a parasitical space stigmatized for encroaching on the purported legitimacy of state-sanctioned spaces and ignored for its supposed exteriority to these spaces.

I posit Tepito as a point of reference for understanding piratical spaces because of its privileged position within the Mexican imaginary for informal and illegal consumption practices. Other piratical markets exist across Latin America, with similar fraught relationships to the state and to authorized forms of media consumption. Since the ethnic video stores discussed from Houston allude to a Mexican heritage, the most famous pirate market in the country functions as a point of connection, symbolically if not literally, for consumption of video and other consumer-targeted media. Tepito serves as a blueprint of a piratical space for a number of reasons. For one, it is the biggest, best known, and most centrally located informal market in Mexico City. The stories and legacies attached to this place lend it a privileged position in certain formulations of Mexican heritage, particularly in relation to indigenous and lower-class populations. Famed writer Carlos Monsiváis characterized Tepito as an "unrivalled synthesis of [Mexican] communities before they were massified" (qtd. in Sa 89). It also holds a privileged position in the Mexican imaginary that signifies a space outside the norms and logics of authorized media consumption. Crucial to the struggle over Tepito is the use of public space in ways not sanctioned by state officials and urban planners, who would prefer to use the centrally located real estate for other profitable redevelopments. These issues of location within the urban landscape are one central aspect of the spatial dynamics of video stores such as Super Video Latino and MexVideo: their place in the city influences not only the audiences that attend these stores but also the disposition to consumption of such audiences.

Another key aspect is that of internal logistics of distribution since spaces of media consumption are shaped by their architecture. As Daniel Herbert argues, video stores exhibit an "architecture of classification": shelves, aisles, and decorations serve as material markers about how media should be understood and consumed (58). Spatial divisions, visual arrangements, and display sizes can all signal importance and assign evaluation before the fact of media watching. Yet the architectures of places are not determining of the logics of spaces that emerge from these. Herbert makes the point that the video consumer "writes" the video store through a "rhetoric of walking," which may be delimited but cannot be determined entirely by the aisles and shelves of the store (69). These "rhetorics of walking" become a factor both in the streets of Tepito, in the hallways of Super Video Latino, and along the sidewalks of MexVideo. Absent the usual forms of film categorization, the patron of these piratical spaces relies on their own sense of exploration, an embodied practice that speaks to the habitual nature of this type of media consumption.

Upon entering Super Video Latino, one is immediately struck by the visual overload of its decor: a glass counter showcasing various figurines and assorted toys runs along the right and far side. Posters line the walls, leaving almost no space uncovered. On the right corner from the entrance stands a clothes rack with soccer team jerseys while three computer stations are set up on the left (Figure 6.4). If the traditional video store was originally designed to replicate the theatrical moviegoing experience (Greenberg 86–87), then the ethnic video store is set to replicate the trope of the *mercado* (market)—its cacophony of visual

**FIGURE 6.4** Inside Super Video Latino
Source: Author.

stimuli, its intermingling of disparate artifacts of consumption, its unruly busyness. It is among these *informal affects* that the experience of video consumption is rearticulated: going to the video store is no longer about looking for specific films, or even exclusively about the films, but about any number of different things, among which cinema may play a varied and changing role. If the success of video stores was tied to obfuscating the technology of reproduction by emphasizing the film experience, then the continued relevance of ethnic video stores is the obfuscation of cinema's centrality for the habitus of media reception within a larger identity-based sense of consumption. Rather than selling the experience of cinema, the ethnic video store sells the experience of community, and cinema plays just one facet of this experience.

The experience of such embodied explorations also serves as a point of connection between these transnationally separated locales since embodied articulations remain a central feature of the migrant experience. Sara Ahmed argues that migration involves "reinhabiting the skin": the different impressions that a new landscape provides, such as air, smells, or sounds, accumulate like points or lines that create new textures on the surface of the skin (4). The rhetorics of walking engendered by these piratical media spaces may likewise create textures that recall similar experiences across national borders. Immigrants acquiring movies at Super Video Latino or MexVideo re-experience, even if subconsciously, the embodied sensations of buying films at street markets in Mexico such as Tepito. That experience is available to all patrons regardless of whether they have been to Tepito, because in some ways they have all experienced spaces with a similar structure of feeling. "Feeling pirate" across these sites of media consumption is not a subjectivity beholden to legal definitions, but rather an affective relation that emerges from the structures of a place, the organization of media contents, and the comportment of people therein.

## Pirate Affects and the Immigrant Experience

The long history of disenfranchisement of Mexican American populations in the southwest United States reveals the always already precarious conditions this community inhabits. From state laws geared towards discriminating Mexicans, to labor shortages during the Great Depression, to the militarized tactics of "Operation Wetback," the twentieth century marked a contentious push and pull for Mexican migration into the United States. Mexicans in the southwest, like other Latina/o groups across the United States, remain a social reservoir vulnerable to the economic and political whims of the country's dominant elites (Amaya 18–19). The intensified immigrant deportation raids of 2018 and 2019 only reinforce this precarious status as Mexican American *citizens* have also become victims of operations purportedly targeting alien immigrants (St. John and Rubin). Legal definitions remain secondary to the lived realities of such populations. Instead, everyday experiences dictate the always indeterminate status that such populations have within the repressive apparatus of the state.

Indeterminacy itself is a structuring component of identifying, conceptualizing, and studying immigrant communities. Political scientist Nicholas DeGenova argues that "undocumented migrants, as such, do not comprise an objectively or intrinsically self-delimiting domain for anthropological study" (422). To conceptualize the "undocumented migrant" in isolation is therefore to perpetrate "a rather egregious kind of epistemic violence" on the social reality of everyday life for those migrants. By constituting undocumented migrants (the people) as an epistemological and ethnographic "object" of study, scholars unwittingly become agents in the production of those migrants' "illegality." Crucial to DeGenova's critical intervention is the observation that "in everyday life, undocumented migrants are invariably engaged in social relations with 'legal' migrants as well as citizens, and they commonly live in quite intimate proximity to various categories of 'documented' persons," such as spouses, parents, coworkers, and neighbors (422). Within everyday practices, an immigrant's document status resonates less because of legal definitions than because of the beats of social dynamics. The framework of legality depends on clear-cut distinctions between those authorized and those that are not, those in or out, but migrants' daily lives are more complicated than that. The 2018–2019 ICE raids serve a clear biopolitical purpose in that they interrupt the harmonious flow of everyday life in order to execute a clear-cut distinction between subjects "allowed" to exist in the state's territory and those that are not. The fact that unauthorized subjects regularly coexist with authorized ones also implies that oftentimes the latter may be grouped together with the former. Indeterminacy of state subjecthood is a structuring everyday condition for immigrants.

DeGenova's argument further illustrates the inadequacy of legal terminology to account for the spatiality of lived experience. Citizenship is a technology of power that can be mobilized to control populations in ways similar to the various restrictions on media consumption. Like DeGenova's move towards separating "illegality" from the situated experiences of undocumented migrants, this theorization of "feeling pirate" seeks to distinguish "piracy" as a legal term from the everyday *pirate affect* of consuming media outside of corporate-state delimited standards, regardless of whether these media are technically legal or not. Like indeterminacy of state subjecthood plagues migrants' everyday life, the indeterminacy of piratical media practices creates spaces and times where media consumption exceeds the parameters of legal frameworks. The spaces explored in this chapter suggest an indeterminacy of consumption, where legal and illegal goods may be sold in tandem. Because of this, they are key sites to explore the notion of "feeling pirate" as an aspect of subjecthood and media practices, in relation to the construction of media space, urban redesign, and biopolitics.

Indeed, focusing on the case of spaces coded as Mexican American in Houston reveals the issues arising from situated theorizing as well as the loaded complications when seeking alternatives to the Latina/o formulation in US media studies. Undoubtedly, immigrants from other Latin American countries frequent establishments like Super Video Latino and MexVideo. These communities would have different histories of immigration to the United States, and they may be less familiar with the public imaginary of a place like Tepito. Yet the particular here also gestures at the universal. The spaces of these video stores hold the potential to instigate similar forms of "feeling pirate" by virtue of their informal design and similar position within the urban landscape. Although the argument put forth here draws from the specificity of a Mexican American social history and imaginary, its conclusions reveal much about the structures and relations of everyday consumption experiences writ large.

For example, the shopping complex PlazAmericas came about in 2009 when, following the loss of its anchor businesses and declining sales, Sharpstown Mall was forced to rebrand in order to capitalize on the changing demographics of the area (Gonzales). Part of the mall's renovation and community reorientation included a newly built *mercado*, an 83,000 sq. ft. open space occupying one-quarter of the second floor of the building populated by stands that sell clothes, food, and electronics, among other things. Among these is Latin-Mex Video, a 6 x 4 ft. stand where only one attendant can fit, and there is no cashier. Despite its size, the locale was remarkably similar to Super Video Latino and MexVideo: it featured classical Mexican films, contemporary Latin/Spanish films, DVD sets of telenovelas, recent Hollywood films, and narco films, arranged haphazardly without any formal signage; and it sold other goods, such as candy and tchotchkes, in addition to media. I first visited the stand in 2012. When I went back in 2016, it was gone.

The fate of Latin-Mex Video illustrates the far too common failure of physical retail spaces in the face of online shopping. Ephemerality increasingly shapes media experiences given the disappearance of video stores and the rise of streaming platforms that value algorithmic enclosures, limited licensing agreements, and procedural generic categories. Ephemerality is also a component of "feeling pirate." Affect instigates forms of belonging shaped by spatial formations and consumption habits. The *mercado* structure of PlazAmericas's second floor afforded this 6 x 4 ft. stand similar affective attachments as those described earlier as tied to the imaginary of a piratical space. While that structure of feeling persists within the space of this *mercado*, it may disappear as suddenly as the Latin-Mex Video stand once did. If the experience of community fostered by video stores depends on infrastructures, spatial dynamics, and social practices, then that experience is subject to the contingency of every one of these elements.

In *Cartographies of Diaspora*, Avtar Brah suggests that diasporic space does not merely emerge when migrant subjects arrive at a place, but rather becomes constituted as these subjects' bodies remain "out of place" (16). The piratical spaces explored in this chapter represent one such instance where migrant subjects can remain "out of place." These spaces allow for the sense of "out of place"-ness to be articulated with and embedded in everyday practices. The transnational orientations fostered by ethnic video stores and their experiential similarities with piratical markets in Mexico are what "feeling pirate" attempts to capture and foreground. It is a sense of being out of place by virtue of falling outside of normative categories of belonging and hegemonic standards. Muñoz succinctly reminds us that "the world is not ideologically neutral. The organization of things has much to do with the way capital and different cultural logics of normativity that represent capital's interests give normative citizen-subjects advantageous distance" (209). Feeling pirate, therefore, is not only about how cultural logics that favor certain citizen-subjects create its "other" (the pirate that remains outside the bounds mandated by laws and mores) but also about how this "other" operates with its own affective register.

The relational constitution between normative cultural logics and subject formation requires understanding how the very terms of recognition will condition *in advance* who counts as a subject and who does not. Questioning the norms that dictate what is permissible—what is legal and illegal, piratical or not—should guide the critique of normative structures. The stakes of "feeling pirate" lie in the fact that, if compliance to the norms of recognition grant subjecthood, then "non-compliance calls into question the viability of one's life, the ontological conditions of one's persistence" (Butler iv). Feeling pirate is one structure of feeling that emerges from the condition of indeterminacy where systems that would delimit subjectification are tenuous and in flux.

Legal frameworks fail to capture the vicissitudes of everyday habits and embodied subjectivities of those deemed piratical. In this regard, thinking through media practices allows for a parallel construction of subjectivity through habit. Media in these piratical spaces functions as a "public thing" that gathers a set of people together, materially and symbolically, so that they may come to "see and experience themselves—even if just momentarily—as a common in relation to a commons, a collected if not a collective" (Honig 119). Ultimately, feeling pirate allows us to recognize how media practices habituate forms of living, including precarious ones, because it is through habit that particular migrant experiences emerge. Indeterminacy of status within the policing mechanisms of the state and industry remains tantamount to erasure or repression. Attending to media practices that persist despite such policing mechanisms reveals the uncontainable creative reservoir that resides in piratical spaces.

## Conclusion

This chapter seeks to recognize piratical practices by drawing attention to their sites of consumption, particularly foregrounding how such a cinema is materialized and experienced before the encounter with the film text. If for Barbara Klinger the concept of "home film cultures" points to "the ideological and institutional formations that exert pressure on how cinema is consumed in the domestic space," I hope that the pirate film cultures found in these video stores will further push the boundaries of these formations, illustrating the repurposed forms of film categorization, the relation of cinema to emergent and residual technologies, and "the vicissitudes of ordinary [film] viewing" and consumption (12). Pirate film cultures represent an accented cinema in that its "accent" refers to how the spaces of consumption undermine normative forms of film distribution and categorization in favor of uncertainty and affect. In doing so, they suggest how exclusion from such normative forms can also become a structuring component of the migrant experience.

This argument thus participates in a broader strategy of reclaiming lowbrow forms of media and their reception practices as loci for understanding the social experiences of disenfranchised populations. For instance, Adan Avalos reclaims the pejorative "naco" cinema to make the case for how low-budget border cinema speaks to the experiences and histories of working-class Mexican immigrants living in the United States (Avalos 185). Part of "feeling pirate" could feed into the enjoyment of a "naco" aesthetic as Avalos describes it, but in this chapter I have suggested that this affect extends further back to the moment before media reception. Doing so reveals how media consumption not only permeates everyday experiences but also remains indicative of how certain populations navigate such experiences.

Affective belongings are historically contingent yet powerful connections for communities with precarious standings. Understanding these attachments should complement our view of identitarian belonging as structured by institutions and governing logics, such as law. Still, both identitarian and affective forms of belonging exist only insofar as their conditions of possibility endure. Feeling pirate should not be read as a utopic exile from all oppressive mechanisms of identity regulation. It is a respite from the restrictive modes of being enabled by legal frameworks, but this affective experience does not undo those systems that regulate legal belonging. In offering a window to a form of belonging otherwise, it unlocks the potential for such an undoing.

In conclusion, feeling pirate may be short-lived, may recur, may endure endlessly, and may ebb and flow across a variety of sites. Like the migrant experience, feeling pirate holds within itself the potential for its own dissolution, because the spaces, structures, and practices that engender it may themselves morph or disappear altogether. The transitory quality of affect and migration, though indicative of precarity, also suggests both a sustained structural critique and a latent liberatory potential. Things need not be like they are at the moment. Feeling pirate, learning to live and thrive in a state of indeterminacy, lays bare the impoverishment of currently existing norms of legality and exclusion and the urgent need for alternative norms to emerge.

## Bibliography

Ahmed, Sara. *Strange Encounters: Embodied Others in Post-Coloniality*. Routledge, 2000.

Amaya, Hector. *Citizenship Excess: Latino/as, Media, and the Nation*. Duke UP, 2013.

Avalos, Adan. "The Naco in Mexican Film: La Banda del Carro Rojo, Border Cinema, and Migrant Audiences." *Latsploitation, Exploitation Cinemas, and Latin America*, edited by Victoria Ruetalo and Dolores Tierney, Routledge, 2009, pp. 185–200.

Brah, Avtar. *Cartographies of Diaspora: Contesting Identities*. Routledge, 1996.

Butler, Judith. *Bodies That Matter: On the Discursive Limits of "Sex."*Routledge, 1993.

Cross, John C. "Pirates on the High Streets: The Street as a Site of Local Resistance to Globalization." *Street Entrepreneurs*, edited by John C. Cross and Alfonso Morales, Routledge, 2007, pp. 125–144.

DeGenova, Nicholas. "Migrant 'Illegality' and Deportability in Everyday Life." *Annual Review of Anthropology*, vol. 31, 2002, pp. 419–447.

Gonzales, J.R. "Sharpstown Shopping Center: 50 Years Later." *Houston Chronicle*, September 14, 2011.

Greenberg, Joshua. *From Betamax to Blockbuster: Video Stores and the Invention of Movies on Video*. MIT Press, 2008.

Herbert, Daniel. *Videoland: Movie Culture at the American Video Store*. U of California P, 2013.

Hilderbrand, Lucas. *Inherent Vice: Bootleg Histories of Videotape and Copyright*. Duke UP, 2009.

Honig, Bonnie. *Public Things: Democracy in Despair*. Fordham UP, 2017.

Klinger, Barbara. *Beyond the Multiplex: Cinema, New Technologies, and the Home*. U of California P, 2006.

Larkin, Brian. *Signal and Noise: Media, Infrastructure, and Urban Culture in Nigeria*. Duke UP, 2008.

Lobato, Ramon, and Julian Thomas. *The Informal Media Economy*. Polity, 2015.

Lomax, John Nova. "I Am a Pedestrian Report: Bellaire." *Houston Press Blog*, May 25, 2007.

Muñoz, Jose Esteban. "Feeling Brown: Ethnicity and Affect in Ricardo Bracho's 'The Sweetest Hangover (and Other STDs).'" *Gay Latino Studies: A Critical Reader*, edited by Michael Hames-Garcia and Ernesto Javier Martinez, Duke UP, 2011, pp. 204–219.

Sa, Lucia. *Life in the Megalopolis: Mexico City and Sao Paulo*. Routledge, 2014.

St. John, Paige, and Joel Rubin. "ICE Held an American Man in Custody for 1,273 Days. He's Not the Only One Who Had to Prove His Citizenship." *Los Angeles Times*, April 27, 2018.

Sulski, Jim. "Video Stores as Diverse as the City." *Chicago Tribune*, April 12, 1991.

Sundaram, Ravi. *Pirate Modernity: Dehli's Media Urbanism*. Routledge, 2009.

# 7

# FROM PIRACY AS A CRIME TO PIRACY AS A NECESSITY

## Territorial Inequalities and the Socially Necessary Market in Brazil

*Fábio Tozi*

### Introduction

We will begin with the important task of defining terms (Bosi 11). Etymologically, the word "pirate" stems from the Latin *pirate* (*praedõ* or *praedõ maritimus* in Portuguese), a "mariner that intercepts ships to plunder them." However, the Latin word derives from the Greek *peiratês*, which meant spoiler, thief, or evildoer (Chantraine; Corvez). Some modern languages use different terms for actions for the misappropriation of material goods versus immaterial property, including French (*contrefaçon* and *piraterie*) and English (*piracy, forgery*, and *counterfeit*, which all have different meanings). In Portuguese, *contrafação* (counterfeiting) is classified as a crime and restricted to legal usage, although this word is rarely used, whereas *pirataria* (piracy) is used indiscriminately in colloquial language to qualify practices related to the misappropriation of materiality and content, giving this word a common, though false, sense of "crime." The increasing use of the word "piracy" in everyday life—which has both retained its original connection to naval pirates and expanded to include other, more commonplace forms of appropriation—is just as important to this investigation as the official legal framework, which is continually updating to adapt to societal changes.

As seaborne trade gradually increased throughout twelfth-century Europe, maritime navigation broke the dominance of ancient forms of rural life. At the same time, maritime piracy appeared as a practice and as a word. Merchant sailors, organized in guilds, were the first to adopt a code of conduct at sea. The thirteenth century attests to the birth of the *privateer*, who represented the institutionalization of piracy carried out by empires, boasting their symbols, flags, and laws. Privateering was a tool used to weaken trade competition.

This brief reconstitution of historical facts is important because privateers and pirates have historically been granted different social and legal status: the former are considered part of society and worthy of a trial; the latter deserve nothing more than the gallows. However, there is another fundamental difference between them, as outlined by Duran (157–163): while early privateers of the thirteenth century reproduced the rigid hierarchies of military tradition and merchant culture, pirates used to have an "anarchistic ideal" expressed in a pirate council in which the captain, elected by the crew, did not make decisions without consulting his subordinates. Additionally, pirates did not have a strong culture of physical punishment, and they had a greater commitment to sharing whatever was captured, distributing it fairly among themselves. Many crews also maintained a common fund to disburse to injured crew members.

Throughout history there has been a contradictory movement that actualizes, in each period and space, the senses of pirate, from the original Greek sense to the one it has in contemporary Brazil: the pirate as the one who does not comply with established norms—i.e., a subject who pursues a diverging social project—and the pirate as a criminal, predestined to be a culprit before a court trial that has not even been convened. As I discuss in the second and third sections of this chapter, there has been a historical and geographical update of this dialectic between rigid norms and freedom of action in Brazil. As the laws protecting intellectual property (IP) multiply, benefiting a select group of private agents, ways of circumventing them are revamped, as I address in my discussion of the unauthorized production of music in the Tecnobrega circuit—"cheesy techno," a musical style characterized by electronic versions of popular, "corny" songs, as well as by Brazilian versions of foreign hits. Even though the criminal definition of "pirate" has never existed in Brazil, a historical overview shows that legal prohibitions are continually reformulated to include stricter control of the reproduction and circulation of objects and information, including music and books.

The Philippine Code—or Ordinances and Laws of the Kingdom of Portugal—imposed on the Brazilian colony by the Portuguese metropolis in 1603, prohibited the reproduction of books and certain merchandise. The Ordinances were repealed in 1916 with the approval of the first Brazilian Civil Code, whose Chapter VI addressed the "protection of literary, scientific, and artistic property." Revised in 2002, the Civil Code no longer addresses authorship, reproduction, or counterfeiting—themes that have become the central topics of specific laws, notably the Intellectual Property Law, no. 9,279 (Regula direitos e obrigações relativos à propriedade industrial) and the Copyright Law, no. 9,610 (Altera, atualiza e consolida a legislação sobre direitos autorais).

Here, following a geographical methodology, i.e., considering society through its use of the territory, I propose a definition of the phenomenon of piracy that is different from that used in legal and economic approaches, without, however, denying their importance, as stated by Tozi ("Pirataria, piratarias" 47; *Rigidez normativa* 25). That said, this chapter will consider the term "piracy" as referring to any action of reproducing objects or information without paying for IP. I believe that it leads to an expropriation of works and knowledge that, in turn, allows for new creative interventions. In offering this definition of piracy, I seek to avoid the reduction of complex socio-spatial situations to overly simplistic structures. Under this definition, pirates are not first and foremost criminals, but individuals, companies, governments, and institutions who take possession of somebody else's property, as it will be shown in the Tecnobrega case study in Belém do Pará, Brazil.

In order to understand the contemporary use of the word pirate, I present three different senses, all of them pertaining to criminal behavior. None of them exists in isolation. On the contrary, the convergence of technique and information creates endless hybrid relations among them, even if each of the different social agents involved has a distinct capacity to use territory, resulting in different levels of social action. The Tecnobrega DJs' case, presented below, illustrates how the entry of the Internet into areas of precarious urbanization creates a new technical milieu in which DJs can create songs, even if, in doing so, they deprive others of their copyrights.

## The Pirate Who Lingers in the Seas

Containers are the primary means of shipping in the global trade of goods. Their adoption, coupled with the size of merchant ships, was essential for reducing transportation costs and managing global interfaces, as argued by Monié (307) and Frémont and Soppé (188). Preserving the international shipping channels through which all kinds of goods—legalized or not—pass is essential to the effective functioning of the geo-economic connections that links large Asian industries with large consumer markets in Europe and North America. In this context, maritime pirates are an active risk to the movement and safety of the vessels, especially in the Gulf of Aden near Somalia, a notorious site of naval piracy, even though the country does not actively participate in the global logistics system. The pirate is personified here by the pauperized image of the Somali assaulter, countered by sophisticated armed forces of European countries, the United States, and China. This maritime piracy is virtually nonexistent in Brazil, but the urban Brazilian popular economy is entirely dependent on global circuits of maritime distribution via containers. These containers circulate the commercial products (mostly Chinese) that reach Brazil's main ports, Santos and Paranaguá, and the customs-free zone in Ciudad del Este.

## The Pirate Who Replicates Materiality

Unauthorized reproduction of objects often involves a kind of reverse engineering, which requires sophisticated technical and logistical knowledge. These specialized processes tend to focus on an object's form and appearance more than its content. Copies and fakes are increasingly common in everyday life due to new technological processes that enable "fast fashion" and other high-speed mass production of common consumer goods like clothes, bags, footwear, eyewear, housewares, and electronics. In turn, peddlers, hawkers, street fairs, and shopping malls provide a venue for the sale of these copies. For most consumers, the imitation of the design and the brand is more important than any possible deviation in quality between the original and its copy. Though Brazil has opened its national borders to global brands in recent decades, replicas have become an especially lucrative commodity there because the high price of the original goods makes them inaccessible to many consumers. Thus, a circuit of production and distribution of copies has emerged in Brazil, with two main hotspots. Foz do Iguacu and the Paranaguá Port, on the border with Ciudad del Este (in Paraguay), have become major entry points for goods, while São Paulo performs a complementary function: national distribution. The final step in this circulation of counterfeits, consumption, takes place in a more dispersed geography: the metropolis, midsized cities, and small towns all over the country.

## The Pirate of Digital Contents

While the technical and regulatory development of the internet was based on guidelines from states and corporations, its massive reach and ability to generate endless global connections has made digital piracy a continually expanding practice with state, corporate, and domestic participation. This generates new debates surrounding the national and international regulation of piracy and updates metaphors that associate it with the verbs of maritime origin such as surfing or navigating the Internet. Since Brazilian society is quickly becoming digitally engaged, there is growing tension between the expansion of the Internet and connection devices (computers, smartphones, and tablets) with the holders of copyrights and patents. The result is a strong police state disseminating an inefficient and criminalizing discourse. On the other hand, these pirates have a great deal of information available to them, which they use creatively under the conditions of poverty. In the final section of this chapter, I examine the Brazilian musical phenomenon Tecnobrega to reveal the relationship between poverty, piracy, information technologies, and new forms of local and regional production. This creative use occurs despite Brazil's increasing normative control of piracy, which will be described in the next section.

## Knowledge as Property and Piracy as Crime: The Geopolitics of Innovation

Another important fact to understand contemporary piracy is the creation of the same planetary technical base, followed up by global norms that control its circulation. Simultaneously, there is a steady reduction in the diversity of productive technical systems as they have progressively expanded geographically. If, in the past, each local or national place had its own particular technical set, successive globalizations led to the creation of more homogeneous technical standards. In geographical terms this globalization could be translated by Santos as the expansion of a "technical-scientific-informational milieu" ("Universal reason, local reason" 108). So, while the socioeconomic process has materialized the bases for piracy, new forms of control have become increasingly centralized by means of laws and of selective and partial practices for the regulated diffusion of innovation.

Some events are paradigmatic of the expansion of regulatory rigidity, like the first International Convention on Patents in 1879; the Berne Convention on the Protection of Literary and Artistic Works in 1886 (extended by the Rome Convention of 1961), approved by Brazil in 1922, and ratified in 1933 when it entered into force; the creation of the World Intellectual Property Organization (WIPO) in 1967; and the International Treaty of Patents, adopted in Washington in 1970. In 1947 the International Organization for Standardization (ISO) and the General Agreement on Tariffs and Trade (GATT) were born, while the Geneva Convention of 1952 (revised in Paris in 1971) represented the adoption of copyright (©) by signatories of the Berne Convention. Divergences tapered; decisions flourished.

In 1994 market protection was coupled with the adoption of the Trade-Related Aspects of Intellectual Property Rights (TRIPS) Agreement. In 1995 the World Trade Organization (WTO) was finally created. The notion of IP sets in motion a new phase of globalization, eliminating old distinctions and divergences between the agreements dedicated to industrial property and those dedicated to copyright and artistic rights. As Gille (1352) notes, the purely national norms became the minority. This can be considered a crucial moment in the relations between nation-states and global corporations. Meanwhile, the national policies for innovation have become international geopolitical disputes. The late industrialization in Brazil, associated with a nonautonomous insertion in international trade, has put the country in a fragile geopolitical position in relation to the holders of IP, as it will be shown in the Special 301 Report discussion late in the chapter. Geopolitics, understood as the political action of public and private agents within the force field of space, provides an overall view of modernization in an unequal and peripheral society.

Legally, one thus finds a hybrid policy among states and corporations at a time when science and information have become productive forces and their control has become a major point of dispute in monopolistic or oligopolistic branches of the economy. As Väyrynen (342) highlights, patents are a way of monopolizing information, and, thanks to this monopoly, the metapower (*métapouvoir*), or the power to determine relationships between metropolises and technical peripheries, of multinational companies is bolstered. In this same vein, Bognár (47) addresses the efforts of the colonizing powers to ensure what he defines as *intellectual monopolies*. Moreover, for Santos (*A natureza do espaço* 144), neoliberalism articulates both technique and politics, propagating productive and labor flexibility in what is, in fact, an organizational toughening of the capitalist accumulation model.

The state characterizes itself as a central agent in this new geopolitics based on patents and copyrights, as is evident in Brazil–US relations. Important in this regard is the so-called Special 301 Report, which imposes technical censorship on Brazilian society. Since 1974, with the creation of the Office of the United States Trade Representative (USTR), the United States has applied targeted sanctions to countries that do not comply with IP protection. Starting with the Omnibus Trade and Competitiveness Act (1988), annual reports were produced about the countries with which the United States maintains more sustained trade relations. Such reports are discursive manifestations of the attack on piracy in contemporary geopolitics.

The Special 301 Report connects to the General System of Preferences (GSP), a program designed to promote the economic growth of developing countries through preferential import tariffs associated with 5,000 products. The GSP is therefore an exception to articles of the WTO, which determine commercial equality among countries and were implemented in the United States in 1976 with the Trade Act of 1974. Since 1984, the renovation of this benefit is subject to the protection of IP, the main objective of the reports. The reports rank countries into the following categories: (i) watch list; (ii) priority watch list; (iii) monitoring; and (iv) priority foreign countries. The American classification for Brazil is shown in Table 7.1.

From 1989 to 2018, Brazil has been receiving varied classifications, sometimes being relegated and other times promoted. These rankings can be seen as either an award or a punishment in relation to piracy. Since 2007, the country has been on the *watch list*. In 1993, Brazil was placed in the *priority foreign countries* category. As a result, between 1994 and 1998, Brazil was excluded from the reports. These years coincided with important events regarding amendments of Brazilian laws: in 1994 the country signed the TRIPS Agreement, in 1996 Brazil approved the new Patent Law and, in 1998, the new Copyright Law. As

**TABLE 7.1** Brazil: classification in the *Special 301 Report* (1989–2017)

| *Year* | *Classification* | *Year* | *Classification* | *Year* | *Classification* |
|---|---|---|---|---|---|
| 1989 | Priority watch list | 1999 | Watch list | 2009 | Watch list |
| 1990 | Priority watch list | 2000 | Watch list | 2010 | Watch list |
| 1991 | Priority watch list | 2001 | Watch list | 2011 | Watch list |
| 1992 | Priority watch list | 2002 | Priority watch list | 2012 | Watch list |
| 1993 | Priority foreign countries | 2003 | Priority watch list | 2013 | Watch list |
| 1994 | Excluded from the list | 2004 | Priority watch list | 2014 | Watch list |
| 1995 | Priority watch list | 2005 | Priority watch list | 2015 | Watch list |
| 1996 | Watch list | 2006 | Priority watch list | 2016 | Watch list |
| 1997 | Watch list | 2007 | Watch list | 2017 | Watch list |
| 1998 | Excluded from the list | 2008 | Watch list | 2018 | Watch list |

Source: *Special 301 Report* (between 1989 and 2018) (USTR). Organized by the author.

a direct result, the fight against piracy multiplied at several levels of the Brazilian Federation (states and municipalities).

The criminalization of piracy has been translated into the criminalization of individuals and places—notably the poorest ones—on which police and military control have been imposed. In the city of São Paulo, the fight against piracy was used as an argument for the militarization of urban territories and their management. In 2011, São Paulo's mayor, Gilberto Kassab (from the extreme right-wing party DEM), appointed servicemen in the military reserve to various positions. Among the 31 commanders appointed, 25 were officers of the reserve.[1] Since then, private agents have sometimes acted in partnership with the city, as in the "Projeto Escola Legal" ("Cool" School Project),[2] financed by AMCHAM Brazil (American Chamber of Commerce). The project, a partnership with the State Department of Education, was supported by other private associations and sought to develop an "IP culture" among students and teachers of public schools. According to Tozi, the project ignored the economic reality of those involved, as the purchase of counterfeit products or the illegal download of music and video were the only forms of consumption within their reach (*Rigidez normativa* 190).

From this, one can observe how Brazil's demotion in the Special 301 Report translates into a geopolitical pressure that crosses national, state, and municipal borders. The report is, then, an emblematic geopolitical instrument for understanding the contemporary mix of state and corporate policies. With the national legal frameworks already aligned to the principles of the WTO, especially to those of American foreign trade policy, one can notice, in recent years, pressure on specific sectors. Examples include the function of ANVISA (National Agency of Health Surveillance) in processes of patenting medicines, the permissiveness of book copying in Brazilian universities, and the sale of pirate CDs and DVDs (with movies, music, and computer programs) on the streets with minimal legal intervention.

However, despite the norms imposed on the territory, the territory also imposes itself as a norm (Santos *A natureza do espaço*). In Brazil, historical and contemporary inequalities create a geographical milieu characterized by: (i) a regionally fragmented territory (the northeast with its colonial urbanization; the midwest, an important location for agribusiness; the north, poorly integrated with the rest of the country; and the south and southeast, where one finds a concentration of places selected by the state and corporations for deeper global integration); (ii) selectively distributed infrastructure, goods, services, and public and private information (invoking the idea of the "four Brazils," conceived by Santos and Silveira [268]); (iii) high-income inequality and low wages; and (iv) rapid dissemination of new informational goods, boosting a consumerism encouraged by advertisement. In this context—to which one should add the high price of the "original" goods—piracy of all kinds proliferates. Let us now turn to the productive spatial circuit of music in Tecnobrega, where we can observe one of the ways territory itself responds to the IP control system.

## From Crime to Necessity: Tecnobrega and Creativity

In contrast to the rigid geopolitics of innovation, the development of piracy allows a distinction between "imitative piracy" and "adaptative piracy" as proposed by Tozi ("Pirataria, piratarias" 55). Imitative piracy is a dense and organized set of technical, scientific, and informational knowledge that requires territorial and economic investments, occurring within the corporate spaces of globalization. This piracy, practiced by states and corporations, is intended for effective reproduction of capital. Adaptative piracy, on the other hand, is linked to the conditions of the geographical milieu where it manifests itself, adopting less modern techniques for production, distribution, circulation, and consumption. Diffused across cities throughout the country, this second type of piracy is typical of places and people in the lower circuits of the urban economy.[3]

Adaptative piracy, associated with everyday survival rather than with the reproduction of capital, carries elements of what Ribeiro (93) defines as the "socially necessary market": the price variation depends on negotiation, so that the needs (of sellers and buyers) become more important than costs and profits, as in a market driven by capitalism. Practiced in homes, in small shops, and on the streets and sidewalks of Brazilian cities, adaptative piracy is based more on curiosity and needs than on skilled labor according to the institutionalized conception of technical-scientific professionalization.

The fact that many agents in society practice piracy does not mean that they all do so in the same manner or with the same access to the territory's technical systems. In Brazil the forms of production, circulation, distribution, and consumption of piracy gravitate between the legal and the illegal in a wide spectrum that can neither be reduced to illegality or the informal sector, nor to a hidden or underground economy.

The city of Belém do Pará, in the state of Pará, is where Tecnobrega vigorously manifests itself. Located in northern Brazil, in the Amazon tropical rainforest area, the municipality has an urbanization rate of 99 percent and a population of 1,500,000 inhabitants according to the Brazilian Institute of Geography and Statistics (Instituto Brasileiro de Geografia e Estatística, IBGE). However, Belém and its metropolitan area have a less modernized geographical environment than the richest region of the country (the so-called "concentrated" region, which includes, roughly, the south and southeast regions).

On the one hand, Tecnobrega feeds from productive spatial circuits that manifest the connections between culture, society, and territory. On the other hand, traditional record companies, pursuing territorial concentration, left the state of Pará and settled in the central parts of the country. So, while the territory acts as a haven for certain musical cultures, within the music industry corporations, including Tecnobrega, the territory is also a "resource" for obtaining surplus value, following the dialectic laid out by Gottmann (37). Figure 7.1 synthesizes the hybridism between agents and objects found along the paths covered from production to the actual listening of Tecnobrega songs.

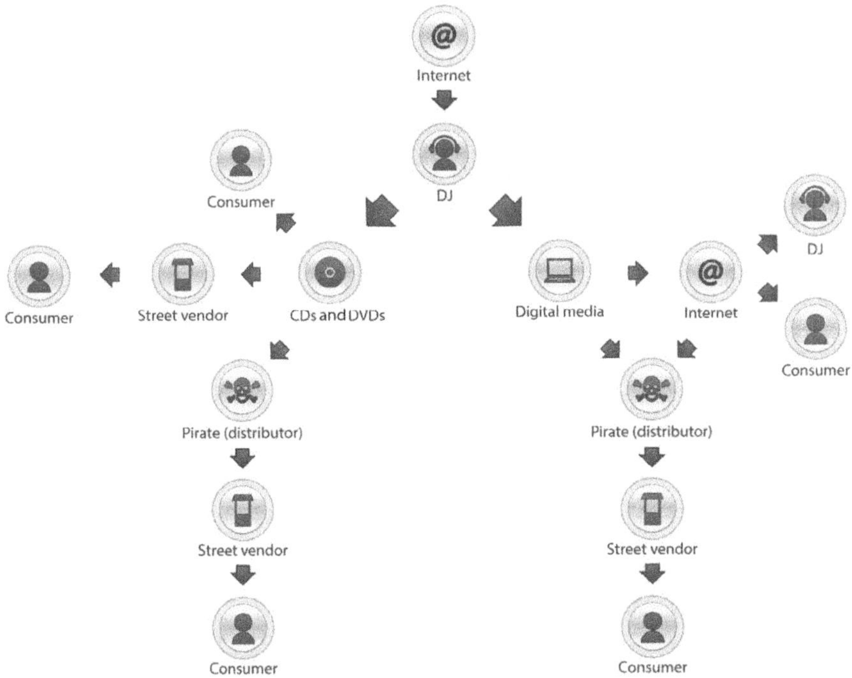


**FIGURE 7.1** Belém do Pará: production, distribution, and consumption of Tecnobrega music
Source: Author's fieldwork.

Lacking contracts with large record labels, Tecnobrega groups reinvented traditional ways to produce, circulate, and consume music (through physical and/or digital media) by relying on new information technologies. Produced in small semi-professional or home studios (Figure 7.2), digital files, CDs, and DVDs are created, distributed, and sold by the bands themselves. Or, with support from "*pirateiros*," who reproduce copies in large quantities, they invade the street markets through the work of peddlers. As argued by Oliveira (219), it is a productive circuit of music—guided by counter-rationalities that reinvent the music industry through horizontal actions—whose strength lies in its creativity, solidarity, and proximity to the public.

This circuit relies on piracy through the expropriation of copyright, enabling the creation of new relationships among musicians, sellers, and buyers (listeners). Often, bands donate their albums to be pirated in exchange for a dissemination that only piracy can provide, considering that the diffusion of music has become more important than copyright. This indicates that copyright law does not always meet the peculiarities of all areas and forms of creativity in Brazil. Hence, the free distribution of music through various media emerges as the connecting element for an entire circuit that becomes a local and regional economic space.

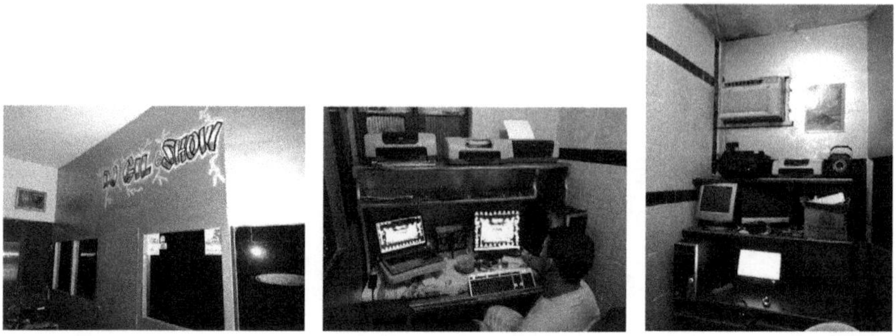

**FIGURE 7.2** Belém do Pará: Nova Dimensão (New Dimension) Aparelhagem (2010). From left to right: an *aparelhagem* (or studio) set up in a home garage, followed by two internal pictures that highlight the use of computers and home printers to download and record music and to print covers or advertising material. The tasks that require expertise and bureaucratic division of labor in a label are here carried out by the DJs (two brothers), who are also the owners of the *aparelhagem*

Source: Photo by author, September 2010.

Consequently, the analytical focus should not be simply the benefit to musical groups or DJs but the urban economy as a whole, formed by a complex social division of labor.

Legal systems based on copyright and authors' rights create disadvantages—without any attendant advantages—for this region of Brazil, where—and this is important to emphasize—ancestral indigenous philosophies characterize key aspects of social life. These expropriation processes fostered by soft information technologies via use (and not property) call into question the definition and the dissemination of corporate knowledge amassed over the last two centuries. As argued by Gaudin (15), it is necessary to challenge the prevailing misconception that protecting an idea is of the utmost importance when, in fact, it is how the idea is created, propagated, and transmitted that really molds our society.

The Calypso band from Belém is an example of a symbolic social agent of this pirated productive process. Their story demonstrates the visibility of this locally conceived music scene. Even without a label, the group has sold over five million copies of their CDs without having ever been on national television. This success challenges the importance of an agent previously considered essential: the record companies. Production and distribution functions were taken over by members of the group, who sold their own CDs during their shows or provided them to street vendors, all supplemented by local and regional radio advertisement. When Calypso became nationally famous, the band went on to appear in large-audience programs on national television, such as the well-known *Domingão do Faustão at Globo*, [4] where they received gold, platinum, and diamond records in 2005 without the representation of a label.

A similar process occurred with Gaby Amarantos. In 2002, the female singer formed a band called Tecno Show. In 2003, her band also received an invitation to take part in the *Domingão do Faustão* show. However, it is Gaby Amarantos's solo career that really took off when, in 2010, she launched her hit "Today I'm Single" ("Tô solteira"), a Tecnobrega version of Beyoncé's "Single Ladies." Faustão is known for having coined the nickname for which she became famous: the Beyoncé of Pará.[5] Copyright is a recurring theme in Gaby's interviews and songs. She claims that her success is due to her preference for disseminating her songs rather than protecting them with copyright. In her song "Xirley" (2011), the chorus repeats "I'm going to sample, I'm going to steal you," and the music video, which relies upon the services of Greenvision Films and is directed by Priscilla Brasil, includes an image of Jesus Christ with the caption:

> The practice of piracy is a sin according to the word of God, and a violation of legal rights entails sanctions provided for in the Criminal Code Act 9610. Piracy is a crime and a sin. Do not violate the law of God. (Amarantos)

In a profoundly Catholic society, the association between piracy, sin, and the Copyright Act demonstrates, in a hybrid mix of irreverence and social criticism, how the ubiquity of norms of unknown origin ends up being a form of censorship. Xirley, the main character in the song, describes the spells she will cast to get the love she wants. In Belém, despite its indigenous and African background, one finds the famous "Cirio de Nazaré," known to be the largest Catholic procession in the world. Tecnobrega, with its colors, abundant lights, clothes, dances, and sexy lyrics, depicts, in its own way, this social tension between Catholicism and other faiths, between national copyright laws and local economies of production and cultural diffusion.

While a few artists get money and labor contracts that guarantee national recognition, most artists only take part in a pauperized local and regional economy marked by the absence of state support. In general, the most visible, continuous, and steady presence of the state is that of the military police, surveilling and oppressing, especially at the entrances of balls in Belém's peripheries. Traditional music and media markets often choose only a few artists to be transformed into exotic products and sold as novelty. YouTube, for one, has shown itself to be a skillful global business player when it comes to benefiting from local peculiarities, transformed into millions of views and likes.

With the advance of technology, the distribution of digital files via the Internet has proven faster and more efficient for Tecnobrega than the traditional circuits, despite the northern region having the lowest presence of Internet services among Brazilian regions, not to mention much lower connection speeds. Therefore, modernity and speed, very common in the discourse on technology innovation, are not the *sine qua non* of social progress in its broadest sense. The less modernized geographical milieu and the existing digital slowness in Belém still manages to meet the needs of the processes of expropriation (piracy) and creation associated with Tecnobrega.

Here we see that creativity is not just a technological variable. Place, as a synonym for communication circuits and infrastructures, has an active influence on creation and creativity. Despite the relatively low-speed Internet in Belém, there is a frantic speed in creation: new songs, CDs, and DVDs are released daily from groups and DJs whose range is local or regional[6] rather than national. Another DJ[7] reported hearing a new song at night and calling a colleague, who immediately downloaded it for him from the Internet (without paying royalties, of course). By the following afternoon, the DJ had received the Tecnobrega version of the song, remixed in a pirate program. Thanks to technique and piracy, a new song was created. From there stems a dense communicational—and increasingly digital—network through which DJs broadcast their music to other DJs and, particularly, to producers. Social networks and instant messaging applications are paramount to the process. Initially it was MSN, Orkut, 4Shared, and Dropbox. Subsequently, WhatsApp, Facebook, Instagram, and Snapchat became crucial sites of communication and exchange.

The songs are also available for free on *aparalhagens'*[8] websites and blogs. In this circuit, there is a necessary and forced socialization, since no music remains unique to a DJ or an *aparelhagem*, and any attempt to prevent its reproduction is an attack against the productive circuit itself. Once released, a song is available to everyone and can be remixed several times, thereby increasing its chances of success.

In the dispute for popularity, a seemingly trivial but essential action is to make the DJ's name and phone number visible (in addition to email, website, and social media) by adding them to the name of the digital file, be it within the images or in the information section of chat applications and social networks. This way, one-click sharing of a single song can disclose a comprehensive database (the DJ's repertoire), thereby boosting its advertising. It is important to note that communication applications—notably WhatsApp, Facebook, and Instagram—have increasingly become work instruments, especially due to the high telephone tariff rates since privatization in 1998. In other words, the Internet has created a new and expanded means of communication, one that simple telephone calls could never match. Moreover, as the speed, quality, and price of Internet connections make them still inaccessible for many in Belém do Pará, it is common to see the sale of USB flash drives (pen drives) with discographies of various DJs and studios, for prices ranging from R$60 (US$18.00) to R$80 (US$24.00) in 2017. The same goes for CDs and DVDs, whose unit prices range from R$3 to R$10 (US $1.00 to US$3.00), with promotions when purchasing higher quantities. These disks still supply the demand of many consumers who are not used to computers or surfing the Internet (or are not even connected yet). Through this we see how practices derived from piracy serve the different communication speeds in Brazilian communities.

Since the DJ's or the band's fame—and survival—does not come from the sale of records but from having a broad audience of listeners who play and share the music, each new song is accompanied by the hope of being massively reproduced. Once taken into studio parties, a song—if it turns out to be a success—becomes part of collections and finally makes its way to radio stations. In Tecnobrega, more important than producing—an activity that has already been banalized—is achieving wide circulation and ensuring the dissemination of the music, at which point the studios become really powerful. But as the speed of creation is vertiginous, the same acceleration that benefits this process is also a threat. Since songs are rapidly created and disseminated, they disappear as quickly as they appear. The success and, of course, the financial returns become ephemeral, maybe even impossible.

As for the party houses, it is important to highlight their popular and peripheral character. They are establishments usually installed in some form of "underground" environment but accompanied by expensive and sophisticated technology: big LED screens, powerful speakers, lasers, fireworks, and other special effects (Figure 7.3). While Tecnobrega challenges the dominance of previously hegemonic agents in music production and distribution (record companies and producers), it also bolsters others, such as big sound and light companies that have a presence in Belém. This is the case for São Paulo-based company Tec.Luz, which even sends its employees to some of the parties in order to monitor the operation of the equipment they provide. Similarly, DJs and sound/light technicians from Belém visit trade fairs specialized in musical instruments and audio equipment, such as Expomusic (International Fair of Music), which takes place in São Paulo. This constitutes a new social and territorial division of labor within the circuit of Tecnobrega: while piracy holds less sophisticated occupations and a local or regional circulation of small amounts of money, skilled workers and consultants, and expensive services and products tend to gather in selected places of the national territory.

The complex network involving Tecnobrega feeds on pirate practices allowed in their own geographical environment. The city houses and provides the elements necessary for their reproduction. Maffesoli (92) asserts that "far from economic or political structures, communication, an essential function, is part of the most humble places, in the most mundane situations." From home-made music to the sale of pirated discs in the old downtown streets (e.g., João Alfredo Street, a pedestrian boulevard filled with stalls from vendors of various pirated products) or neighborhoods, the city, with its networks and relationships, is a constant celebration: there are parties every day, especially between Thursday and Monday. DJing, a line of work usually linked to a profound knowledge of music, has become a common occupation carried out by people lacking the technical and aesthetic knowledges typically required.

**FIGURE 7.3** Belém do Pará: Ruby Aparelhagem 2010. Supported by modern sound and light systems, this party (Rubi Saudade) takes place at Metropolis every Monday, starting at 3 p.m., and is known for playing the *saudade* music style, which recovers and recreates old songs of the *brega* (corny, tacky, cheesy) music style

Source: Author, October 2010, photo taken from the Rubi Saudade Facebook page, www.facebook.com/pg/LendarioRubi/photos/?tab=album&album_id=690687734274932.00 Accessed August 27, 2017.

## Final Thoughts: Piracy as a Use of Technique

As discussed earlier, for centuries and in many different locations, pirates have been seen as criminals. In Brazil today, this concept is based on a legal framework for the protection of IP. Parallel to that, however, there has also always been a libertarian aspect inherent in the pirate's activity, understood, in this case, as the ability to work, create music, present it to the public, and allow the circulation of money under local control, thus breaking with the rules of the oligopoly of the music industry in Brazil. This study of Tecnobrega is an attempt to analytically understand this transfiguration of crime into creation, satisfying local cultural expression needs, and sustaining a market that is socially necessary in Belém. These "pirate" markets that meet local or regional needs are disseminated across the country.

In major Brazilian cities such as São Paulo, Rio de Janeiro, or Belo Horizonte, the cost of taking a family with two children to a movie theater illustrates another relationship between territory, poverty, and piracy: the family will spend R$24 (US$6) on public transport (considering a round trip and that students pay 50 percent of the full price) and R$75 (US$18.75) on tickets (considering an average price of R$25 (US$6.25) per ticket and two children entitled to a 50 percent discount). Disregarding any meals, drinks, or other extra expenses, the total cost of the movie theater trip amounts to R$99 (US$24.75). The minimum monthly wage in Brazil, which represents the income of a significant percentage of households, is R$954 (US$238.50).[9]

Thus, the simple act of watching a movie at the theater represents almost 10 percent of the income of a lower-class family in Brazil. However, with R$10 (US$3.00) one can buy three to five pirated DVDs from a street vendor. In addition, once bought, DVDs can be loaned, exchanged, or donated. These objects—pirate objects according to the law—create alternative market and nonmarket relationships between people. Their circulation and price don't have a single capitalist pattern, a fact that gives additional political meaning to the actions that generate them. Besides, most cities in Brazil do not even have a movie theater. Piracy—digital or physical—is, in practical terms, the only way in many areas to watch a film.

The same argument is valid for another sensitive topic for families and book publishers in Brazil: the copying of books. Even though illegal according to successive copyright laws, as previously shown, unauthorized reproduction legitimizes itself in view of the precariousness of the geographical milieu, characterized by the absence of public libraries and bookstores in most of the colossal Brazilian peripheries. Indeed, it is notable that even the most important universities in Brazil could not exist without an "on-demand" system of unauthorized copies of books, manuals, articles, and fragment of texts. The advent of distributive technologies in informational peripheries such as Brazil enables practices that function, perhaps, against the rationality of the creators of these technical systems.

However, these strategies of technical improvement based on piracy are not exclusive to peripheral places. The technical censorship imposed by the innovations' owners completely ignores the findings of Béaur et al. (14), which prove that counterfeiting and fraud have always been a necessary lubricant to all economic systems. The same line of argument is followed by Stanziani (577), who maintains that if innovation is the engine of economic growth, fraud and counterfeiting are its pistons. One can thus argue that contemporary Brazilian piracy is not an aberration in the historical process of innovation but one of its most extraordinary manifestations.

Moreover, when space is incorporated as a category of analysis, digital pirates are not only found among the poor. From a legal point of view, more than half of the population would be considered criminal if existing laws were strictly enforced. In this sense the association between piracy and poverty—proposed by the state and by corporations—is incorrect or misleading. Territorial inequalities are striking in Brazil. It is the rich and middle classes—who possess modern computers and live in neighborhoods with the best network and Internet providers—who are the predominant agents of digital piracy. Protected within the privacy of their homes, however, they are not bothered by policemen or inspectors, who, by contrast, haunt the daily lives of street peddlers trying to sell pirated media in public spaces. The crime is the same, the treatment different. The practices of piracy and its policing together remodel public spaces as sites of differential political practice.

Rather than reproducing such discriminating moral judgments, it is imperative to understand this criminalization of the everyday survival tactics of the poorest in the context of geographical environments, which often do not provide a broad spectrum of possibilities. In large, intermediary, and small cities around the country, creativity takes advantage of the possibilities and limitations of geography and social spaces.

Landscapes full of stalls packed with pirated products reveal a strategy for how to use the city, taking advantage of its spaces, itineraries, and schedules. Choosing the right place and time is a fundamental form of economic knowledge. Bus stops, subway stations, colleges, factories, gas stations, and other geographical fixtures are generators of abundant flows. Clients are located in a daily commute between work and the bus stop, a trajectory that becomes an economic and social circuit. This is the true Brazilian *smart city*, even if it does not have all the glamor of the projects offered by international consultants. In opposition to the normative rigor, the poor enforce a *tropical flexibility*, as defined by Santos (*A natureza do espaço*). They are constantly engaging in new debate, sometimes quiet and sometimes noisy, with people and things that already exist.

Ingenuity and wit negotiate the distance between the resources and precariousness of concrete places. The fragility of the available means in Belém do Pará, for example, reveals the importance of the cardboard boxes, plastic tarps, strings, tapes, and iron frames employed by these street sellers. While fragile, these materials fulfill their functions: sell, hide, flee from supervision, shelter from bad weather, and, in some cases, provide a little rest. These are provisional forms that are, nevertheless, reproduced multiple times, in a great diversity of ways of acting and thinking, and are supported by the surroundings and the city itself. These workers, known as *pirates*, constitute the fragile end of larger circuits. Goods produced in China, distributed through containers, and purchased to wholesalers, are finally available to the consumer. Through so-called piracy the circuit comes to a close, even if that requires resting on top of a simple cardboard box. While more sophisticated, Tecnobrega also transforms the infrastructure of daily life on the periphery into a means of production, such as the small garage that becomes a music studio.

Given the conditions of urban economies in Brazil, piracy is an unavoidable practice. Twice abandoned, by the state and by the capitalistic market, much of the population in impoverished places find in piracy one of the only ways to access objects and content that are essential for their social lives, work, study, and knowledge, thereby characterizing a socially necessary market. Even though their insistence on benefiting from globalization's promises of abundance results in their criminalization, such labels do not stop pirates and their customers from daily practicing and creating new and necessary piracies.

## Notes

1 The city of São Paulo had 11.3 million inhabitants in 2011. Its huge territory is divided into 31 subprefectures, whose subprefects are appointed directly by the mayor.
2 The title of the project makes use of a pun on the word "legal" that has two meanings in Portuguese: it refers to the "legality" of something, but it also means something "cool."
3 According to Santos (*The Shared Space* 13), there are two interconnecting and interdependent circuits of the urban economy that differ from the combinations of capital (intensive or not), technology (advanced or simple), organization (bureaucratic or rudimentary), and information (strategic or banal): the upper circuit refers to the modernized parts of the city, creating a division of skilled labor. In the lower circuit, activities and agents live with a nonmodern urban environment.
4 One of the most watched television programs in Brazil. See www.youtube.com/watch?v=HFrbmvdOkTQ. Accessed 11 March 2017.
5 See "Beyoncé do Pará (Gaby Amarantos)—1° vez no Faustão," www.youtube.com/watch?v=g2b2i0G8vJs. Accessed 11 March 2017.
6 During an interview in September 2010 with DJ Anderson Melo, the presenter of a radio program called *Batidão do Príncipe* (*Prince's Beats*), he reported that he had received nine new songs that day. The visibility as a broadcaster gave him a social function equivalent to that of a music producer.
7 DJ Edielson, from the *Príncipe Negro* (*Black Prince*) *aparelhagem*. Interview conducted during a *Batidão do Príncipe* program at Radio Marajoara (100.9 FM), September 30, 2010.
8 *Aparelhagens*, according to Costa, would be "sound companies geared especially for the realization of 'brega' (tacky, cheesy) parties. Usually family-owned and managed by families … The aparelhagens are generally classified as small, medium or large … Strictly speaking, the studio is the sound equipment consisting of a control unit and its operator (DJ), which enables the use of various resources and high quality in the music emission, and its speakers, which comprise several speakers and tweeters, grouped in the form of columns 3–5 meters high, approximately" (3).
9 Based on the exchange rate as of August 2018.

## Bibliography

Amarantos, Gaby. "Xirley." YouTube, uploaded by Greenvision Films, October 3, 2011, www.youtube.com/watch?v=niGt6fhwMtA. Accessed March 11, 2017.

Béaur, Gérard, Hubert Bonin, and Claire Lemercier, editors. *Fraude, contrefaçon et contrebande de l'Antiquité à nos jours*. Publications d'Histoire Économique et Sociale Internationale, no. 21. Librairie Droz S.A., 2006.

Bognár, Jozsef. *Economic Policy and Planning in Developing Countries*. Akadémiai Kiadó, 1968.
Bosi, Alfredo. *A dialética da colonização*. Companhia das Letras, 1992.
Chantraine, Pierre. *Dictionnaire étymologique de la langue grecque. Histoire des mots*. Kincksieck, [1968] 1999.
*Código Philippino ou Ordenações e Leis do Reino de Portugal, recopiladas por mandado d'El Rey D. Philippe I* [facsimile]. Fundação Calouste Gilbenkian, [1603] 1985.
Corvez, Pol. *Dictionnaire Marin des sentiments et des comportements: les mots issus de la mer et de l'eau*. Éditions Cristel, 2009.
Costa, Antonio Mauricio Dias da. "Festa na cidade: o circuito bregueiro de Belém do Pará." *Revista TOMO*, vol. 6, no. 1, 2003, pp. 107–136.
Duran, Leandro Domingues. *A construção da pirataria: o processo de formação do conceito de 'pirata' no período moderno*. PhD dissertation. Universidade de São Paulo, 2000.
Frémont, Antoine; Martin Soppé. "Transport maritime conteneurisé et mondialisation." *Annales de Géographie*, vol. 114, no. 642, 2005, pp. 187–200.
Gaudin, Thierry. *L'écoute des silences: les institutions contre l'innovation*. Union générale d'Éditions, 10–18, [1978] 2005. Electronic edition available at Université du Québec à Chicoutimi, http://classiques.uqac.ca/contemporains/gaudin_thierry/ecoute_des_silences/ecoute_des_silences.html. Accessed April 4, 2010.
Gille, Bertrand. *Histoire des techhniques*. Encyclopedie de la Pléiade, [1948] 1993.
Gottmann, Jean. "The Evolution of the Concept of Territory." *Social Science Information*, vol. 14, no. 3/4, 1996, pp. 29–47.
Instituto Brasileiro de Geografia e Estatística (IBGE). "Estimativas populacionais para os municípios e para as Unidades da Federação brasileiros em 01.07.2017," www2.ibge.gov.br/home/estatistica/populacao/estimativa2017/default.shtm. Accessed September 11, 2017.
Maffesoli, Michel. *La Conquête du présent. Pour une sociologie de la vie quotidienne*. PUF, 1979.
Monié, Frédéric. "Globalizalação, modernização do sistema portuário e relações cidade-porto no Brasil." *Circulação, transportes e logística—diferentes perspectivas*, edited by Márcio Rogério Silveira, Outras Expressões, 2011, pp. 299–330.
Office of the United States Trade Representative (USTR). *Special 301 Report*. 1989–2018, https://ustr.gov/issue-areas/intellectual-property/Special-301. Accessed April 4, 2017.
Oliveira, Anita Loureiro de. *Música e Vida Urbana: encontros e confrontos na cidade do Rio de Janeiro (1990–2008)*. PhD dissertation. IPPUR/UFRJ, 2008.
Presidência da República. Law no. 9.279, May 14, 1996. Casa Civil, Subchefia para Assuntos Jurídicos, www.planalto.gov.br/ccivil_03/leis/l9279.htm. Accessed April 4, 2017.
Presidência da República. Law no. 9.610, February 19, 1998. Casa Civil, Subchefia para Assuntos Jurídicos, www.planalto.gov.br/ccivil_03/leis/l9610.htm. Accessed April 4, 2017.
Ribeiro, Ana Clara Torres. "Território usado e humanismo concreto: o mercado socialmente necessário." *Formas em crise. Utopias necessárias*, edited by Roberto Carvalho Arruzzo, Julia Adão Bernardes, Catia Antonia da Silva, and Ana Clara Torres RiberioEdições Arquimedes, 2005, pp. 93–111.
Santos, Milton. *A natureza do espaço. Técnica e Tempo. Razão e Emoção*. HUCITEC, 1996.
Santos, Milton. *The Shared Space: The Two Circuits of the Urban Economy and Its Spatial Repercussions*. Methuen, 1979.
Santos, Milton. *Técnica, Espaço, Tempo: Globalização e meio técnico-científico informacional*. HUCITEC, 1994.
Santos, Milton. "Universal Reason, Local Reason, the Spaces of Rationality." *GeoJournal*, vol. 36, no. 1, 1995, pp. 108–110.

Santos, Milton, and María Larua Silveira. *O Brasil: território e sociedade no início do séc. XXI*. Editora Record, 2001.

Stanziani, Alessandro. "La fraude: un équipement juridique de l'action économique." *Fraude, contrefaçon et contrebande de l'Antiquité à nos jours*, edited by Gérard Béaur, Hubert Bonin, and Claire Lemercier, Publications d'Histoire Économique et Sociale Internationale, no. 21, Librairie Droz S.A., 2006.

Tozi, Fábio. "Pirataria, piratarias: imbricações entre espaço e técnica na contemporaneidade." *Revista Ecopolítica*, vol. 1, no. 8, 2014, pp. 41–61, https://revistas.pucsp.br/index.php/ecopolitica/article/viewFile/19463/14423. Accessed October 10, 2017.

Tozi, Fábio. *Rigidez normativa e flexibilidade tropical. Investigando os objetos técnicos no período da globalização*. PhD dissertation. FFLCH/Universidade e São Paulo, 2013, www.teses.usp.br/teses/disponiveis/8/8136/tde-30042013-094602/pt-br.php. Accessed October 10, 2017,

Väyrynen, Raimo. "Les brevets internationaux, moyen de domination technologique." *Revue Internatinale de Sciences Sociales*, vol. XXX, no. 2, 1978, pp. 332–356.

# 8

# BOOK PIRACY IN CHILE AND THE PROLETARIANIZATION OF LITERATURE IN PEDRO LEMEBEL

*Juan Poblete*

I would like to start with two vignettes that place the issue of book piracy in the context of recent Chilean history. The first one comes from the history of resistance of the shanty-town dwellers in población La Victoria in Santiago during the Pinochet dictatorship in the 1980s. It is told by Jennifer Ashley, in an article on what she calls "Honorable Piracy":

> "Pirate" media became a central component of the resistance efforts of activists in La Victoria during this time period. Accessing clandestine copies of audiovisual material of protests and detentions through their socio-political networks, they organized public screenings to provide neighbors with news censored by the military regime. During the late 1980s, they also drew on a series of publications printed by the Chilean NGO ECO entitled *Honorable Pirates* (*Piratas Honradas*) for their counter-communication efforts. In this series of publications, ECO compiled examples of cartoons and other drawings of Latin American artists and encouraged those who wanted to design posters, pamphlets, and other sorts of small media opposing the dictatorship to copy the models provided in order to communicate their message ... Copying the work of others, in this case, was considered "honorable" because it was done not for individual economic benefit, but rather for the collective political good. In this way, piracy for these Chilean activists has a specific socio-historical resonance with ties to media democratization. (Ashley 10)

The second vignette is connected to one the biggest best-sellers, and thus, some of the most pirated books, in the recent history of Chilean publishing: the three volumes of *La Historia Secreta de Chile* by Jorge Baradit published between 2015 and 2017. The author—whose books have sold more than 250,000 copies in the formal circuit, and many thousand more in the informal one—points out:

> Many people are mistaken when they think of piracy as a form of social justice. They think they are participating in a counter-cultural gesture or a form of cultural vindication, when in fact what they do is to finance the truck of a cultural narco-trafficker, an "entrepreneur" operating in the most brutal form of capitalism, one that exploits the work of others without proper compensation or regard for their rights. I do not feel honored when I see one my books pirated on the curb. I feel robbed and I feel for others too: designers, illustrators, publishers, proof-readers, writers and the whole big chain of effort and labor that goes into publishing a book. Lemebel is great but he did a lot of damage when he validated a form of stealing from cultural workers. Because this is not the case of an old lady with a mimeo at home trying to survive. This is a shark with a full clandestine operation, with machinery, distribution networks and corruption that robs writers, themselves one of the weakest cultural and artistic producers in Chile. (Baradit)

In these two accounts, piracy appears in two very different lights. In the first, as an important part of the historic struggles for the democratization of Chilean culture and against the dictatorship and its neoliberal economic model. In other words, piracy is seen there as one of the subversive tactics of the subaltern against the powers that be. In the second case, however, piracy is considered the ultimate example of the corrupting logic of that model of domination. In other words, the "cultural narco-trafficker, an 'entrepreneur' operating in the most brutal form of capitalism" emerges as an embodiment of power and dominance. For Baradit, piracy could, in fact, be connected to the deep ideological or mental transformation dictatorial neoliberalism operated on Chileans:

> I believe that in the great narrative arch of our history we are facing a terrible moment. Not because the [political] right is coming but because we are confronting ourselves … When the social reforms begun—free education, tax reform—people showed they did not want their state-subsidized high-school affected. They did not want tax hikes in order to pay for pensions. I believe that shows how deep neoliberalism's roots are in Chile. After seventeen years of the chemotherapy Pinochet subjected us to, that model penetrated the bones of Chileans and is now an integral part of the soul of our society … The dictatorship accomplishment in Chile was a mentality change, a redefinition of success. We now believe that in order to have better health or better education you must pay. Pinochet managed to change Chilean mentality. That is his triumph. (Benavides)

In the first case, piracy is a collective rebellious reaction against an unjust political and economic system; in the second, it is presented as a most developed form of the violence and selfishness that would define that system. It is not an accident that Pedro Lemebel—who, before Baradit, was one the great pirated authors in what he himself called "the curb or sidewalk mall" ("el mall de la cuneta") in order to refer to the wide variety of books on offer in the streets of Santiago—makes a cameo appearance. In a 2006 interview, Lemebel, connecting the two stories above, stated: "The capitalist fever generates parallel forms of commerce, incites to piracy. And those people who have never walked into a bookstore, find me at a great price on the side-walk" (Budassi 7).

In this chapter, after a contextualizing section, I study the case of Pedro Lemebel and book piracy in Chile. I propose that Lemebel's careful position on book piracy in the country is directly linked to his concept of literature, his self-understanding as a cultural producer, and his relationship with literature as a market-mediated activity. In other words, it is a discourse directly responding to the economies of production, circulation, and consumption of literature in the nation. Moreover, I think that his ideas on the issue are related to what could be called the special status of book piracy and the history of mass publication in Chile. They are, in other words, linked to the trajectory of the concept of national culture that goes from the presidency of Salvador Allende (1970–1973), with its extraordinary plan of massification of printed culture and its proposal for a deep national-popular culture, to the privatization of social life and publishing culture during the dictatorship and post-dictatorship period.

## Book Piracy in Chile

On February 3, 2010, *La Nación* of Santiago included an article with the following headline: "Chile a Nation of Pirates." The piece declared that, at the time, Chile was the country with most piracy of all those included in the Organization for Economic Cooperation and Development (OECD). According to its source, the Business Software Alliance, software piracy in Chile had reached 67 percent of the market (*La Nación*, "Chile, Una Nación de piratas").

Even though Chilean experts immediately questioned both the data and their source, the fact is that the situation of book piracy in Chile is, to say the least, special. It is so, not only because of its alleged causes, but also because its dimension within the publishing market compared to other areas affected by piracy and underground commerce—in a country that regularly boasts of being one of the most open and transparent economies in the world and thus one of the most willing to comply with international standards promoted by the World Trade Organization and Washington—is significantly higher. In 2003, an article in the Chilean press referred to the complaints of Grupo Editorial Planeta, one of the big international publishing houses operating in the country. According to them: "One of every five books sold in Chile is a pirate copy. This data point places us, along with Peru, as the Latin American country with the highest degree of informality in that industry." Jesús Bardenes, at the time the director of the publishing division of Planeta, added that "Chilean companies 'lose' (fail to earn) every year around 42 million dollars, which represents 20% of overall sales." This fact—itself already peculiar in a country that had made so many efforts to, first, position itself as a global defender of international commerce, and then, join the OECD, practicing their standards in many other areas—became even more interesting when Bardenes added that, "The Chilean case is very particular, since the causes of this high degree of book piracy are not comparable to those in countries with high levels of informality, such as Peru and Colombia." Unlike the Peruvian and Colombian cases, in which a lack of clearly defined and fully operative legal structure, and overall levels of poverty, are mentioned as the roots of the problem, in Chile, always according to Bardenes, the culprit is the high sales taxes applied to books: "Chile has the highest sales tax on books in the world, more than 20%, a case without comparison anywhere in the globe." The article concludes by pointing out: "It is estimated that within this [publishing] sector, piracy may represent 40% of all sales in the Chilean market, which is twice as much as in other sectors in the country" (*La Estrella*).

Still in 2017, after years of negotiations and pressure, the Special 301 report on Chile by the US Office of the US trade representative, which is, from an American perspective, the annual account of piracy of all kinds in most countries around the world, stated: "Chile remains on the Priority Watch List in 2017" and

> The United States continues to have serious concerns regarding longstanding implementation issues with respect to IP provisions of the United States–Chile Free Trade Agreement. The United States continues to urge Chile to implement both protections against the unlawful circumvention of T[rade] P[rotection] M[easure]s and protections for encrypted program-carrying satellite signals. (USTR 53)

The question then emerges: Why, in a country like Chile, is book piracy not only a common practice but also widely accepted by the public and by many of the intellectuals allegedly affected by it? One possible answer, as already mentioned, has been the price of books in the country.

"With the piracy of books in the streets of Chile," adds Hernán Rivera Letelier—another popular writer and author of literary novels, such as *La Reina Isabel cantaba rancheras*—"I do not lose a client but gain a reader." For Rivera Letelier, "Piracy is proof that people want to read." He criticizes authorities who "abuse and do nothing to bring down the price of books" while they wrap themselves in the discourse of cultural diffusion.

> The person who buys my book on the sidewalk does so because she cannot allow herself the luxury of going into a bookstore and buying it at the price

> it is being sold. No matter what, people still make an effort to read, that is the reason why pirates exist, there is a hunger for reading. (*Revista Panorámica*)

Rivera Letelier is not alone in this view among Chilean writers. Even those who united against piracy expressed similar ideas. On September 7, 2000 the Sociedad de Gestión de Derechos Literarios de Chile (SADEL, Society for the Administration of Literary Rights in Chile) was created with renowned writer Jorge Edwards at the helm. The purpose of that society would be "to defend their intellectual rights before the diverse forms of piracy and technological dissemination that are so common now." One of the founding members, the poet Raul Zurita, stated that "among the first task of the new association should be to combat book piracy." However, he also added that such effort must consider the real roots of such illicit activity:

> My starting point is that piracy stems from the fact that books are too expensive. Then we must understand that that is precisely the bottom line problem, and that the tax on books is a crucial factor in this situation. Here books are twice as expensive than in Argentina, thrice as much as in Colombia or Mexico. (Castillo 47)

In March of 2017 and from a different perspective, Arturo Infante Reñasco, editor and director of Editorial Catalonia and founding member of the Corporación del Libro y la Lectura, stated at a seminar on intellectual property (IP) and the right of authors:

> Chilean publishers must be among the few producers of goods who know that they must take into account piracy as a factor in their economic calculations. And if they have a bestseller in their catalog, sooner rather than later, they must give part of their earnings to a shadow partner, who, without even saying thank you, will capitalize on all the effort that goes into the production of a bestselling book, and will continue to enjoy full benefits on it, without any risks, with no taxes, within a true fiscal paradise. (Infante)

Then—referring to this peculiar and *sui generis* status of book piracy in a country that is as obsessed with and interested in convincing the world that it is an ideal place, especially in the Latin American context, for foreign investment, due the clarity and efficiency of its legal norms and practices for all areas of commerce—he added:

> The sidewalk-bookstore[s] ("librería cuneta") [those that operate on the sidewalk and mostly with pirated books] have existed for thirty years and enjoy absolute impunity. They are still located in the same places, in

> front of universities, the main bookstores, right in front of the offices of the Ministry of Education or Economy, and just a few yards from police stations. This has always been a very difficult to understand situation, even more difficult to explain to authors, especially foreign ones, who cannot understand the abandonment and the impotence affecting local publishers and booksellers. This image of the authorities' tolerance of the free exercise of piracy as an activity has given us a truly negative reputation as a country of piracy, which has significantly affected our publishing industry, making our local licensing more expensive. (Infante)

After complaining that the lack of compliance with intellectual property rights (IPRs) and the relative normalization of piratic behavior goes well beyond book piracy in the streets of Santiago, and in fact, includes universities, private and public, religious and secular high schools—which are quick to digitize books in PDFs without permission as a way of complying with regulations requiring them to have available for their students a certain number of copies per capita in order to keep their accreditations—and, even the Supreme Court itself, which, at the time, had recently used a legal loophole to digitize its full library and make it available to its 12,000 members, Infante recommended the development of an educational campaign to promote the values of IP and against piracy.

In fact, in January of 2008 the Brigada Investigadora de Delitos de Propiedad Intelectual (Bridepi, Investigative Brigade for IP Crimes), had been created in Chile. It defined itself as "the only specialized brigade in the Latin American context dedicated exclusively to combat such crimes" and as independent from the Jefatura Nacional de Delitos Contra el Patrimonio y el Medioambiente (National Office on Crimes Against Patrimony and the Environment). Bridepi sought a specialization and deepening of the war against piracy, and was itself an answer to "the free commerce treaties signed by Chile, that invite the country to fight against piracy." According to the Brigade, crimes against IP are regulated in Chile by "Law No. 17.336 on Intellectual Property (rights of authors, literary and artistic works, software, sculptures, dissertations, music, video games, films, photography and documentaries, among others)." With that mission in mind, Bridepi developed, first, the campaign "Ayúdanos a combatir la piratería" (Help us to Combat Piracy) and, then, the campaign "Compra Original, Compra Seguro" (Buy an Original, Buy Safely), some of whose videos can be seen on YouTube. In general, and unlike previous campaigns, and specially unlike the heavy moralizing tone of anti-film piracy efforts, these new campaigns highlighted the pragmatic reasons for preferring the original and avoiding the copies. Thus, they mentioned the integrity of the work, the quality of the binding, proper pagination, and avoided the criminalization of users (Policía de Investigaciones).

## Pedro Lemebel and Book Piracy in Chile

In denouncing book piracy in Chile, Jorge Baradit had directly mentioned Pedro Lemebel. Lemebel—the author of the novel *Tengo miedo torero* and many very popular books collecting his magazine or newspaper texts in the hybrid genre of *crónicas*, half way between journalism and literature—had himself often referred to those who sold illegal copies of his books on the street, complaining half-heartedly and with humor, but also sympathizing with them, given his own past as a street peddler and his efforts to develop a countercultural literary discourse capable of reaching a huge public. In 2008, for example, Lemebel said:

> My *crónica* writing is like a pamphlet, published in the newspaper, and it makes possible a relation with [literary] writing for regular people, much more than with the book, bookstore, library, … etc. The pirates in the street tell me: "Pedro, when are you going to publish another book?" It is not my issue to persecute pirates, but publishers' and the authorities'. I am not going to attack people who are trying to make a living (García 52)

In 2002 and responding to the question,

> You have said many times that book piracy seems legitimate to you. Now that you have signed a contract with a publishing company as big and important as Planeta, and being yourself one of the authors most affected by piracy, have you changed your mind on this issue?

Lemebel stated:

> I don't have moral right to attack or censure the sellers of pirated books. I also worked in the area. I sold on the sidewalk ("cunetié"), run from the police … It is touching to see my texts on the streets, go on a taxi and have the driver show it to me—the book, that is—in a pirated version. This allows my book to have a different trajectory, less predictable. There [are] a lot of people who are afraid of going into a bookstore. In fact, I have never bought a book at a bookstore, at best I have stolen some … I would love to make a Pirate Anthology of Pedro Lemebel, selecting my best texts, and publish it so it could be itself pirated. (Morales Alliende 47)

Another profile of the author and his city, included the following story between Lemebel and a street peddler selling pirated books:

> In Lyon [Street], Lemebel comes to a full stop: "You didn't even give me a month to earn some money," he tells a woman selling pirated copies of *El Zanjón de la Aguada*. "I only sell them," she says … The woman notices how

> he looks at her … "Please sign one for my son." And Lemebel, forgetting about the mafias behind book piracy and imagining the young reader, says: "We are not going to betray our fellow pirates" ("Entre piratas no nos vemos la suerte"). He concludes remembering his own past as a street peddler. (Matus 76)

In fact, Lemebel had not only manifested multiple times his understanding but also expressed his support for book piracy:

> I also am a pirate and download free music from the internet, what is the big deal? My books cost eight thousand pesos, keep in mind that that sum is bread for a whole week in the case of a poor family. (Matus 76)

Finally, in a text from *Serenata Cafiola* (2008) titled "Tu pirata soy yo" (I Am Your Pirate) the author walks through the boulevard Ahumada in Santiago "when the pirate night of street peddler's commerce transforms the downtown into a cauldron of big sales" (Lemebel, "Tu pirata soy yo" 231). He then runs into a lady selling books on the sidewalk, including "the latest from Isabel Allende, Marcela Serrano, Bolaño and Coelho," and Lemebel's own books. The *crónica* continues:

> "Would you believe that we are not selling much," says the woman, blushing a bit, thinking that I am going to demand money from her. And rather than getting upset, a rush of tenderness reaches me from the lady who, at that time and with that much cold out there, is trying to make ends meet by selling pirated copies, while keeping an eye on the police … "It's just that we love you so much," says another seller, next … You better not love me this much or we will all end up selling right here, together. "And when is another book coming don Pedro?" What! Do you think I am a bunny, you are already pirating my books before they make it to a bookstore … "Take care don Pedro." And I keep on walking among the shouts of approval that the pirate fan base produces. It is not my duty to persecute my long-suffering people, I think, and I remember the year 1984, in the midst of the dictatorship, when with a few friends we decided to publish a pirated version of the book [from Sandinista comandante Omar Cabezas] *La Montaña es más que una inmensa estepa verde* … [since] the Frente Patriótico Manuel Rodríguez needed money. And what could be better than pirating that book that so many comrades wanted to read. (232)

Lemebel concludes this text, adding:

> Now, while I walked through Ahumada Boulevard, remembering my times as a guerilla pirate, I looked back to see again the ladies selling on the sidewalk, but they were no longer there; as a wave responding to the first police wind, they had sailed away, disappearing among the human sea of Boulevard Ahumada, without a trace, not even a tricolor one. (233)

This *crónica*—which summarizes well Lemebel's position on book piracy and leaves us with the image of the pueblo/people chased by the repressive apparatus of its own state—makes visible how book piracy touches, at different levels of specificity and generality, on political, cultural, and economic forces operating in a given society at a given time. They do so precisely through a series of related economies: the first is an economy of cultural circulation and consumption; the second is an informal economy that establishes relationships with the formal one; and the third goes well beyond culture and the economy themselves, and encompasses the forms of social life of the actors involved in these formal and informal economies, and the forms of inclusion and exclusion that define them.

In *The Informal Media Economy*, Ramon Lobato and Julian Thomas insist on the interaction and degrees of continuity between formal and informal media systems instead of the more common radical contrast that pits legitimate versus illegitimate or pirate business, and produces a culture of policing and lawsuits. For Lobato and Thomas, informal tinkering, experimentation, market and demand development, are all practices often performed first in the informal economy. These activities in turn make possible and precede corporate engineering and profiting. Rather than a simple black-and-white opposition between formal and informal economies then, Lobato and Thomas insist on their interdependence. They define the informal economy as follows:

> A basic definition of the informal economy would be something along the lines of "the sum of economic activity occurring beyond the view of the state." This includes activities like unregistered employment, domestic homework, street trade, non-market production, and backyard tinkering. (Lobato and Thomas 8)

Matias Dewey, trying to think the relationship between sociology and informal economies, and between the notions of legality and illegality, insists on the porous borders between them, an approach that is directly counterposed to the dominant criminalizing and reductive view of the illegal and informal. Thus, rather than using the idea of a condition of illegality, Dewey refers to processes of illegalization whose sociohistoric and political contexts are crucial to their understanding. He also invites us to de-staticize and historicize our idea of legality and illegality in formal and informal economies. Faced with the illegalization of certain markets by the laws of the state, participants recognize or deny the legitimacy of such decisions, depending on what is the history of that state, and depending on the goods involved. Marijuana may be a good example of how these distinctions are historically variable. Both legal and illegal markets have an architecture, with their institutions, their participants and their own forms of mediation of social perceptions on them (Dewey).

Although there has always existed an economy of survival and reproduction in Latin America, running parallel to the what economists conceptualize as the productive formal economy, the arrival and implementation of neoliberalism in the continent involved the proliferation and systematization of a different and more complex form of this phenomenon of survival. While at the level of the street peddlers that multiplied in Latin American cities during the 1980s the experience was similar to previous ones in the past, the fact is that it did not simply respond to the forms of self-organization of popular sectors, but, instead, to the 1980s region-wide uncontrolled opening to international commerce and the massive importation of consumption goods of dubious quality, often from Asia, that could then be sold cheaply on the streets. Even though the products were legitimate, the forms of selling them in everyday life escaped the forms of control and taxing imposed by the state. On the other hand, it is undeniably the case that this was an extended and informal way of making less socially explosive the high levels of unemployment among the poorest citizens that the neoliberal economic restructuring had generated. Another way of identifying this paradox, i.e., the legal production of illegalization, is to point out that the multiplication of informal economies in the region, including the explosion of piracy, was due to macroeconomic decisions made at the highest levels of government. Neoliberalism was both the ultimate culprit for this proliferation of informal commerce at the national level, and the one in charge of, then, persecuting it, responding at the international level to the dictates of metropolitan countries' policies for the application of their IPRs laws and the protection of their interests. The historical consciousness of this clash between the strategies of political and macroeconomic power, on the one hand, and the tactics of survival of the unemployed and marginalized who suffered the consequences of their application in Chile, on the other, is part of the answer to the question I posited earlier about the strange degree of tolerance towards book piracy in neoliberal and post-dictatorial Chile. Another aspect of that answer has to do with the status of the book as a good in the market and as a cultural good in the history of contemporary Chile. Both partial answers may be seen as examples of the lack of fit between the law and social practice, both at the level of the formal and informal economies, Hernando de Soto spoke of in his book *The Other Path: The Economic Answer to Terrorism* (originally published in Spanish in 1985). Pedro Lemebel's work insists, precisely, on connecting the erasure of the official production of the expansion and incorporation of structural informality (what one could define as neoliberalism as a form of accumulation and subjectification based on dispossession and criminalization) and the need to remember other historical forms of conceiving of the people, popular culture, and with it, the book and literature.

## Lemebel, the Economies of the Literary, and their Proletarianization

For Lemebel the technological factor—the new technologies that widen the possibilities of production, reproduction, and circulation of discourses today—and the historical factor—that reminds us of, on the one hand, the structural causes of the radical informalization of the life of the urban poor, forgotten by a state deeply engaged in a violent process of self-reduction, and, on the other, the ways the marginalized found to survive in this dictatorial context in Chile—are both important aspects of what I have called his strategy for a proletarianization of Chilean literature.

In my recent book on the work of Lemebel, I have explored in greater detail the three forms of proletarianization to which Lemebel subjects Chilean culture and literature (Poblete). These forms of proletarianization involve, first, a redefinition of what politics may be and, thus, of what may be considered political in the country. Sexuality is key here, as a revolutionary practice that expands the limits of the political. Second, his systematic work in the media (mostly alternatives ones, but occasionally media of national range) against the hegemonic forms of mass mediation using, first, the resources of the *crónica* with its blurring of the line dividing the literary and the journalistic, the fictional and the nonfictional, and, then, what I have called a "re-farandulización" or counter-spectacularization, which reacts against the everyday banalization of communication in the dominant media. Finally, Lemebel's forms of proletarianization involve, at a more general level, a redefinition of what it means to do cultural work in Chile at the time of its neoliberal globalization, by way of the critical and creative use and overcoming of the cultural binaries that patrol the borders between popular and high culture, literature and mass media, the intellectual and the masses, the cognitive and the affective, the sexually constituted subject and a more just and freer society. In order to do this, Lemebel recuperates the forms of social memory and the tools for thinking and action available at his time and within his society.

Among those resources and memories is his own experience during the Allende years. Asked whether he wanted to go college, Lemebel responds:

> I don't know if college exactly. It was something else. It was a deep, vortex-like, desire to know that took hold during the Popular Unity years. What everybody now talks about are the lines ["colas"], the strikes, but not the cultural renaissance that took place then, and young people like me participated in that vortex. That is why I loved March 1 this year, at the Forestal Park, because [that open air book fair] resonated with the nostalgic echo of the multitudes occupying a city that belonged to them, and not this foreign and always surveilled territory in which we have lived. (Donoso 84)

What Lemebel was referring to included, among many other aspects, the radical change in the status of the book before and after the 1973 *coup d'état*. As Bernardo Subercaseaux and Paulo Slachevsky have shown, that transformation can be summarized as the transition from the book as a public good, crucial to the formation of citizens and the development of national culture, to the book as both ideologically suspicious first, and then as another product in the market, a fact clearly marked by the application since 1976 of the same tax as every other item sold commercially.

In fact, in another *crónica*, this one from the book *El Zanjón de la Aguada* (2003), referring to three moments of the Feria del Libro (Santiago's yearly book fair), Lemebel contrasted the free and open-air fair at the Parque Forestal during the last years of the dictatorship with its much more commercial, bigger, enclosed, and entrance-charging fair of the post-dictatorship era. Notably, he emphasizes the fact that the first one allowed for the "parallel fair of artisans and street-peddlers" to settle by its sides and "despite everything, was a fiesta where it was possible to pirate ['se pirateaba'] a certain clandestine cultural effervescence" (Lemebel, "La Feria" 292).

Lemebel's position on copyright and piracy is, then, a complex one. Its roots are many: some are political, some are historical, some are experiential. At the political level, Lemebel, as he does in most of his written work, explicitly or implicitly, is constantly contrasting a moment of full, massively popular socialization of political energies—in fact two of them, first, the truly revolutionary moment of the Unidad Popular under Allende with its own understanding of what a national-popular culture ought to mean, and, second, the counter-reactionary moment of the struggles against the dictatorship and its program for radical individualization of the social—with the fragmentation produced by the market's overall mediation of the social, which turned citizens into consumers and politics into technical problems.

Historically, Lemebel contrasts the people as the actor of national-popular politics during the Allende years and during the anti-dictatorial struggle, with its disaggregation into the sea of consumption and conformism that succeeded them in the so-called transition and post-dictatorship years.

Experientially, Lemebel was himself a street peddler at some point in his life and suffered directly the operations of a hypocritical state that, first, created the conditions for the informalization of a significant sector of Chilean workers—expelling them from their locations in a downgraded system of production, and thrusting them into the streets for survival—while it, to keep the still surviving formal commerce happy, persecuted those informals selling in the streets.

Moreover, one of the more important factors explaining Lemebel's discourse on piracy has to do with the complex connections between his idea of a national culture, his own position as outsider turned insider in the Chilean literary market, the forms of discourse and the forms of dissemination of that discourse that his whole *oeuvre* privileged, and his own understanding and relations with the general intellect or the overall sociality from which both his topics, resources, and language—what I have called his popular baroque—stemmed.

Lemebel was biographically and politically inclined to suspect the origins of all manner of privatized value and the unequal forms of appropriation of labor that went into them. IP, in its dominant version as a universal discourse, with no exceptions and harsh conditions of imposition, was naturally repulsive to an author who fully understood he was writing from the social experience and with the socially generated language of those lacking representation in order to critically reconstruct the capacity of written discourse to transform those forms of representation and, in so doing, widen its circles of readers or publics. Thus, he was placing himself at the border between a standard conception of IPRs, which conceive them as emanating from single individuals and as private property, and cultural rights that are based on commonly held and produced goods (Strathern 449). He was then placing appropriation, socialization, and historicity at the center of his discourse on IP and piracy.

This tension between different understandings of IPRs has manifested in contemporary Chile in what Pablo Latorre calls two governmental sides, with two different views of copyright, its nature, and function in society. While for the last 200 years copyright has been on the side of the cultural institutionality in the country, there has been a strong push lately to move it to the economic or industrial side of that institutionality. The latter conceives copyright as another manifestation of IP industries, like software and entertainment, whose goal is to maximize profit and minimize free use, and, thus, wants to extend the duration and degree of protection for all its products. The cultural institutions, on the other hand, consider copyright in cultural industries as linked not simply to profit but to the expansion and cultivation of culture. While the economist side insists on protecting the original creator and individual proprietor, the culturalists highlight the collective source of all creation and the need to protect and expand the public domain for the benefit of all (Latorre 33).

Lemebel's work manifests, in the end, as a project seeking an alternative form of thinking the relationships between different forms of the production and meaning of written discourse, formal and informal economies, and the people as a historical construct and as a reading public. This project also points towards another big conceptual area piracy is related to: the problems of the relationship between the original and its copies, and the sources of innovation, creativity, and the diffusion of culture. Circulation, diffusion, and innovation refer to the macro concept of culture that is at stake. In the Chilean case, this involves two contrasts: first, between the national-popular Chilean culture promoted by the cultural apparatuses (and specifically the publishing ones) of knowledge socialization during the Popular Unity government and today's dominant relationships between the interests of the new transnational capitalism of informational base, bent on privatizing and patenting all knowledge; and, second, between this neoliberalism and the interests of states and communities of citizens to make them publicly available. Cognitive-based capitalism—i.e., the one that uses information, design, and discourse itself as the source of value—is faced with the contradiction between the diffusion of knowledge, which it promotes globally (as access and use of software, for instance), and the socialization of those knowledges (access to the production and reproduction of that same software), which it is so intent on controlling (Rullani 103). If for the informational capitalist the key to profit is to accelerate the commercial diffusion and slow down the socialization of the production of knowledges, the new technologies of material reproduction and the new forms of production and circulation of written discourses tend to reduce the temporal distance between both processes. Informational diffusion and participatory socialization are, in this latter case, simultaneous. As Salvador Millaleo and Hugo Cadenas explain in their overview of the problems and conflicts affecting the history and current situation of IP in Chile, an otherwise modern country with a high level of social inequality produces what, from the normative viewpoint of the center, are seen as anomalies. In the case of book piracy, there is a dual deregulated inclusion of two different actors: first of the informal pirates into the economy, and then of the consumers of pirated goods as members of the cultural public. For both groups, these may be the only forms of participation available in these specialized circuits of communication (the economy and culture, respectively).

The *crónica*, with its close dependence on direct observation of everyday life in the city, was an especially well-placed genre to understand the tension between originality and ownership, on the one hand, and the general intellect of the living labor of collectivities, as the proper public source and destination of all discourses, on the other. Then we can say that, especially in developing countries—where the divide between the importance of the product, its price, and the levels of income of the consuming public are greater—there is a sort of structural inclination towards piracy and the informalization of national production in certain areas. If to that one adds one the biggest taxes on books in the world, and a previous national history of radical socialization of culture and its products, the conditions for book piracy in Chile today seem particularly ripe and the so-called paradox of its dominant presence in Chile much easier to understand.

## Bibliography

Ashley, Jennifer. "'Honorable Piracy' and Chile's Digital Transition." *Popular Communication: The International Journal of Media and Culture*, vol. 13, 2015, pp. 6–17.

Baradit, Jorge. "La cruzada de Baradit contra la piratería y los "narcos" de la cultura." *Diario Concepción*, August 14, 2016.

Budassi, Sonia. "Pedro Lemebel." *Suplemento Cultura Perfil*, August 27, 2006, p. 7.

Benavides, Sofía. "Jorge Baradit. La alameda de Santiago debería llamarse José de San Martín y no Bernardo O'Higgins." *Infobae*, May 7, 2017.

Castillo, Rodrigo. "La piratería une a los escritores." *Las Últimas Noticias*, September 8, 2000, p. 47.

de Soto, Hernando . *The Other Path: The Economic Answer to Terrorism*. Basic Books, 1989.

Dewey, Matías. "Porous Borders: The Study of Illegal Markets from a Sociological Perspective." Max Planck Institute for the Study of Societies Discussion Paper 16/2, 2016.

Donoso, Claudia. "Lemebel." *Revista Paula*, vol. 821, July 2000, pp. 82–85.

García, Javier. "No soy la Eva Perón de las locas." *La Nación*, September 13, 2008, pp. 52–53.

Infante Reñasco, Arturo. "El desolador panorama de la piratería de libros en Chile." *Corporación del Libro y la Lectura*, March 2017.

*La Estrella*, "Chile es el país con más piratería de libros en toda América Latina." vol. 83, no. 24.278, June 14, 2003.

*La Nación*. "Chile, Una Nación de piratas." February 3, 2010, p. 17.
Latorre Tallard, Pablo. "Reivindicar el lugar del derecho de autor en la institucionalidad cultural." *Revista de Gestión Cultural*, Edición Especial, vol. 11, 2018, pp. 32–33.
Lemebel, Pedro. "La Feria del libro en tres actos." *El Zanjón de la Aguada*. Seix-Barral, 2003, p. 7.
Lemebel, Pedro. "Tu pirata soy yo." *Serenata Cafiola*, Seix Barral, 2008, pp. 231–234.
Lobato, Ramón and Julian Thomas. *The Informal Media Economy*. Polity Press, 2015.
Matus, Alvaro. "El Patiperreo urbano de Lemebel." *Revista Qué Pasa*, vol. 1685, July 25, 2003, pp. 74–76.
Millaleo, Salvador, and Hugo Cadenas. "Intellectual Property in Chile: Problems and Conflicts in a Developing Society." *The Sage Handbook of Intellectual Property*, edited by Matthew David and Debora Halbert, Sage, 2015, pp. 130–147.
Morales Alliende, Pilar. "Entrevista Pedro Lemebel." *Intramuros*, vol. 3, no. 9, September 2002, pp, 44–47.
Office of the United States Trade Representative (USTR). *2017 Special 301 Report*. USTR, 2017.
Poblete, Juan. *La Escritura de Pedro Lemebel como proyecto cultural y político: Crónica, ciudadanía y literatura bajo el neoliberalismo*. Cuarto Propio, 2019.
Policía de Investigaciones de Chile. "Brigada Investigadora de Delitos de Propiedad Intelectual (Bridepi)," www.pdichile.cl/instituci%C3%B3n/unidades/delitos-econ%C3%B3micos. Accessed December 18, 2019.
*Revista Panorámica*. "El Secreto a voces de los locatarios de San Diego." November 30, 2014.
Rullani, Enzo. "El Capitalismo cognitivo. ¿Un déjà vu?" *Capitalismo cognitivo. Propiedad intelectual y creación colectiva*, edited by Olivier Blondeau, Nick Dyer Whiteford, Carlo Vercellone, Ariel Kyrou, Antonella Corsani, Enzo Rullani, Yann Moulier Boutang, and Maurizio Lazzarato, Traficantes de sueños, 2004, pp. 99–106.
Slachevsky, Paulo. "El Libro y la lectura, un asunto público. La participación de los editores en la Política Nacional de la Lectura y del Libro en Chile," 2017, www.cultura.gob.cl/wp-content/uploads/2014/08/libro-lectura-asunto-publico-paulo-slachevsky.pdf. Accessed December 18, 2019.
Strathern, Marilyn. "Intellectual Property and Rights. An Anthropological Perspective." *Handbook of Material Culture*, edited by Chris Tilley, Webb Keane, Susanne Küchler, Mike Rowlands, and Patricia Spyer, Sage, 2006, pp. 447–462.
Subercaseaux, Bernardo. *La Historia del Libro en Chile*. Lom, 2010.

# 9

# PIRATE BOOK AESTHETICS IN CONTEMPORARY ARGENTINA

*Víctor Goldgel-Carballo*

The book was the first mass-produced cultural commodity, and piracy has followed it ever since as its shadow. Long before the invention of copyright, practices of appropriation branded as piratical became such a fundamental component of print culture that no intellectual history of the modern period would make much sense without them. During the eighteenth century, for example, the editions of Voltaire or Rousseau commonly available in France were the ones pirated abroad and smuggled into the country. As Adrian Johns has succinctly observed, "No piracy, we might say, no Enlightenment" (Johns 50; Karaganis 407). But the same could be argued about almost any other modern time and region, even after new media eclipsed print in discussions of intellectual property (IP). Having been unable to either find or afford most of the books I needed to finish college in Buenos Aires and a doctorate program in the United States at the turn of the twenty-first century, I can attest to the following: no photocopiers, scanners, or illegal downloads, no higher education.

Beginning in the seventeenth century, the word pirate was used to refer to a person who "unjustly prints another person's copy" (Johns 23). Now in the twenty-first century, it invokes first and foremost the notion of IP. In this chapter, however, I am less interested in the legal, moral, and economic dimensions of piracy than in what it brings into existence from an aesthetic perspective—in other words, the sensible properties of books-as-objects and the judgments of taste that they elicit. Focusing on the book production of contemporary Argentine literature, I begin by examining piracy in its relation to two literary phenomena that have also been part of the world of letters for centuries—plagiarism and parody. With the figure of Jorge Luis Borges at its center, Argentine literature grants both concepts a particularly important role. Along with piracy, I argue, they emerge from the same abstruse distinction between proper and improper ways of copying. In the second half of the chapter, I explore the contours of what I call pirate aesthetics, characterized by "improper" forms of reproduction, anti-elitist access, cheapness, and the perception of the "fake" as "real" in its own way.

As scholars have argued, the very legitimacy of the formal market, brands, and "originals" only exists in relation to its constitutive outside—that is to say, to piracy (Dent 32). Beyond the small circles of activists and academics who care about the issue, however, this mutually constitutive relation remains neglected. IP regimes have become so prevalent as to enclose our thinking almost completely, always referring us back to a normative framework and a mythical point of origin (the author, the brand) that obscure the *positive* dimension of piracy. Studying this dimension, which I call *positive* in the philosophical sense of the term—as something that *is* rather than not; as something possessing qualities rather than lacking them—presents a number of challenges, among which reflexes conditioned by moral, economic, and legal norms are the most obvious. For those who frame piracy as a parasitic activity, there's simply nothing worth studying, while those who champion a stronger public domain often have loftier goals in mind—such as affordable access to life-saving drugs—and therefore meet the profit-driven actions of media pirates with an uncomfortable silence (Liang 168). This, combined with our fascination with ever-newer media technologies, explains why the aesthetics of contemporary pirated books is a completely understudied phenomenon.[1] As I will try to show, however, the type of aesthetic experience that such books generate is comparable to those taking place around other contemporary pirate products and affords specific possibilities around practices of writing, reading, and interpreting.

If any culture would be unthinkable without piracy, those in the Global South help us see this more directly, as several scholars working on new media in Africa and Asia have shown. In his groundbreaking study of Nigerian pirate video, for example, Brian Larkin observes that "piracy creates an aesthetic, a set of formal qualities that generates a particular sensorial experience of media marked by poor transmission, interference, and noise" (291). As he demonstrates, the failure of formal infrastructures in developing nations is usually matched by the emergence of informal ones "marked by cheapness, faulty operation, and constant repair" (308).[2] Though Larkin focuses on distorted sounds and blurred images in a context in which videocassettes were still mainstream, his analytical lens can be productively borrowed to understand the aesthetics of other piratical practices. The semiotic distortion that he studies—fuzzy video images, bad audio, rickety recording machinery—can be compared, as I will show in the pages that follow, to that affecting pirate books, with their marks of bad Xeroxing, faulty spines, and improvised design. Even if disappointment, aversion, and distrust are part of the experience, the pirate book also has an intriguing allure—the allure of the cheap and fake.

## Pirate Borges

In 2009, the Argentine writer Pablo Katchadjian published *El Aleph engordado* (*The Fattened Aleph*), a fattened or engorged version of "El Aleph" (1945), one of Jorge Luis Borges's most famous short stories. Known in literary circles for other similar experiments, Katchadjian interpolated 5,600 words in the original 4,000. He also added an epilogue explaining his procedure. From a commercial perspective, this was an irrelevant endeavor, like most experimental literature anywhere in the world. The book came out with a minor independent press and only 200 copies were printed. But it did catch the attention of major players in the field of Argentine letters. Two years later, María Kodama, Borges's widow and estate heir, sued Katchadjian for IP fraud, and the work became a *succès de scandale*. The courts dismissed the charges twice. Kodama kept appealing and, in 2015, a judge prosecuted Katchadjian. As the case came back to public attention that year, a pirate publisher made a new edition. It only took him 32 hours to download the text, design the book, print it, and bring it to Buenos Aires, where it was sold at book fairs and in a handful of bookstores amenable to the informal publishing network that emphasizes open access and a strengthened public domain. As he explained when I interviewed him in 2016, this publisher's goal was to make

> a prohibited book available for all. Even though it was online, it was not in the streets, in people's hands. It was a piratical, anarchist, countercultural action. A lot of people had not read the book and now they could do it at a very accessible price.[3]

The copies he made were sold at 60 pesos each (about 7 US dollars at the time). They were 6 x 4 inches, less than 100 pages, and printed on 80 g/m2 paper (a little bit over 50 lbs. in the US system), and included a title page displaying author, dates, and publisher: "Pablo Katchadjian, 2009/Ediciones Pirata, 2015." In all of these respects, the book was just one more in a catalogue of over 20 pirated titles with a focus on Argentine literature. More conspicuously, however, the cover showed Kodama's smiling face and situated her in a grotesque scene of Pantagruelian spaghetti eating.

Throughout history, prohibited books have nurtured piracy in a wide array of ways—from the Enlightenment-inspired literature feared by European monarchies in the wake of the French Revolution to twentieth-century modernist novels banned for obscenity by US judges to poems written by communist sympathizers under Latin American dictatorial regimes to books imported into countries with weak currencies. While the Argentine courts never banned *El Aleph engordado*, its author faced up to six years in jail and was forbidden from leaving the country, thus making the prospects of a new edition practically nonexistent. When Ediciones Pirata published the book, the "prohibition" mentioned by the editor had already gripped the attention of countless writers, lawyers, publishers, and university professors. On July 3, 2015, more than 300 of them met at the National Library to read an open letter in solidarity with Katchadjian, arguing that both Kodama and the 1933 IP law still in place today missed the very essence of Borges's literary work, thereby implicitly declaring themselves more legitimate heirs, if not of his estate and rights, certainly of his insights. From their perspective, Katchadjian's literary experiment—based on creative appropriation—was very much in the spirit of Borges. As the critic and fiction writer Alan Pauls recently pointed out, thanks to Borges "we Argentines disbelieve the idea of private property"; we rather believe—and here Pauls plagiarizes Borges—that "the universe is our birthright." Even the director of PEN International sent a message in solidarity that was read that day (Friera). Other than her lawyer, there were no voices defending Kodama's position in public. She was, however, winning the trial. By transgressing it, Ediciones Pirata foregrounded an IP regime that seemed to have no legitimacy among the very same intellectual actors that it was supposed to protect.

Even though he did not show an explicit interest in the topic, Borges and piracy were destined to meet. To a great extent, he occupies the position of Argentina's most revered and original writer precisely because he was a champion of irreverent citation who mocked originality as a fantasy. As major critics have observed, his works are generally marked by intertextuality, recontextualization, and an effort to blur the limits between authorship and reading practices (Molloy; Sarlo; Wells). Borges, as Sarlo points out, "constructs his originality through quotations, copies, the rewritings of other texts"; in other words, through parody, intertextuality, and even plagiarism (6). He famously once declared, in reference to his mentor Macedonio Fernández, that he had imitated him "to the point of impassioned and devout plagiarism" (Borges, "Macedonio" 146). Correspondingly, few authors have been as adamant as he was about both the derivative nature of their writing and the dangers of monumentalizing literary works. His "Pierre Menard, autor del Quijote" ("Pierre Menard, Author of the Quixote") has become one of the most cited texts in global discussions of plagiarism and intertextuality (Genette 374; Perromat 121; Randall 4). Pierre Menard, the reader might recall, intended to write a text identical to Cervantes's *Don Quixote*, not by copying it or by becoming Cervantes, but as the minor French symbolist poet that he himself was. The chapters he produced were verbally identical to those of Cervantes's novel, but also different and equally original. Reading, Borges notes, is a creative and dynamic act that constantly transforms the text, making it a true palimpsest in which previous meanings are preserved. Following this reasoning, one could conclude that, had Katchadjian not fattened "El Aleph" but published it verbatim under his name, readers would have found his text clearly different from the one published at the end of World War II by Borges. But all of the above also implies that any text can become impoverished and ossified, if that's how readers relate to it. In that sense, Borges's narrator observes that Cervantes's work, once "a pleasant book," had been reduced to "an occasion for patriotic toasts, grammatical arrogance, obscene *de luxe* editions" (Borges, Collected Fictions 94). Plagiarizing, from these combined perspectives, is both futile (as any text will be different anyway, even if verbally identical) and refreshing (as classics are often reduced to objects of patriotism and pedantry). Not surprisingly, in the 1954 prologue to his *Historia universal de la infamia*, Borges coyly admitted to having amused himself "with the falsification and distortion (sometimes without aesthetic justification) of the stories of others" (Waisman 93). Referring to this passage, Sarlo has gleefully identified "more insolence than shyness in the idea of pilfering the stories of others, altering them, adding details, Argentinizing them in his own vocabulary, and confiding them to irony and parody" (qtd. in Waisman 93). Now, all of these literary actions—pilfering, altering, adding, ironizing, parodying—have also been used, in turn, to describe Katchadjian's text; even that of "Argentinizing" makes sense, if we understand the concept as making vernacular something that is perceived as remote and excessively sophisticated (in this case, the work of a canonical author, Borges). Katchadjian not only explained his experiment in relation to these practices, but also declared that his main motivation had been the fact that Borges had become "sacralized" and "monumentalized"—in doing so, he may have been plagiarizing literary critic Sylvia Molloy, who had pointed out the same three decades earlier (Molloy 9; "Pablo Katchadjian").

Something very similar can be argued about the editor who, going against the law and the "propriety" demanded by Borges's widow (more on the concept of propriety below), not only republished the fattened version of "El Aleph" but also fattened Kodama herself. Extending the desecration drive in an openly carnivalesque direction, the cover of the pirate edition shows Kodama gorging on a mound of spaghetti served by Katchadjian with a shovel, with a blind Borges merrily witnessing the scene from across the table (the collage was made out of a photogram from a famous scene in the Beatles' film *Magical Mystery Tour* in which John Lennon as the waiter bears the shovel and Ringo's auntie greedily gets the serving). Due to permission rights specific to the Global North, I am not allowed to include the image here, but it can be found online at bit.ly/2m9oegr or by emailing me.

The editor described the image in the following terms: "Kodama is fattened by the situation; she is anxious, greedy for what Katchadjian could give her" (interview with the author). In this sense, the pirate book intervened not only in debates on intellectual property rights (IPRs) and access but also in the Argentine literary system and its ongoing conversation about how to deal with the legacy of Borges—who, far from being one important writer among others, is perceived as "the canon itself" (Ludmer 289). All this to say, in making Katchadjian's "prohibited" text accessible and defacing both author and copyright holder, the pirate editor buttressed a specific understanding of the dialectics of canon and parody.

Borges's "El Aleph," in fact, has been read as a parody of Dante's *Divine Comedy*, and the last name of its main character is, one may say, a "thinning" of Dante Alighieri: Daneri. Although my focus is on the pirate copy issued by

Ediciones Pirata rather than on Katchadjian's literary experiment, it is worth pointing out that his "fattening" can be read in reference to this "thinning"—and, more broadly, to Borges's reputation as a writer who never used a single excessive word. As critic Juan Caballero put it, while Borges's writing is "genteel, tasteful, and self-contained," Katchadjian ridicules it through a kind of "uncanny bodily parasitism," which makes Borges's story swell with sex and politics; "engorged," in that sense, might be a more accurate translation than "fattened" (1–6). From this perspective, Katchadjian's experiment pertains to a well-established tradition that can be framed globally in terms of appropriationism and what Marilyn Randall has called "guerrilla plagiarism," which also has a specifically Argentine articulation (neither Katchadjian nor the pirate editor were the first to "remix" Borges; to name just one example, in 1985 Rodolfo Fogwill entitled his own parody of "El Aleph" with an anagram: "Help a él").[4]

Because we usually approach parody, plagiarism, and piracy as disparate concepts, we may easily overlook the fact that "El Aleph" (a parody of Dante), its fattened version (a parody of the parody, indicted as plagiarism), and its pirate instantiation (an unauthorized copy in which the pirate injects his own parody paratextually, especially in the book cover) are all part of a sequence with more commonalities than differences. We overlook, in other words, our continuous participation in a culture of the copy that, while taking different forms at different social junctures, is marked by a similar understanding of (or confusion about) the difference between proper and improper ways of copying. As the IP director of Cambridge University Press once admitted, the question—fundamental to defining "fair use"—is, to say the least, slippery (Taylor 261). Because piracy is generally understood as relating to *property*, copyright, and legal persons, we usually miss the key ethical-aesthetic component that "propriety" entails (Johns 12; Randall 77).

## Property and Propriety

Mark Rose has shown that centuries before the emergence of copyright and notions of property rights in terms of economic interest, there already existed an increasing individualization of authorship that generated "a general sense that it was improper to publish an author's text without permission" (214). Even if irrelevant from a legal perspective, this sense is still very much present today, as Kodama's comments on Katchadjian's work clearly demonstrate. The dispute, according to her, was primarily about propriety, respect, and honor; or, put differently, it was about ethics and aesthetics. In several interviews with the press, she insisted that her motivation had never been economic. At an early stage, indeed, she offered to withdraw the lawsuit in exchange for an apology and a symbolic payment of one Argentine peso on the part of Katchadjian—who, in turn, also seemed to have considered his honor more important than the legal and economic consequences he could potentially face, because he refused. A few years later she declared that Katchadjian had

> taken the whole short story without asking for permission. We have lost respect for ourselves—that is why we don't respect others. If someone uses something that does not belong to him ("que no es *propio*" in Spanish), the least he can do is ask for permission.

Having invoked her Japanese father in other interviews to explain why she had codes of honor, she also declared that in protecting the integrity of Borges's work she behaved like a samurai ("Kodama vs Katchadjian"). Far from circumscribing her arguments to the legal sphere, she moved in a wider, familiar, and traditional moral galaxy in which piracy is perceived as dangerous for the soul (in this case, the spirit of Borges). Albeit in a different context, this moral galaxy was fittingly expressed by the Presbyterian pastor Henry van Dyke in his 1888 sermon against the sin of pirate books, which provoked, he argued, "the perversion of national taste and manners" (17). All this to say that underneath modern notions of property, there is still propriety: a rich ethico-aesthetic dimension characterized by an aversion to unregulated forms of copying—one so strong that it may determine if a copyright holder goes to court or not.

Although slippery and undertheorized, propriety is articulated through laborious rituals and weighty unwritten rules that inform the way in which we relate to books and evaluate piracy. In contrast with economic and legal principles like IP, propriety is an aesthetically, morally, and affectively grounded concept that guides our judgement and defines the difference between "good" and "bad" behaviors. There is a good way to make and consume books, and then there is the perverse one that keeps pastors of strong IP awake. This can be readily understood through high-culture reflections that link books to refined behavior and polite society. George Steiner's "The Uncommon Reader," first published in 1978, constitutes a paradigmatic example. In this text, he explores a concept closely related to that of propriety and key to his understanding of book history: that of *cortesia*. Through an analysis of Chardin's *Le Philosophe lisant*, a 1734 painting that shows a man wearing a hat and a furred cloak in the very solemn act of reading, Steiner observes:

> The motif of cortesia, of ceremonious encounter between reader and book, implicit in the costume worn by Chardin's philosophe, is now so remote as to be almost unrecapturable … Informality is our password … Current literacies are diffuse and irreverent. (12–16)

Steiner's nostalgia stems from a relatively recent moment in book history, the era of paperbacks: "As object, the book itself has changed … The paperback is, physically, ephemeral … both a marvel of packaging and a denial of the largesse of form and spirit expressly stated in Chardin's scene" (17–18). He is, indirectly, lamenting the expansion of the reading public, as paperbacks are not just convenient but also cheaper and printed in greater quantities. In the same essay, he links this "courteous, almost ... courtly encounter" to the related concepts of "tact" and "civility," which bridge our sensuous experience and the world of manners or *mœurs* (2, 6, 15).

Piracy clearly undermines notions of *cortesia* and propriety. In fact, Ediciones Pirata defines itself against them, celebrating instead vulgarization. Rather than reenacting the ceremonious and deferential encounter described by Steiner, the pirate editor uses the cover to stage a wretched-of-the-earth revenge against the legal hegemony of those forms of tact and civility that ennoble and protect the status of only those who don't need to resort to the informal economy. The result looks something like one of those "poor" images theorized by Hito Steyerl. Derivative, with substandard resolution, it deteriorates as it is "squeezed through slow digital connections, compressed, reproduced, ripped, remixed, as well as copied and pasted into other channels of distribution" (Steyerl). It participates in an alternative visual economy associated at a global level with Dziga Vertov, the Tricontinental, and a "genealogy of carbon-copied pamphlets, cine-train agit-prop films, underground video magazines and other nonconformist materials, which aesthetically often used poor materials" (Steyerl). In the Latin American context, this was represented most distinctly by movements such as Tercer Cine ("Third Cinema") and the *estética da fome* (aesthetics of hunger). The copyright holder, the pirate editor tells us, will eat all the spaghetti in the world if she can, leaving the rest of us with nothing. His poor image is thus part of an ostensibly pirate aesthetics that—contrary to the moral or economic-utilitarian justifications of those who defend strong IP regimes—rebukes large-scale regulations of property and propriety as detrimental to the well-being of the majority.

## Organizing Piracy

Before focusing on the works in which pirate aesthetics is most palpable, I will differentiate four main types of pirate books: (1) the ones that are materially identical to the legal edition (produced, for example, in the same printing press in excess of the number contracted by the publisher); (2) copies that are made using different materials and/or production process but are intended to resemble the legal edition as much as possible; (3) books that pretend to be part of a different legal edition and make reference to an imaginary but believable publisher (which is usually presented as the copyright holder) and place of publication (often unreachable or in a foreign country); and (4) books that are open about their piratical status. A quick comparison with the world of pirate clothing can help differentiate these four categories. Type 1 and 2 books violate not only copyright but also trademark laws by reproducing the logo and the name of the original publisher; in that sense, they are similar to surplus-export T-shirts that the factory owners put into the market without authorization (type 1) or to the almost-identical ones produced with equivalent machines, materials, and techniques (type 2). Type 3 and 4 books, on the other hand, include a different signature that aims to either authenticate them in reference to a fictional legality or present them as piratical in an explicit way. Type 3 can be compared to those T-shirts whose producers, rather than counterfeiting brands, work on the basis of "brandedness"—or a style that participates in the aesthetic universe of brands without making reference to any one in particular.[5] In Buenos Aires, for example, a pirate entrepreneur recently came up with the name "Una pluma ediciones" to publish texts by Judith Butler, Gilles Deleuze, and other writers equally ubiquitous in higher education, claiming to be a Mexican company. While the price, the unheard-of name of the publisher, the quality of the cardboard used for the cover, and other factors may suggest its piratical status to some readers, others might not notice; and, regardless, a type 3 book looks more legitimate than type 4 typically does. This leads us to the last category, which has overlapping qualities with the previous ones but is defined by its explicit and open piratical nature. Type 4 publishers express their piracy in a variety of ways. For example, Ediciones Pirata presents itself as an anti-brand, in the same way that some sea pirates raised the pirate flag rather than leaving the pole empty. A different pirate editor, however, chose to name their editions "No te tomes tan en serio" (literally, "Don't take yourself so seriously").

As with the concept of piracy itself, all four categories depend on the underlying assumption that there is a meaningful difference between the authorized copy and the illegal one—a difference that is quite often hypostasized and presented as one between the real and the fake, or the authentic and the inauthentic. But while in many cases we can distinguish "authentic," authorized copies from their "inauthentic," nonauthorized rivals, the social life of books—or T-shirts, for that matter—demonstrates on a daily basis that, quite often, this is actually not possible and that, moreover, authenticity can also be a quality of the fake and the illegal (Crăciun, "Rethinking Fakes" 859). In the simplified classification I presented above, type 1 goods are authentic from the point of view of their materiality but pirate because of the way in which they enter into circulation; type 2 and type 3 look authentic but, under closer scrutiny, are revealed to be fake; and type 4 books dispense with the question of authenticity altogether by proclaiming their pirate nature. But doesn't the inauthenticity of type 1 disappear—like laundered money—if booksellers or readers are not aware of its origins as excess printing? Similarly, don't type 2 and type 3 collapse whenever a person is unable to successfully perform this putatively universal "closer scrutiny"? One may even argue that type 4 goods are the only ones that truly achieve authenticity, by founding an alternative legitimacy outside of the legal and not making any claims to be something that they are not. And while they apparently break with the genealogical logic of IP that guarantees the authenticity of a product by verifying its legal origin, they simultaneously establish alternative forms of authorship and agency that may, in turn, establish a new kind of authenticity (a desire commonly expressed by anarchist editors, who perceive IP regulations and economic disparities as obstacles to a truly authentic relationship to texts). Like any publisher, the type 4 pirate usually groups titles as coming from a single source, thus guaranteeing their "authenticity" in very much the same way that sellers of clothing may personally guarantee the quality of their counterfeits (Crăciun, "Rethinking Fakes" 851; see also Dewey, Chapter 11 in this volume). Whether they reappropriate the skull and bones (as in the case of Ediciones Pirata) or avoid the copyright/piracy dichotomy by advancing an anarchist agenda that posits access to texts as a universal right (as in Ediciones Cospel, from northeastern Argentina), type 4 publishers usually go by a certain name and proudly display it in their title pages.

Acting as originators as well as imitators, type 4 creators and publishers transform what they reproduce. Opponents of piracy usually present this as a pitfall: the reader who buys a pirate copy, it is commonly argued, risks reading an adulterated version and thereby missing the "true" text, which can only be guaranteed by the author-as-sole-originator. But type 4 books show that this argument has a blind spot. *El Aleph engordado* is, once again, a telling example. Whereas the first pirate edition included 12 completely blank pages at the end of the book (a sign of its improvised, rushed, and low-quality production), later ones use that empty space to print a short satire of María Kodama by the Argentine writer Cristian Di Nápoli ("I was," his narrator says, "one of the few whom Kodama had not subpoenaed"). As it happens with other pirate media, such as the PlayStation soccer games that are hacked to include local sports teams (Lobato and Thomas 153), Ediciones Pirata customized Katchadjian's book according to new consumer preferences—in particular, the interest aroused by the lawsuit. Creative agency was thus shared by new actors in ways that could be productively compared to both Katchadjian's and Borges's literary endeavors. Pirate publishing, in other words, does with books something akin to what Borges did with Dante, Katchadjian did with Borges, or other appropriation artists regularly do with the works they seize: they recreate.

## Pirate Aesthetics

The question of reproduction is at the core of pirate aesthetics. When viewed from this perspective, the irreverence shown by pirate editors constitutes a counter-hegemonic form of copying that generates value rather than reducing it. This irreverence, in other words, prompts a number of modifications that become materially constitutive of the pirate copy. We see this most clearly in the aesthetics associated with type 4. Far from having the style associated with higher-class patterns of consumption, type 4 books are unstylish and shoddy (Nakassis 710). Rather than being made with the same materials, machines, and methods used in the formal market, they are made on the cheap. Their small format, usually under 5 x 7 inches, and sometimes as tiny as 2.5 x 4; the stains left by Xerox machines; the low-grade paper; the just slightly thicker cardboard for the cover; the hand-glued binding that gives away after little use; these are some of type 4's most noticeable signs. While they are technologically superior to unbound photocopies, in the realm of published books they are readily perceived as poorly made. This is also true of types 2 and 3; readers of best-selling novels, for example, often buy pirate copies that they describe as "uglier" than the legal ones ("Cinco esquinas—Mario Vargas Llosa"). Only type 4 books, however, display this cheapness to its full extent, even proudly, thereby producing a pirate aesthetics in which being a "fake" becomes part of the allure. Cheapness is in this sense a category that brings together economic, moral, and aesthetic values.

There is no established vocabulary or standard set of analytical tools to engage with pirate aesthetics. However, in addition to the relevant ideas offered by Larkin, Manuel, Sundaram, and Liang cited above, there are a number of critics whose work rethinking aesthetic categories is useful to consider. Among contemporary thinkers, Sianne Ngai is a prominent example, particularly her recent analysis of the gimmick. Whereas traditional aesthetic categories such as the sublime or the beautiful are seemingly disconnected from the economic value of the object, Ngai argues that,

> One cannot think or even perceive a gimmick without a judgment of cheapness immediately attending that perception; that is, without a gestalt of a commodity's cost of production based on a rapid synthesis of sensory and conceptual cues (materials, design, location of manufacture). (495)

The aesthetic experience elicited by a pirate book, one may say, is also inextricable from a perception of its lower cost. Gimmicks and pirate copies both deliver something we are actually looking for, but they do it in a way that we deem illegitimate: too easy, too quick, too cheap (Ngai 475). Our very aesthetic rejection of a pirate object may have to do with this, as the cheap access it grants us is inextricable from a violation of propriety and *cortesia*. In that sense, cheapness might be a trait of even type 1 pirate books—derived not from the quality of their materials or manufacturing but from their price tags and the location in which they are sold. Similarly, both pirate goods and gimmicks strike us not as the products of authentic artists and professionals, but of crafty artisans and improvisators; not as impeccably finished objects (with the exception of type 1) but as contrived artifacts that force us to grapple with their composition and operation. Because they are noticeably cheap, most pirate books reveal the astonishing fact that *somebody made them*. In that sense, they interrupt the abstract logic of commodity exchange and make us aware of the labor and the social relations behind them. In a time when almost any title can be downloaded for free, they also remind us how messy, unnecessary, and nevertheless desirable a printed book can be. If IP laws commodify the text and demarcate ownership, a pirate book constitutes a unique opportunity to recognize the rich social life of a text beyond its existence as a commodity and as somebody's property. As a poorly made product, it reminds us of the alienation involved in commodities in general; and as a successful breach of property/propriety, it demonstrates that the text, after all, can belong to other people as well and participate in alternative modes of civility.

Even aside from economic or labor considerations, the manufactured nature of print books is readily manifest in pirate publications, especially as we get closer to type 4, where traces of a book's construction often remain as markers of cheapness and part of a celebrated low-budget aesthetic. In Argentina, openly pirate books are often part of an informal network of small publishers who champion open access and a DIY approach whose main expression is the Feria del Libro Independiente y Alternativa (FLIA, Independent and Alternative Book Fair; the "A" sometimes stands for "autogestiva," i.e., "self-managed"), where self-publication is encouraged and taught (Taller de autopublicación). Far from the *cortesia* of Chardin's reader as described by Steiner, the FLIA tells us that anybody can be the author of a book (Borges knew this well: his first one was self-published), that beer and plastic cups next to an inexpensive home printer can be part of the production ceremony, and that a floor covered with failed page proofs is as good for décor as expensive fabrics. Also, as technology and algorithms are increasingly black-boxed (in the sense of having an obscured inner functioning), seeing how a book is made (pirate or not) becomes an extraordinary experience. In this context, an "operational aesthetic" comes to the fore: the excess binding glue spilling onto the first page; a design so simple that almost anyone could have done it; sometimes even a printed URL at the bottom of the page indicating where the text was downloaded.[6] Whereas, in its efforts to compensate for the loss of personhood in the alienated commodity, a brand may try to convince us that an animated tiger named Tony had something to do with the sugar-coated cereal we eat (Newell 150), spaces like the FLIA and publishers such as Ediciones Pirata bring us surprising news: commodities are indeed made by human beings. They also show that, rather than belonging exclusively to that mythic point of origin we call the author (Coombe 8), the copyrighted text can be appropriated by writers, publishers, or readers and begin to operate differently.

An additional, unavoidable question in any understanding of pirate aesthetics is that of deception, or of the putative difference between fake and real. After all, don't most pirate copies (other than type 4) try to deceive us into thinking that they are something they are not? Here, it's worth looking to the rich body of reflections about a realm of art usually characterized as derivative, fake, and cheap: kitsch. Very much like pirate goods, kitsch products are generally defined as those that pretend to be good by merely copying the "really" good ones. First used in the 1860s to refer to trashy or cheap art, the concept of kitsch, as described by Matei Călinescu, centers around "imitation, forgery, counterfeit, and what we may call the aesthetics of deception and self-deception" (229; see also Kulka 43–44). Here, Călinescu renders clear a distinction that is fundamental for the comparison of kitsch and piracy—that between kitsch and forgeries. While forgeries pretend to *be* the original, kitsch deceives by promising "to supply its consumers with essentially the same kinds and qualities of beauty as those embodied in unique or rare and inaccessible originals" (Călinescu 252). As I have argued, type 2 pirate books can be compared to counterfeits—and, we may now add, to forgeries (of paintings by great masters, for example).[7] Types 3 and 4, however, can be more accurately compared to kitsch; by presenting themselves either in the guise of an alternative legal edition (type 3) or as existing beyond the constraints of copyright laws (type 4), they insist on their capacity to grant an experience equal to the one afforded by "originals." In that sense they possess what Călinescu calls an "anti-elitist availability," indexed first and foremost by their price (252). Of course, the boundary between types 3 and 4 is as murky as our relationship with authenticity and self-deception, or, from a social angle, as the heterogeneous ways in which a single pirate object may be experienced by different actors. While critics of piracy see it as fraud and ask us to not lie to ourselves by thinking that buying a pirate copy is not a bad thing, consumers might actually perceive deceptive type 3 goods and openly fake type 4 as authentic in their own way. This is what, in her study of fake clothing, Magdalena Crăciun defines as "authenticity writ small"—here meaning "good enough" for consumers who are aware of and indifferent to the distinction between brand and knock-off (*Material Culture* 12).

In addition to those afforded by kitsch, we may introduce an additional, properly improper concept that illuminates how paradoxical deception might be when it comes to piracy: bullshit. In his small treaty on the topic, and taking into consideration Wittgenstein's distrust of "nonsense," Harry Frankfurt writes that the essence of bullshit is disregard for the difference between true and false statements, or an "indifference to how things really are" (34). Inasmuch as it affects how we experience the copy, the question of truth and falsehood is necessarily part of pirate aesthetics. In Argentine Spanish, for example, the most widely used word to refer to pirate goods is "*trucho*," which means both cheap and fake (Falco; Pedroso 81–114). Their cheapness is here inseparable from the judgement that determines their untruthful status, as fakeness involves a discrepancy between what something says it is and what it truly is. But what kind of missing "truth" is at play here? It would be misleading to simply conflate truthfulness with originality and to treat pirate copies as lies. While the person who lies asserts a falsehood deliberately, the pirate may or may not want the copy to be taken for the original—broadly speaking, this would be the line dividing types 1, 2, and sometimes 3 from type 4, or what scholars have defined as "deceptive" and "non-deceptive counterfeiting" (Grossman and Shapiro). It would make little sense to say that pirates who don't present their books as legal or authorized copies, or who do so in a half-hearted or perfunctory way, are lying or trying to deceive us. Rather, they simply show disregard for IP laws—a disregard for the difference between true and false (or for a correct representation of the world, as Frankfurt would put it) that in the case of type 3 and 4 pirate books takes the form of an indifference toward the distinction between legal and illegal copies.

## Concluding Remarks

Pirate aesthetics finds itself at the center of the long-standing struggle over the historically contingent and politically motivated question of mimesis—or the question of how we represent the world. Even though they have been compellingly challenged by contemporary philosophy, binaries such as real/fake and original/copy continue to bolster hegemonic understandings of representation, thus heavily conditioning our understanding of piracy (Deleuze). Our aesthetic experience of pirate goods, however, also exceeds and contradicts what we supposedly know about them in ways that an ever-growing number of scholars have tried to pin down. "Culture of the copy," "modernity as bluff," "fake globalization": the critical idioms to understand this excess are many. Hsiao-hung Chang, for example, observes that "fake" means "'counterfeiting' as well as 'appropriating.' (In Chinese, 'Jia' means both 'fake' and 'by a particular means')" (233). In this way, she stresses not just that some fakes are now materially indistinguishable from the official products but also, more crucially, that the proliferation of fakes—or the global phenomenon that, riffing on Jacques Derrida, she names "fake dissemi-nation"—forces us to move beyond the understanding of mimesis prevalent in Western thought since Plato (231). Similarly, drawing from the work of Michael Taussig, Sasha Newell examines brands as masking devices and argues that they are "not mere deceptions but rather performances that produce meaningful fictions, and since our very social reality is a fabric of such everyday fictions, our truths are masks" (247). Like Chang, she tries to grasp the reality of the fake. But the task is daunting, as there are very good reasons why we continue to believe in originals, brands, and other markers of authority and authenticity—among them, the preservation of social status. As Barton Beebe argues, IP laws have begun to fulfill the function of sumptuary laws, in the sense that they allow for a type of social distinction based on consumption patterns at a time when "our increasingly powerful copying technologies threaten quickly to dilute the rarity and thus the distinctiveness of otherwise distinctive goods" (815). What Raymond Williams observed 60 years ago in his analysis of advertising as a magic system also functions today as a compelling explanation of why certain people would rather be dead than buy a pirate copy: when you make a purchase, "[y]ou do not only buy an object: you buy social respect, discrimination, health, beauty, success, power to control your environment" (189). How do we go about critiquing this kind of magical thinking, especially when social status is also at stake? As I have tried to argue, an old-fashioned paper pirate book might be a good tool.

The pirate book, as I pointed out earlier, illuminates its origin by ostensibly hiding it. By naming a series Ediciones Pirata, an editor can simultaneously question and defend its legitimacy; he can posit a clear point of origin while at the same time withholding the information necessary to reach it, or to find the person behind the mask. If, as Newell argues, we don't see brands as masks for mass-produced, indistinguishable copies but as the "real" face and origin of consumer goods, the pirate signature pokes a hole in this illusion. Their "improper" way of copying; their cheapness; their production in milieus that embrace an operational aesthetic; their anti-elitist availability; their disregard for the difference between true and false, or real and fake, through which they undermine common notions of authenticity; all of these traits give pirate copies the power to prompt a number of questions—such as how they are made, who reaps the profits, or why the formal economy does not offer them at affordable prices—that might awaken us to the fact that IPRs, brands, originals, and single authors are neither magical nor natural, but rather politically and economically motivated social forms that regulate our access to art and knowledge.

## Notes

1 While they don't focus on piracy, two recent studies of Argentine book production illuminate important aspects of the phenomenon, especially in regard to materiality and modes of production: Magali Rabasa's *The Book in Movement: Autonomous Politics and the Lettered City Underground* and Craig Epplin's *Late Book Culture in Argentina.* For a recent collection of critiques of IP by Argentine intellectuals, see Beatriz Busaniche's *Argentina Copyleft.* Although fragmentary, *The Piracy Project* by AND Publishing and Andrea Francke offers a quick look at the variety of forms that pirate books published globally may take.

2 Similar arguments have been made by Ravi Sundaram in his work on "pirate modernity" in urbanscapes saturated by new media, Peter Manuel in his analysis of audio cassettes in India, and Lawrence Liang in relation to pirate DVDs. They have all demonstrated that, as soon we take our legal and economic blinkers off, the pirate copy reveals its complex social life and the forms of creativity that are involved in apparently slavish acts of reproduction.

3 For obvious reasons, the editor wishes to remain anonymous. Interviews conducted on May 20–24, 2016 via Facebook Messenger.

4 Randall understands guerrilla plagiarism in relation to the changing notions of subjecthood and authorship characteristic of the late twentieth century (218–252). See also Perromat. On legal notions of authorship, see Woodmansee and Jaszhe. In 2017, after consultation with Graciela Montaldo, Annick Louis, Julio Premat, and other literary scholars, the court established that *El Aleph engordado* "is a contemporary literary experiment with numerous precedents in the twentieth century" ["es un experimento literario contemporáneo con numerosos antecedents en el siglo veinte"].

5 In his study of the urban Tamil Nadu market, anthropologist Constantine Nakassis defines this "aesthetic of brandedness" as one "having the qualitative and material look and feel of a brand commodity" (704) and, in that sense, "reanimating them, citing them, refashioning them" rather than replicating them exactly (717).

6 The expression "operational aesthetic" proceeds from Neil Harris's study of Barnum's American Museum. According to Harris, the objects held at P.T. Barnum's American Museum in New York City invited the mid-nineteenth-century public "to learn how they worked. They appealed because they exposed their processes of action" (57). But there was of course another side of the coin: "Deception, hoaxing, humbugging, cheating, those were some of the words Americans commonly associated with Barnum" (57).

7 This comparison, of course, has clear limits, as it is generally understood that there is a big difference between allographic and autographic arts. While in the latter (painting, for example) copies of originals are forgeries rather than genuine, in allographic arts such as music and literature copies can be exactly like the original (Goodman 113, qtd. in Hick 120).

## Bibliography

Francke, Andrea. *The Piracy Project.* http://andpublishing.org/the-piracy-project. Accessed September 1, 2019.

Beebe, Barton. "Intellectual Property Law and the Sumptuary Code." *Harvard Law Review*, vol. 123, no. 4, 2010, pp. 810–889.

Borges, Jorge Luis. *Collected Fictions.* Translated by Andrew Hurley. Penguin, 1998.

Borges, Jorge Luis. "Macedonio Fernández." *Sur*, vol. 209–210, 1952, pp. 145–147.

Busaniche, Beatriz. *Argentina copyleft. La crisis del modelo de derecho de autor y las prácticas para democratizar la cultura*. Ediciones Boll Cono Sur, 2010.

Caballero, Juan. "The Borgesian Monad Contaminated and Buenos Aires Photobombed: Pablo Katchadjian's 'El aleph engordado' and Pola Oloixarac's 'Las teorías salvajes.'" *Lucero*, vol. 22, 2012, pp. 1–17.

Călinescu, Matei. *Faces of Modernity: Avant-Garde, Decadence, Kitsch*. Indiana UP, 1987.

Chang, Hsiao-hung. "Fake Logos, Fake Theory, Fake Globalization." *Inter-Asia Cultural Studies*, vol. 5, no. 2, 2004, pp. 222–236.

"Cinco esquinas—Mario Vargas Llosa." March 2016, 0enliteratura.blogspot.com/2016/03/cinco-esquinas-mario-vargas-llosa.html. Accessed September 1, 2019.

Coombe, Rosemary J. *The Cultural Life of Intellectual Properties. Authorship, Appropriation, and the Law*. Duke UP, 1998.

Crăciun, Magdalena. *Material Culture and Authenticity: Fake Branded Fashion in Europe*. Bloomsbury, 2014.

Crăciun, Magdalena. "Rethinking Fakes, Authenticating Selves." *Journal of the Royal Anthropological Institute*, vol. 18, no. 4, 2012, pp. 846–863.

Deleuze, Gilles. *Difference and Repetition*. Translated by Paul Patton. Columbia UP, 1994.

Dent, Alexander S. "Piracy, Circulatory Legitimacy, and Neoliberal Subjectivity in Brazil." *Cultural Anthropology*, vol. 27, no. 1, 2012, pp. 28–49.

Epplin, Craig. *Late Book Culture in Argentina*. Bloomsbury, 2014.

Falco, Federico, editor. *Lo trucho*. Traviesa, 2013.

Fogwill, Rodolfo. *Pájaros de la cabeza*. Catálogos, 1985.

Frankfurt, Harry G. *On Bullshit*. Princeton UP, 2005.

Friera, Silvina. "Esto pertenece al rubro de lo cómico." *Página/12*, July 5, 2015. www.pagina12.com.ar/diario/suplementos/espectaculos/17-35986-2015-07-05.html. Accessed September 1, 2019.

Genette, Gérard. *Palimpsests: Literature in the Second Degree*. U of Nebraska P, 1997.

Goodman, Nelson. *Languages of Art: An Approach to a Theory of Symbols*. Hackett, 1976.

Grossman, Gene M., and Shapiro, Carl. "Counterfeit-Product Trade." *American Economic Review*, vol. 78, no. 1, 1988, pp. 59–75.

Harris, Neil. *Humbug: The Art of P. T. Barnum*. U of Chicago P, 1973.

Hick, Darren Hudson. "The Nature of Copying and the Singular Literary Work." *The Aesthetics and Ethics of Copying* [Kindle ed.], edited by Darren Hudson Hick and Reinold Schmücker, Bloomsbury, 2016.

Johns, Adrian. *Piracy: The Intellectual Property Wars from Gutenberg to Gates*. U of Chicago P, 2010.

Karaganis, Joe, editor. *Media Piracy in Emerging Economies*. Social Science Research Council, 2011.

Katchadjian, Pablo. *El Aleph engordado*. Imprenta Argentina de Poesía, 2009.

"Kodama vs Katchadjian: la paradoja borgeana." *Los Andes*, July 21, 2015, www.losandes.com.ar/article/la-paradoja-borgeana. Accessed September 1, 2019.

Kulka, Tomas. *Kitsch and Art*. Pennsylvania State UP, 1996.

Larkin, Brian. "Degraded Images, Distorted Sounds. Nigerian Video and the Infrastructure of Piracy." *Public Culture*, vol. 16, no. 4, 2004, pp. 289–314.

Liang, Lawrence. "Beyond Representation: The Figure of the Pirate." *Making and Unmaking Intellectual Property: Creative Production in Legal and Cultural Perspective* edited by Mario Biagioli, Peter Jaszi, and Martha Woodmansee, U of Chicago P, 2011, pp. 167–180.

Lobato, Ramon, and JulianThomas. *The Informal Media Economy*. Polity, 2015.
Ludmer, Josefina. "¿Cómo salir de Borges?" *Jorge Luis Borges. Intervenciones sobre pensamiento y literatura*, edited by William Rowe, Claudio Canaparo and Annick Louis, Paidós, 2000, pp. 289–300.
Manuel, Peter L. *Cassette Culture: Popular Music and Technology in North India*. U of Chicago P, 1993.
Molloy, Sylvia. *Las letras de Borges*. Sudamericana, 1979.
Nakassis, Constantine. "Counterfeiting What? Willful Ignorance and the Brand in Tamil Nadu, India." *Anthropological Quarterly*, vol. 85, no. 3, 2012, pp. 701–722.
Newell, Sasha. *The Modernity Bluff: Crime, Consumption, and Citizenship in Côte D'Ivoire*. U of Chicago P, 2012.
Ngai, Sianne. "Theory of the Gimmick." *Critical Inquiry*, vol. 43, 2017, pp. 466–505.
"Pablo Katchadjian: 'Borges está sometido a una sacralización.'" www.lavoz.com.ar/ciudad-equis/pablo-katchadjian-borges-esta-sometido-una-sacralizacion. Accessed September 1, 2019.
Pauls, Alan. "De Duchamp a Pierre Menard, el apropiacionismo en arte y literatura." *Telam*, February 26, 2017, www.telam.com.ar/notas/201702/180868-de-duchamp-a-pierre-menard-el-apropiacionismo-en-arte-y-literatura.html. Accessed September 1, 2019.
Pedroso, Osvaldo, editor. *Debates en la cultura argentina, 2005–2006*. Vol. 4. Emecé, 2007.
Perromat Augustín, Kevin. "Plagiarismo: ¿estética o movimiento contemporáneo?" *Revista electrónica de teoría de la literatura y literatura comparada*, vol. 5, 2011, pp. 115–127.
Rabasa, Magalí. *The Book in Movement: Autonomous Politics and the Lettered City Underground*. U of Pittsburgh P, 2019.
Randall, Marilyn. *Pragmatic Plagiarism: Authorship, Profit, and Power*. U of Toronto P, 2001.
Rose, Mark. "The Author in Court: Pope v. Curll (1741)." *The Construction of Authorship: Textual Appropriation in Law and Literature*, edited by Martha Woodmansee and Peter Jaszi, Duke UP, 1995, pp. 211–230.
Sarlo, Beatriz. *Jorge Luis Borges: A Writer on the Edge*. Verso, 1993.
Steiner, George. *No Passion Spent: Essays 1978–1996*. Faber & Faber, 1996.
Steyerl, Hito. "In Defense of the Poor Image." *e-flux*, vol. 11, 2009, www.e-flux.com/journal/10/61362/in-defense-of-the-poor-image. Accessed September 1, 2019.
Sundaram, Ravi. *Pirate Modernity: Delhi's Media Urbanism*. Routledge, 2009.
*Taller de autopublicación F.L.I.A. Feria del Libro Independiente, Autogestiva, Asimétrica, Amorfa, Andrógina, Amorosa*, www.fliarosario.blogspot.com. Accessed September 1, 2019.
Taylor, Kevin. "Plagiarism and Piracy: A Publisher's Perspective." *Learned Publishing*, vol. 19, no. 4, 2006, pp. 259–266.
van Dyke, Henry. *The National Sin of Literary Piracy: A Sermon*. C. Scribner's Sons, 1888.
Waisman, Sergio. *Borges and Translation. The Irreverence of the Periphery*. Bucknell UP, 2005.
Wells, Sarah Ann. *Media Laboratories. Late Modernist Authorship in South America*. Northwestern UP, 2017.
Williams, Raymond. *Culture and Materialism: Selected Essays*. Verso, 1980.
Woodmansee, Martha, and Peter Jaszhe, editors. *The Construction of Authorship: Textual Appropriation in Law and Literature*. Duke UP, 1994.

# 10

# BETWEEN ABUNDANCE AND APPROPRIATION

## Indeterminate Critiques of Global IP Schemes

*Zac Zimmer*

Intellectual property (IP), by its very nature, attempts to identify ownership in an intangible idea.[1] An author owns a story, an inventor patents an idea, a company trademarks a signature flourish, a chef guards their secret recipes: in these four examples—representing the four major categories of Anglo-American IP law—a creator is granted an ownership stake in the expression of an idea. If the author's story is published without consent, or the inventor's process is used without permission, or if a non-licensed logo is reproduced on a commodity, or if you steal my secret sauce: in every case the IP holder's rights would be violated.

There are many wonderful histories about authorship (Woodmansee and Jaszi), patents (Biagioli, "Between Knowledge"), trademarks (Coombe, The Cultural Life), and trade secrets (Lobel), and much recent scholarship on IP in the age of digital reproduction (Benkler; Fuchs; Kelty; Lessig). Almost overwhelmingly these studies all conclude that our current concept of IP insufficiently describes creative action, and those problems have only been further amplified by technological developments in global communication.

New innovations have allowed us to see anew how creativity works; in that sense, digital culture is like a telescope, or a microscope, allowing us humans to see again, with new eyes, how we create, share, appropriate, improve, mimic, and monetize the previous fruits of our creative endeavors. IP law is scrambling to catch up, but new existential challenges arise—*who owns IP created by artificial intelligence?*—before current problems, like *at what point is a pharmaceutical patent detrimental to the promotion of public health?*—can be successfully addressed.

These ever-more visible instances of conflict between cultural production and global IP norms have turned the fora where such norms are codified into sites of worldwide resistance. Those who protest, whether on-site at meetings of supra-national organizations or online during the negotiation of free trade agreements

(FTAs) or treaties, represent a wide and even motley collective. Varied as these groups may be, their complaints all share a common core issue: the current IP regime does not work for the way we experience cultural and scientific knowledge. And yet beyond the core postulate that the contemporary globalizing IP regime is insufficient, two very different paths emerge. One path seeks to advance an ethos of free culture and experimentation, while another seeks to advance an ethos of protection and patrimony.[2] Although those two paths seem clearly at odds, thinking them together will reveal the true limits of IP discourse. And by insisting that we *must* think them together, I will suggest a different, complementary metaphor for describing human creativity: indeterminacy.

In what follows, I will first outline the two strands of resistance mentioned as they've expressed themselves in global movements against FTAs and IP treaties. Then I will focus on two ethnographic studies of local entanglements in global IP norms, Anita Say Chan's *Networking Peripheries: Technological Futures and the Myth of Digital Universalism* and contributor to this volume Kedron Thomas's *Regulating Style: Intellectual Property Law and the Business of Fashion in Guatemala*, in order to further draw out the contradictions and complications of IP norms in global contexts that are both digital and indigenous. I conclude, borrowing from Karan Barad's *Meeting the Universe Halfway: Quantum Physics and the Entanglement of Matter and Meaning*, by proposing the concept of indeterminacy as a necessary complement to IP.

## Contradictory Impulses

In a recently published anthology, *A Critical Guide to Intellectual Property©*, Callahan and Rogers highlight "social movements" and "piracy" as two social rubrics used to understand the growing opposition to global IP norms enacted by international trade agreements. Callahan and Rogers code the "low intensity civil war" unfolding globally as an uneasy alliance of, on the one hand, "the young and the educated flagrantly disobeying the law and declaring those authorities charged with enforcing it illegitimate," and, on the other, "farmers and indigenous people throughout the world" who have "risen in defiance not only of government and corporations but against privatization as a way of thinking" (5).

It must be acknowledged that these two impulses can easily generate conflict, even if both take exception to the reigning global consensus on IP as codified in the international regulatory structure. The ethos celebrated by the "young and the educated" applauds creative appropriation and denigrates corporate privatization, while defenders of cultural patrimony precisely resist appropriation, and use ethnic-based relative privatization as a defense of traditional knowledge. So to define the social movements as being against privatization is not fully accurate; many of the movements Callahan and Rodgers reference are against appropriation, but are in favor of conservation. Sometimes this position leads movements to strategically adopt a logic of privatization that effectively advances their more fundamental conservationist commitments.

In order to better reflect such nuances, I will provisionally call these two impulses the "free culture" impulse (based on a celebration of creativity and the circulation of knowledge) and the "cultural patrimony" impulse (based on a resistance to cultural appropriation). To reiterate: both impulses share a fundamental rejection of existing global IP norms, and only engage such norms from a position of radical skepticism in order to make a profound demand for reform. But each impulse leads to different, and even mutually exclusive demands. Let's compare the two.

## *Free Culture Ethos*

Over a centuries-long timeline of development, the IP regime has worked to reduce the generative mess of inspiration and obligation into a simple metaphor that *ideas behave like things*, in order to codify human creativity and convert its products into commodities. The conventional solution in Anglo-American IP law has been to divide an idea from its expression: ideas circulates freely, while any expression fixed in a determined medium enjoys legal protection. But as the *immaterial* world of ideas has taken an ever-more *material* form—rendered into the ones and zeros of binary code written on hard drives and global servers—we find the traditional objects of IP forced out of their cozy metaphorical slumber and into the world of tangible things: the digital file, the sequenced genome, the archives of traditional knowledge. As *ideas*, these artifacts are nonrivalrous and nonexcludable, meaning that my IP is not consumed when someone else thinks it, and it is near impossible for me to prevent someone else from using or thinking my IP once it enters into circulation. What the growth of digital technology and networks adds is that now—as *things*—these artifacts are also nonrivalrous and nonexcludable: as never before, today they can be copied for near-zero cost and distributed simultaneously to any user with capable technology.

Technology, in other words, has called IP's bluff. Before the objects of IP were digital—that rosy dawn when books were bound in leather—the particular expression of any given idea found itself trapped in a material form. This allowed legal theorists to posit the object of intellectual labor: *she wrote a book*. This reasoning is analogous to that expressed in the sentence: *he plowed this field*. Both set up a workmanship model of production, with labor serving as the mechanism to appropriate an otherwise common resource. As the romantic genius pours his labor over the seedling of his idea thus allowing it to flower, so the farmer tends the field to produce the melons he will harvest. Both farmer and genius produce things that will ultimately be sold in a market (Woodmansee).

Now that creators manipulate the very material expression itself—the digital file in binary code—we see the creative process revealed as a web of connected iterations of reinterpretation. Thus the displacement of *ideas* by *things* is an awkward fit when talking about the objects of IP, given that these *things* are no longer singular objects invested with an "aura," but rather infinitely and simultaneously reproducible manifestations of creative work. The "workmanship" model can also be blind to collaboration and privileges the protection of previous creativity over the potential of unknown future innovations.

The free culture impulse grounds its resistance to the global IP regime in these technological developments. The movement's battle cries demand the free circulation of ideas, and open access to critical information and information and communication technologies (ICT) infrastructure, albeit with more pithy slogans: creative commons, access to knowledge, compulsory licensing, network neutrality, anonymous, etc. The movement's enemies are those—whether corporations, nation-states, organizations or individuals—who advocate an IP maximalist position. Halbert defines the IP maximalist position as when the "government works in tandem with corporate entities to facilitate the increased concentration of IP ownership" (84), categorically prioritizing enforcement and incentive over access (74).

If free culture views IP maximalism as its primary antagonist, it understands its own cultural logic to be the remix.[3] Remix culture values creative reuse, parody, second-order commentary and ironic distance. During the pre-Internet era, it was called the postmodern aesthetic; before that, it was pastiche or antropofagia. Thanks to new media technologies it has transcended a single historical moment. Its peak has coincided with an expansion of international human rights, and political movements for decolonization, equality, and free expression. Remix culture traces a global genealogy from the historical avant-gardes to postcolonial masterpieces of postmodernist lyric, its spread following diasporic routes of migration, exile, and captivity. It captures suffering and joy; it simultaneously innovates and recycles.

This remix logic has imposed itself as an undeniable cultural force, captivating global thinkers and tinkerers across all sectors of society. Today it manifests in fan cultures sharing amateur fanfic, but also in maker spaces where the curious play with soldering irons and programming languages. It mainly unfolds at the level of cultural production and consumption, and its acceleration has coincided with expanding consumer access to ICT. Touchscreen supercomputers have shrunk to the size of a mobile telephone, and these black-mirror devices are discarded and replaced in the developed world like fungible consumer items. How people uses those devices—what they can share on them, what they can make with them, and who owns which streams of data—has become a terrain of political and artistic struggle.

But the free culture movement is not restricted to a struggle over the rights of cultural consumers and producers. There are also radical wings of the free culture movement that focus on the means of production of digital culture itself. Hackers defend their ability to reverse engineer systems. Coop movements experiment with the cooperative ownership of digital infrastructure. Global health activists demand access to medicine, and educators demand access to knowledge. Many of these examples adopt anti-capitalist or anti-market positions, and all value the social circulation of knowledge as much or more than any form of incentivized innovation scheme.

Thus free culture advocates and global health activists find themselves together protesting domestic piracy laws and international FTAs, and these alliances are well represented in the *Critical Guide*. In fact, FTAs and the coordinated meetings of agencies that advance maximalist IP positions have become focal points of global resistance, in part because those meetings are the very mechanisms that codify IP regimes as legitimate and legal, and also because they provide the rare venue in which human rights grievances against the current IP regime can be heard by an international audience. There is little consensus whether such meetings represent opportunities for dialogue or if, instead, they represent openings for more disobedient tactics. Furthermore, the IP-focused activists also share the stage with organized labor, environmentalists, and a host of other sectors of civil society.

We can take struggles against the IP section of the recently abandoned Trans-Pacific Partnership (TPP) as exemplary of the contours of resistance to corporate-friendly maximalist IP schemes. The TPP was a multinational trade agreement between 12 different nations who together represented 40 percent of all world trade. The IP section of that agreement sought to consolidate and expand the international legal IP regime previously established by the Trade-Related Aspects of Intellectual Property Rights (TRIPS) Agreement in 1995, and to bring harmony to a series of bilateral and regional trade agreements that proliferated in the late twentieth- and early twenty-first-century heyday of neoliberal globalization. Before its spectacular collapse in the madness of the 2016 US presidential election, where it became at once a cudgel and a strawman, the TPP negotiations had occurred in secret, and the only pubic information about the TPP available were leaked marked-up draft chapters courtesy of WikiLeaks. The draft IP chapter first became available in 2013, with the final version leaked a year later.

The comments to the draft chapter highlight three thematic fields of resistance. In addition to the two fields I've already discussed as falling under the broad impulse of free culture—struggles around piracy, copyright, and anti-circumvention rules and unconditional demands to access any IP necessary for the advancement of global health—there is a third field of resistance, organized around cultural patrimony, dedicated to the protection of traditional knowledge.

## Cultural Patrimony Ethos

The invocation of cultural patrimony has become a tool of indigenous and autochthonous resistance to globalizing IP norms, and the movement to protect traditional knowledge expresses itself in terms antithetical to free culture, especially as it relates to the unlimited circulation of ideas and the nature of creativity. On the contrary, the preservationist impulse behind proclaiming something *cultural patrimony* is precisely the demand to remove that thing from the cultural commons, or to change the terms of access, in order to protect it. The legal literature abbreviates this fight to defend sacred knowledge, traditional culture, and memory across generations as "TK" (traditional knowledge), along with other iterative acronyms like "TIK" (traditional indigenous knowledge) and TEK (traditional environmental knowledge).

Contrast this with the logic of free culture, which understands preservation to arise from reuse, with culture preserved through unlimited reiteration, replication, and proliferation. Free culture views maximalist IP arguments, especially when put forth by corporate entities, as a categorical evil; yet when the indigenous defense of cultural patrimony expresses itself in the legal jargon of traditional knowledge, it makes an extremely expansionist argument. Helfer and Austin, the authors of *Human Rights and Intellectual Property: Mapping the Global Interface*, explain that indigenous IP rights

> are very broadly defined and include past, present, and future manifestations of their cultures, such as archaeological and historical sites, designs, ceremonies, technologies, visual and performing arts, literature, and religious and "spiritual properties"; science and technology, such as "human and other genetic resources, seeds, medicines, health practices, vital medicinal plants, animals, minerals, indigenous knowledge systems and practices, resource management systems, agricultural technologies, knowledge of the properties of fauna and flora, and scientific discoveries"; and "language, music, dance, script, histories, oral traditions, conflict resolution mechanisms, peace building processes, life philosophy and perspectives and teaching and learning systems." (446)

It would be impossible to imagine a more expansive rights claim! And yet when defenders of traditional knowledge present these claims, the nation-state itself feels threatened, as indigenous peoples' claims "question the dominant perception of the nation state as the lynchpin of the international legal order" (Helfer and Austin 445).

Cultural patrimony's uneasy relationship with these state and supranational regulatory bodies leads it to prioritize preservation over the market logic of production. It is a conservative orientation towards culture in the most material sense, given that the articulated goal is to conserve. Yet a left–right political scheme has trouble representing these demands, as if they existed on wavelengths beyond the visible political spectrum.

Even when traditional knowledge delegations intervene at the level of national or international governance to protect cultural patrimony, such interventions demand to be recognized from somewhere beyond the nation-state. Conversely, as Helfer and Austin warn, "those who view systems of property ownership only through Western eyes may overlook the significance—or even the existence—of indigenous systems of control and ownership over traditional knowledge" (455).

That blindness was manifest as recently as the turn of the millennium, when a Canadian IP law textbook from the University of Toronto Press thought it unnecessary to mention traditional or indigenous knowledge as factors in the protection–dissemination spectrum they use to characterized legal IP discourse (Doern and Sharaput 21–22). As useful as Doern and Sharaput's matrix may be, it is not capable of addressing knowledge claims that arise from an ancestral concept of territory. In order to fall anywhere upon that protection–dissemination axis, cultural patrimony must be first translated into modern property; only after a piece of IP is *owned* can the IP regime sort out whether that particular IP should be protected or disseminated.

Cultural patrimony cuts diagonally across that axis, because it advocates for alternative systems of control. It activates temporal connections and genealogies that extend beyond and before any state that grants limited monopolies over the products of individual or contractual labor. It is almost as if it belongs to an additional plane: Not a different wavelength on that protection–dissemination spectrum, but rather a different dimension entirely.

Cultural patrimony fights against the global IP regime's marked tendency to reproduce the *terra nullius* logic inherent in what C.B. Macpherson has memorably called "possessive individualism"; the patrimony ethos demands an accounting for ancestors. It says this: *There were people here before you; if you don't know about them, then listen to me and pay your respects.* Traditional knowledge is not *new*, but its renewed emergence as *visible* challenges the fundamental legal and philosophical premises of any IP regime. Cultural patrimony only seems like something novel or unthinkable from a perspective that seeks to maximize private ownership and profit over other creative values.

To the free culture logic that is still based on the Lockean notion of improvement and enclosure (Hayden 87), defenders of traditional knowledge counter with an insistence more proper to Proudhon than to the possessive individualists: misappropriation is theft. The demand is best demonstrated by the Kimberley Declaration, released at the conclusion of the 2002 International Indigenous Peoples Summit on Sustainable Development in Khoi-San Territory:

> Our traditional knowledge systems must be respected, promoted and protected; our collective intellectual property rights must be guaranteed and ensured. Our traditional knowledge is not in the public domain; it is collective, cultural and intellectual property protected under our customary law. Unauthorized use and misappropriation of traditional knowledge is theft. (Qtd. in Helfer and Austin 460)

When IP protection is used to justify biopiracy or other forms of misappropriation, protection is theft, plain and simple. Even Brown, a polemicist on the limits of political sovereignty in the debates surrounding cultural heritage and patrimony, recognizes that fact: "Underneath property concepts there always lurks the specter of commodification—that is, an inexorable tendency to treat property as fungible and alienable" (Brown et al. 576).

## Expanding the Metaphor: Beyond Protection and Dissemination

The admission that the contemporary IP regime is incapable of escaping the specter of commodification only further highlights how the concept of cultural patrimony troubles global IP norms. The late arrival of indigenous voices and ways of knowing also bears witness to their systematic attenuation or exclusion over the long history of copyright and IP law. As Rosemary Coombe has argued, rights claims based on traditional knowledge

> are voiced in terms of the spiritual meaning these practices have to the fulfillment of specific human forms of well-being. These have cosmological or "religious" dimensions, but are not easily appreciated within a rights tradition that understands religious rights primarily in terms of freedom of belief and practice and privatize and individualize these as matters of choice and conscience. Assertions of [traditional environmental knowledge] are more often made in terms that stress the social understanding of the sacred as a form of belonging, obligation, and reciprocity rooted in systems of human and nonhuman relationships with others across time. ("Protecting" 134)

When taken together, these many failures to account for the spiritual, ontological, and cultural entanglements of creativity and tradition across time remind us, incessantly, that what we call IP is, has been, and always will be an approximation, an attempt to circumscribe the products of human and nonhuman creativity and culture within an easily legalized and commodified ontology. Ideas, whether traditional or innovative, surely exist. IP, as a legal concept that manifests itself in FTAs, also clearly exists, with material traces like takedown notices and licensing-based micropayment networks. So to say that IP is a legal construct is not to dismiss it, but rather to describe it. IP attempts to legally codify the products of human creativity. But creativity, by its nature, behaves in unpredictable ways and can produce unexpected results. As both global human rights discourse and access to consumer ICT have expanded, the empirical experience of twenty-first-century life has diverged from the norms imagined by the contemporary IP regime. The metaphor at the heart of the global IP regime, *ideas are things that can be owned*, is no longer sustainable.

As is becoming clear, there is no single point of failure where the IP metaphor definitively breaks down. Its failures are multiple and distributed. In order to better understand those empirical fault lines, I now turn to two ethnographic investigations of local creative practices that differ significantly from so-called global norms.

Anita Say Chan's 2014 *Networking Peripheries: Technological Futures and the Myth of Digital Universalism* announces its skepticism in its subtitle. Chan does not take self-congratulatory ICT rhetoric about an ever-expanding modernity and a universal networked future as self-evident truths, nor will she allow her readers to think such "universalists myths" without first grounding those myths in the context of globalizing capitalism's expansion across Peru. The book's structure follows, more or less, the two broad critiques of the global IP regime I have provisionally identified as free culture and cultural patrimony, although she uses different labels. The first part, called "Neoliberal Networks at the Periphery," tells the tale of a traditional cultural practice that comes to define itself in the language of global IP norms, thanks to an *entrepreneurial* mindset and a state-sponsored campaign. In other words, it is the study of how one specific example of cultural patrimony is—in the most material and literal terms—commodified for export. The second part, called "Hacking at the Periphery," much more directly engages the free culture logic. It is a multi-threaded study of the Peruvian contours of the cosmopolitan and global free-software movement, moving from political battles between Microsoft and free-software advocates, to civil society networks of coders, teachers, and activists based around educational and bureaucratic ICT.

Decades previous, in an era before omnipresent personal computers and a global consumer market for "traditional" ceramics, Antonio Cornejo Polar had already described Peruvian society as fundamentally heterogeneous. As he outlined in the introduction to *Writing in the Air: Sociocultural Heterogeneity in Andean Literature*, Peru's long history of colonialism and conquest, coupled with a recent history of rural to urban migration, created a culture that is essentially, even constitutively heterogeneous, where every cultural manifestation (he was mainly concerned with literature) was infiltrated by ruptures, fractures, contradictions, and instabilities (Cornejo 10).

As new conflicts arise out of the spread of ICT, Cornejo's heterogeneity also finds new expressions in new media. Chan finds one such example in the workshops producing Chulucanas ceramics for export; these workshops become the anchor point for her wide-ranging ethnographic study of a neoliberal network at the periphery, where traditional ceramic practices interface with the Peruvian government's Center for Technological Innovations (CITE). In Chulucanas, she learns that the question of which workshops produce "traditional" handicrafts (and which do not!) has as much to do with the global supply chain as it does with production techniques handed down across generations. By adopting "DO," the "denomination of origin" IP title aimed at protecting traditional knowledge, artisans orient their workshops towards those supply chains. The global IP regime in turn legitimates certain workshops as producers of legitimate DO products, while a new export-oriented market encourages those artisans to compete for efficiencies in producing now legally defined Chulucanas native products. The most successful producers adopt state-of-the-art technologies, allowing them to create and distribute native products at a scale unthinkable by previous generations. The resulting artifact—a standardized, quality-controlled, market-ready commodity—may be called Authentic®, but it is also something completely new: "Whatever the implications of its name, then, Chulucanas native products stand out emblematically as a unique invention, born out of the dynamic orchestrations of the Peruvian state and its network of transnational partners and refit for the information age" (Chan 28). In Chan's account, the organized efforts of the Peruvian state to recognize native local products is "an honest neoliberal attempt at outreach, incorporation, and assimilation" (32). But, she continues, such entanglements with the global IP regime "comes at a cost, of course: traditional culture is transformed and 'legitimated' into an *exclusionary* logic" (33). She describes what this looks like in practice: "local artisans aren't granted the right to the DO because of their history of local production or maintaining traditional techniques but on the earned ability to demonstrate the 'technical norms' required by the Consejo" (61). In other words, traditional Chulucanas ceramics must be molded into shapes recognizable by the global IP regime. And those artisans who do not participate have little recourse beyond rumor and gossip (or perhaps piracy, on which more soon). Chan is attentive to those critical accounts, and she records complaints that:

> The state's stagings of indigeneity [do not appear] as authentic expressions of a contemporary will to preserve tradition but are exposed instead as strategically engineered essentializations whose purpose leans more towards logics of exclusion or undeserving partners than broad cultural inclusion. (62)

This is the process that Chan calls "native stagings," which has much in common with the demand to "perform ethnicity" studied by the Comaroffs in *Ethnicity Inc.* The Chulucanas native products label creates an "exclusive indigeneity" based around a concept of "authenticity" that itself has been codified by an IP regime, and that demands a very specific performance of indigeneity (Chan 65). These kinds of discursive operations have long been understood to create variations of the cultural simulacra highlighted by Baudrillard: Native products must project and perform a "natural authenticity" that paradoxically conceals the remade production techniques behind the commodity (Chan 71–72). Chan's research highlights the particular orientations and subjectivities that flourish in these conditions: entrepreneurs and go-getters focused on personal achievement, or younger artisans who start new workshops in direct competition with their mentors (112–115).

As is to be expected, other groups of rural artisans reject these market-friendly and export-oriented reforms, and use gossip networks to label those workshops as dishonorable: "Rural gossip's counteraccounts speak of local relations as instead morally compromised, radically individuated, and increasingly promiscuous" (Chan 97). These dissenters refuse to become what DeHart has called the "ethnic entrepreneur," and find themselves accordingly excluded from the cultural patrimony export market: "Why, in the strangest twist of all, would traditional groups have to compete among themselves for authentic entitlement, as if authenticity itself were truly a scare resource?" (Chan 67). When native branding becomes a marketing strategy, cultural patrimony has indeed been dragged down from the peaks of ancestor worship to the grimy workings of a market economy.

It is another player on the neoliberal stage, however, who haunts Chulucanas ceramics: the pirate artisan. During Chan's fieldwork, rumors of an international scandal began to circulate in Peru: some Chulucanas workshops were passing off low-quality ceramics as authentic native products. Whether encouraged by a US chain to sacrifice quality in the interest of consistency, or due to fierce local competition that encouraged unethical practices, workshops replaced the traditional—and recently Traditional®—eight-step process of staining the ceramics with mango leaf smoke and resin with a much faster and less variable single coating of paint. That paint, unfortunately, was chipping off and staining holiday shoppers' fingers in the check-out lines in Pier One stores across the United States.

In Chan's account, the government representatives ignored the scandal, perhaps because the culture ministry's official position could not acknowledge forgeries without also revealing "the unspoken work of displacing native tradition" (Chan 61). Or perhaps the explanation was a bit more immediately scandalous: the forgeries were produced in the very same workshops that the government had designated as DO producers! Even though the pirate artisans reside on the far side of exclusive indigeneity, their "traditional forgeries" were still embraced by less-scrupulous actors in global trade.

Within Chulucanas, Chan documents the sense of betrayal experienced by all those connected to the ceramics trade; even the actors who seem the likely perpetrators of the scandal express shame not at their alleged actions, but rather as arising from the betrayal of community. One can imagine, however, a different cultural logic operating in the pirate workshops: a logic of production focused on immediate survival and direct economic participation, rather than on preservation and tradition.

According to Kedron Thomas, this condition accurately describes the much more common way that indigenous communities experience the global IP regime: "Current property debates do not take into account that indigenous peoples are more and more confronted with IP, not as benefactors of special copyright and patent protections but as producers and consumers of criminalized classes of goods" (25). What happens, for instance, when the "tradition" to be protected by the global IP regime is a swoosh mark adorning a Greek goddesses's name? Thomas's book *Regulating Style: Intellectual Property Law and the Business of Fashion in Guatemala* directly addressed this question through a study of the indigenous production of nontraditional items. The main sections of her book document the knockoff fashion trade in the Guatemalan highlands, grounded in the lived local experiences of one node of the global textile industry. According to some parties, that node—Tecpán—has come to be seen by the IP regime as a hotbed of global piracy, but Thomas also pays attention to how the mostly Mayan Highlanders understand their everyday activities. The IP discourse of brand piracy can easily blind observers to what actually happens in and around the textile industry in Tecpán:

> The idea that brand pirates are simply doing something illegal and immoral discounts the reality that they are doing something innately human by making meaning, producing material culture, and forging an existence in the world in ways that make sense within local worlds where the connotations and politics of culture, identity, ownership, authenticity, and property are not reducible to or the same as those built into globalized IP frameworks. (Thomas 8)

Not only are brand pirates doing something innately human; their customers, other highlanders who range across the social and economic spectrum, are doing something perhaps even more basically and fundamentally human: clothing themselves.

To further complicate matters, this piracy unfolds within the worlds of fashion and apparel, worlds that are governed as much by the whims of fancy as they are by the iron laws of exchange. That is to say: the question of *regulating style* is not at all transparent, precisely because *style* thrives in imitation and repetition. While global IP schemes reduce fashion to trademark disputes—who you need to pay to wear what—style itself can only be understood in motion: circulation, negotiation, and obligation are not secondary characteristics of creative style but rather the fundamental conditions of style's existence. Style works with and against tradition, now representing a timeless design, now using a signature flourish to distinguish itself from the background. Thomas explains:

> In order to be recognizable as style—to have social and aesthetic significance—any expression must refer to a more general patterning and engage a dynamic temporality and historical formation that unfolds across multiple materializations. This theory of style applies equally well to the highland apparel trade and the fashion industry at large. Each "new" design is admittedly, on the part of so many US and European fashion designers and brand owners, an interpretation of extant cultural forms and not an isolated event or a pure creation that comes from nowhere … It is indeed only through acts of interpretation, repetition, association, and differentiation that a design becomes available and recognizable to consumers and critics as "fashion." (14)

Because style is inseparable from the "regional, national, and international structures of difference that have shaped class, gender, race, and ethnicity in the highlands" (Thomas 19), the author's fascinating and profound ethnography spans a geography ranging from North American neoliberalism's trademark *maquiladoras* to local workshops and markets in Tecpán. She weaves thematic threads as diverse as the security state, microfinance organizations, Guatemalan design studios, international legal fora, and prints ads from around the globe into an honest and troubling tapestry.

Although Thomas dedicates one section to highlander indigenous brands that experiment in fashion appropriation without assimilation (a practice she views dubiously as based on some uninterrogated gender dynamics) (137), the vast majority of her book tells the story of indigenous people marginalized not only by the global IP regimes, but also by the state and international institutions writ large. She concludes:

> Late indigenous styles of fashion and business found in highland Guatemala reveal how the neat and tidy narratives of originality, development, economic modernization, formalization, and multiculturalism are fundamentally ideological and misleading. These narratives are not consistent with what is happening on the ground and what people want out of life. The realities of brand piracy in Guatemala show the flaws and fissures in these fables and reveal a different way of doing thing, a different style. (241)

Her book suggests another kind of indigeneity that exists within the global IP regime: not the "exclusive indigeneity" of the Chulucanas ceramics workshops, but rather a "pirate indigeneity" that exists in the markets of Latin American towns and cities. These are indigenous people who migrate to cities and end up participating in the garment economy, either as producers or consumers. This kind of "pirate" indigeneity has little to do with the kind of sanctioned indigenous identity that is performed under the rubric of cultural patrimony. As Thomas's book makes clear, highlanders are excluded, marginalized, and in the case of brand piracy, criminalized, specifically *because* they are indigenous. The global IP regime is incapable of recognizing the highlanders as anything other than trademark pirates, even when this logic is revealed to be profoundly flawed. It is equally blind to history and empirical practice, and will only recognize certain kinds of indigeneity, that of the entrepreneurial variety which is so sympathetic to states and FTAs.

The two ethnographies, read together, cast profound doubts about whether the current IP metaphor is capable of addressing Chan's demand for "an active acknowledgement of past ruptured ties, broken trusts, and unresolved conflicts" (209), or Thomas's demand that it describe the empirical lived experiences of people like the Tecpanecos (241). How, then, to temper the IP metaphor back to a more modest "engaging universal," in the spirt of Dipesh Chakrabarty's *Provincializing Europe*? How to conceive of a global IP regime that, even while aiming towards global extension, would "operate to decenter the totalizing powers of Western universals precisely in [its] ability to enable locally situated encounters and mutations" (Chan 210)?

What if, other than *ideas are like property*, we think through a different metaphor, one that more closely aligns with our current understanding of the world, and that is more capable of describing empirical creativity? In fact, we won't even need to abandon IP wholesale; we only need to understand it as complementary to the dominant way of describing the phenomenon. What if the metaphor becomes *ideas are like light*?

We wouldn't even have to stray too far from the global IP regime's own autobiography to find an example of that alternative metaphor, as none other than the owner of Virginia's most famous slave plantation suggested it in 1813. Thomas Jefferson's famous "candlelight" metaphor—*He who receives an idea from me, receives instruction himself without lessening mine; as he who lights his taper at mine, receives light without darkening me*—has been glossed many times over. Today we know much more about how light behaves than Jefferson did in 1813; indeed, our understanding and domestication of electromagnetic radiation, along with universal suffrage, are arguably the two most significant differences between Jefferson's world and the twenty-first century.

The best contemporary scientific understanding of electromagnetic radiation, which we experience most directly as visible light on the ROYGBIV spectrum, arises out of the two-slit experiment. In the early nineteenth century, Thomas Young used that experiment to challenge the corpuscular understanding of light. The then-reigning understanding, in the Newtonian tradition, insisted that light is made up of tiny particles. Young used the two-slit apparatus, which determines whether something is a wave or a particle, to argue convincingly that light is a wave. The two-slit experiment's role in the history of science ripples out from that moment into the "thought experiments" of Einstein, Bohr, and others at the opening of the twentieth century, with the result that today's consensus in quantum theory (which uses a two slit-apparatus to observe both photons and electrons) is that light behaves like a particle at times, and like a wave at others. That strange truth, that light exhibits a wave–particle duality, is so commonly held as to merit a chapter in most college physics textbooks, and yet complicated enough that I won't be able to succinctly summarize it here.[4]

The value of the wave–particle duality for our metaphorical purposes should be quite apparent already. Although it does not line up exactly with the free culture/cultural patrimony distinction, it suggests some clear similarities. Free culture's discourse of propagation and circulation speaks the language of waves. Furthermore, without extension over time and space, a wave ceases to be a wave; like an idea, it is all momentum and oscillation. When an idea is consolidated into an object available for appropriation or preservation, that idea is turned into an IP particle. Whether that particle looks like a patent or a copyright, it no longer rides the wave of unlimited and unbounded creativity that spans generations. It is fixed by determined three-dimensional coordinates. In the case of cultural patrimony, it could even be said that an IP particle's authenticity rests precisely on the fact that it represents a static, preserved moment. That frozen IP particle won't allow for the ripples of future propagation, for new generative encounters.

It is tempting to line up the wave–particle duality with the previously mentioned protection–dissemination spectrum (Doern and Sharaput 21–22). But beyond the limitations to that spectrum outlined above, the quantum theoretical understanding of the relationship *between* wave and particle reveals that the IP metaphor must be complemented by an additional concept. As Karen Barad's magnum opus *Meeting the Universe Halfway: Quantum Physics and the Entanglement of Matter and Meaning* helps us comprehend, the wave–particle duality is *not* a spectrum, nor is it a trade-off. Such understandings of quantum indeterminacy and entanglement are in fact not accurate.

In order for quantum theory to fully account for the behavior of light, it must be *both* a wave and a particle, although in any given circumstance it will be observed to behave as one thing or the other. An observer can never see it as operating as both things in the same moment, so there is no common ground for negotiation between the two models. It is both of these things, but whenever an observer looks at light, or studies it, or attempts to explain it, it becomes one or the other. Barad summarizes: "For Bohr, the crucial point is in the fact that wave and particle behaviors are exhibited under *complementary*—that is, *mutually exclusive*—circumstances" (108). The two-slit apparatus can be configured to detect light waves, and it will; when the two-slit apparatus is configured to detect light particles, it will detect those instead: "We can't have it both ways at once" (108).

This is the true insight that Barad rescues from Bohr, and her ontological commitment to the ramifications of Bohr's metaphysics leads her to proclaim categorically "concepts are defined by the circumstances required for their measurement" (109). "That is," she continues, "theoretical concepts are not ideational in character; they are specific physical arrangements" (109).

That is an incredibly profound and useful revelation, and has direct applications well beyond the domain of particle physics. For instance, it helps us understand how concepts like the protection–dissemination spectrum create the false impression that the IP regime is simply a negotiation between the two competing demands to protect and disseminate, and that slightly less protection will yield slightly more dissemination, or vice versa. This is not the case, as Chan, Thomas, and so many others have elegantly demonstrated. There is a much more complicated operation at stake.

That said, we must take care in constructing the metaphor, especially because Barad is generally skeptical of the value of making analogies with quantum physics. In *Meeting the Universe Halfway*, she insists that "physics can't be bootstrapped into giving a full account of the social world" (24). But Barad also issues a challenge, both to herself and to her interlocutors: "What is needed is an analysis that enables us to theorize the social and the natural together, to read our best understandings of social and natural phenomena through one another in a way that clarifies the relationship between them" (25).

In that spirit, an observer can either catch light behaving as a wave, or as a particle. Those two states are complementary and mutually exclusive: light is always both, yet I can only observe one state at any one time. It is in this sense that Barad proclaims: measurement as such determines and excludes. If I determine to observe light as a particle, I exclude the possibility of observing it as a wave (19). In more specialized terms, a wave function collapses into a measured particle.[5] This leads to the first restatement of our metaphor: creativity is a wave function that collapses into an IP. To determine a property right in an idea, one must exclude that idea's intellectual momentum, its deep past and its unfettered potential future use.[6]

We are far beyond Thomas Jefferson's taper, but much closer to describing the entangled realities of "exclusive indigeneity," the Kimberley Declaration, and "pirate indigeneity." In her Bohr-inspired vocabulary, Barad defines a phenomenon as the collection of subject, an observation apparatus, and a described object. Quantum physicists can set up a two-slit apparatus and use it to observe either photos or electrons; both exhibit the same wave–particle duality. Those scientists—our subjects—will observe electrons or photons—our objects—passing through the apparatus. If the apparatus is configured a certain way, the objects behave like waves; if the apparatus is configured a different way, the objects behave like particles. The phenomena called "light as wave" names a certain relationship between the subject, the object, and the apparatus; the phenomena called "light as particle" names a different relationship between a different, complementary subject, object, and apparatus (Figure 10.1).

So it is for the indeterminate phenomenon we are naming creativity: In this case, a legal apparatus is constructed to observe creativity, art, science, ideas, style, inventions, and innovations as things to be owned; we've been calling this apparatus the global IP regime. The law observes discrete things and their owners, and calls this IP. Yet the same indeterminate phenomenon, when viewed through an apparatus calibrated for collaboration, observes the circulation of arts and sciences, and calls this creativity and culture.[7] (Figure 10.2)

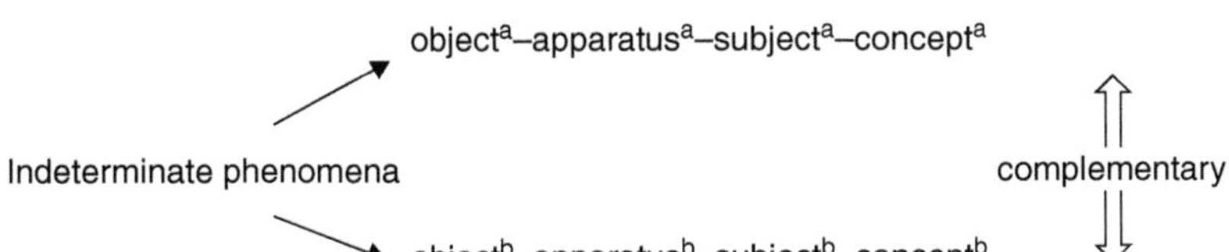


**FIGURE 10.1** Two entangled and indeterminate phenomena
Source: Created by author.

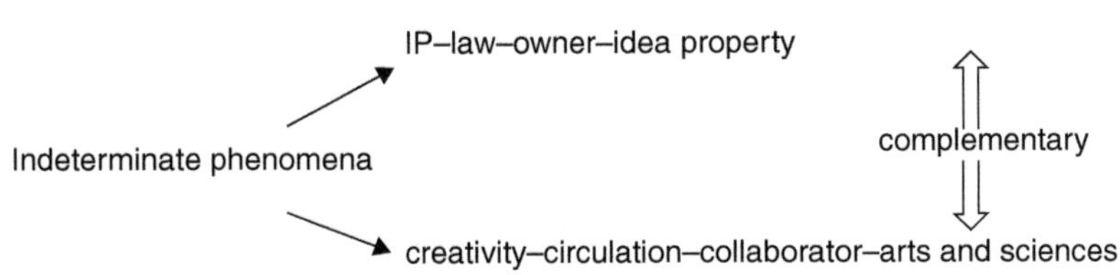


**FIGURE 10.2** Creativity as indeterminate phenomena
Source: Created by author.

Indeterminacy means that it is both things, but it only expresses itself as one or the other. When the phenomenon is defined as a wave, it cannot in that moment be a particle; when it is measured as a particle, it cannot in that moment be a wave. Any codification of an indeterminate phenomenon (be it electromagnetic radiation or creative circulation) misrepresents that phenomenon. IP underrepresents the creative function, much like a wave function underrepresents the quantum behavior of electromagnetic radiation. Due to that underrepresentation, ideas that look novel and original (or derivative and infringing) when viewed through the IP apparatus, may instead—when viewed through a complementary apparatus—express traditional knowledges that travel across geographies and histories, and that disseminate themselves precisely through their sacred protection and social obligations.

With this in mind, we can attempt a second restatement of our metaphor: Like photons and electrons, creative activity expresses a wave function; when that creative activity comes into contact with an IP apparatus, it collapses into a discrete particle of IP. Yet that specific IP is complemented by the wave function, and only together, as indeterminately wave or particle, does it cohere into an accurate and complete description of the empirical phenomenon of an idea.

This expanded, complementary, and indeterminate account of ideas has a direct ramification: the formal recognition that IP is an incomplete metaphor to describe the phenomenon it purports to name.[8] Viewing IP as a wave-function collapse reminds us what is excluded, and insists that it be accounted for. It reminds us that ideas are entangled in fundamental ways. Collapse also reminds us of the precarious state of cultural circulation when ideas fall into the realm of proprietary exclusivity. Perhaps it can suggest an exit from the dialectics of authenticity and copy, or that of preservation and appropriation. It will most certainly present inconveniences to the global IP regime itself, much like the two-slit experiment in its various manifestations troubled and unsettled human understandings of light, electromagnetism, and subatomic particle physics. *Eppur si muove* …

My task in this chapter has been to suggest a complementary metaphor to pair with IP in order to better capture the demands and realities of free culture and traditional knowledge. It would be a presumptuous absurdity for me to conclude by suggesting specific legal reforms to the global IP regime arising from the complementary metaphor. That is a task to be undertaken collaboratively; I hope, however, that the metaphor of the indeterminate nature of creative action will help ground, guide, and advance that collaborative endeavor.

## Notes

1 This argument was originally presented as part of the "Culture of the Copy" roundtable at the 2016 Latin American Studies Association Conference in Lima. My thanks to the organizers Juan Poblete and Victor Goldgel-Carballo for the invitation, and to the panelists and audience, whose comments and conversations contributed greatly to the development of this chapter. I presented previous, preliminary versions of this

argument at the 2014 HASTAC conference in Lima, Peru and on the empyre mailing list associated with that event in April 2014.

2 A third and important strand of resistance gathers around public health: demanding to know how a capitalist pharmaceutical industry based in the overdeveloped world will serve the global health needs of a planetary population. There has been much excellent scholarship using the access-to-knowledge paradigm in this area, along with scientific innovation and technology transfer more generally (see Krikorian and Kapczynski). I believe the concepts of indeterminacy and complementarity that I will develop in relation to IP are very sympathetic to the access-to-knowledge approach, although that will be a project for future study.

3 In *Two Bits: The Cultural Significance of Free Software*, Kelty gives a more nuanced definition, calling this the recursive logic of free software, which focuses on "radical technological modifiability of their own terms of existence" (3).

4 Barad's *Meeting the Universe Halfway* describes the two-slit experiment in depth across several chapters of her book.

5 Barad has a lengthy excursion on the difference between this kind of indeterminacy and the more popular "uncertainty" principle advanced by Bohr's contemporary Heisenberg and popularized in popular scientific circles.

6 Quantum entanglement is also an enrichment to the IP metaphor because it helps us remember that historically property itself has named a web of rights and obligations, and not any particular thing in itself. As C.B. Macpherson explains: "To have a property is to have a right in the sense of an enforceable claim to some use or benefit of something, whether it is a right to a share in some common resource or an individual right in some particular things. What distinguishes property from mere momentary possession is that property is a claim that will be enforced by society or the state, by custom or convention or law" (*Property* 3).

7 The "artists and scientists" in the first scheme are not only anthropological and can include the art of birdcalls and the science of flock behavior, entanglements that foreground subjects other than us humans. Barad explores the entangled ontological consequences of such an inclusive metaphysics throughout *Meeting the Universe Halfway*.

8 This does not seem to be the lesson learned in some law journals, where economics and law theorists act as if classical game theory can simply adopt a "quantum" component without undermining the very subject position and conceptual apparatus that make "game theory" an intelligible concept (see Sichelman).

## Bibliography

Barad, Karen. *Meeting the Universe Halfway: Quantum Physics and the Entanglement of Matter and Meaning*. Duke UP, 2007.

Benkler, Yochai. *The Wealth of Networks: How Social Production Transforms Markets and Freedom*. Yale UP, 2006.

Brown, Michael F. "Heritage Trouble: Recent Work on the Protection of Intangible Cultural Property." *International Journal of Cultural Property*, vol. 12, 2005, pp. 40–61.

Brown, Michael F. "Culture, Property, and Peoplehood: A Comment on Carpenter, Katyal, and Riley's 'In Defense of Property.'" *International Journal of Cultural Property*, vol. 17, 2010, pp. 569–598.

Biagioli, Mario. "Between Knowledge and Technology: Patenting Methods, Rethinking Materiality." *Anthropological Forum*, vol. 22, no. 3, November 2012, pp. 285–300.

Biagioli, Mario. *Galileo's Instruments of Credit: Telescope, Images, Secrecy*. U of Chicago Press, 2006.

Callahan, Mat, and Jim Rogers, editors. *A Critical Gide to Intellectual Property©*. Zed Books, 2017.

Chakrabarty, Dipesh. *Provincializing Europe: Postcolonial Thought and Historical Difference*. Princeton UP, 2000.

Chan, Anita Say. *Networking Peripheries: Technological Futures and the Myth of Digital Universalism*. MIT Press, 2014.

Comaroff, John L., and Jean Comaroff. *Ethnicity, Inc*. U of Chicago P, 2009.

Coombe, Rosemary J. *The Cultural Life of Intellectual Properties: Authorship, Appropriation, and the Law*. Duke UP, 1998.

Coombe, Rosemary J. "Protecting Traditional Environmental Knowledge and New Social Movements in the Americas: Intellectual Property, Human Right, or Claims to an Alternative Form of Sustainable Development?" *Florida Journal of International Law*, vol. 115, March 2005, pp. 114–135.

Cornejo Polar, Antonio. *Writing in the Air: Heterogeneity and the Persistence of Oral Tradition in Andean Literature*. Translated by Lynda J. Jentsch. Duke UP, 2013.

DeHart, Monica C. *Ethnic Entrepreneurs: Identity and Development Politics in Latin America*. Stanford UP, 2014.

Doern, G. Bruce, and Markus Sharaput. *Canadian Intellectual Property: The Politics of Innovating Institutions and Interests*. U of Toronto P, 2000.

Fuchs, Christian. *Culture and Economy in the Age of Social Media*. Routledge, 2015.

Halbert, Deborah. "The Politics of IP Maximalism." *WIPO Journal*, vol. 1, 2011, pp. 74–85.

Hayden, Cori. "The Proper Copy: The Insides and Outsides of Domains Made Public." *Journal of Cultural Economy*, vol. 3, no. 1, March 2010, pp. 85–102.

Helfer, Laurence R., and Graeme W. Austin. *Human Rights and Intellectual Property Law: Mapping the Global Interface*. Cambridge UP, 2011.

Kelty, Christopher M. *Two Bits: The Cultural Significance of Free Software*. Duke UP, 2008.

Krikorian, Gaëlle, and Amy Kapczynski, editors. *Access to Knowledge in the Age of Intellectual Property*. MIT Press, 2010.

Lessig, Lawrence. *Free Culture: How Big Media Uses Technology and the Law to Lock Down Culture and Control Creativity*. Penguin, 2004.

Lobel, Orly. *Talent Wants to Be Free: Why We Should Learn to Love Leaks, Raids, and Free Riding*. Yale UP, 2013.

Macpherson, C.B. *The Political Theory of Possessive Individualism: Hobbes to Locke*. Oxford UP, 1962.

Macpherson, C.B. *Property: Critical and Mainstream Positions*. U of Toronto P, 1978.

Sichelman, Ted. "Quantum Game Theory and Coordination in Intellectual Property." *San Diego Legal Studies Paper*, vol. 10, no. 35, November 19, 2015, pp. 1–41.

Thomas, Kedron. *Regulating Style: Intellectual Property Law and the Business of Fashion in Guatemala*. U of California Press, 2016.

Woodmansee, Martha. *The Author, Art, and the Market: Rereading the History of Aesthetics*. Columbia UP, 1994.

Woodmansee, Martha, and Peter Jaszi, editors. *The Construction of Authorship: Textual Appropriation in Law and Literature*. Duke UP, 1994.

Yúdice, George. *The Expediency of Culture: Uses of Culture in the Global Era*. Duke UP, 2003.

# 11

# THE CREATIVE COPY

## Agency and Fashion at a Market for Counterfeited Garments

*Matías Dewey*

### Introduction

"The important thing is that it is identical," concluded Luis as he looked at the Boca Juniors football shirt the seller was offering him. It was not meant for Luis himself, but for his son, and it cost significantly less than the original version. Having an identical replica was crucial, Luis explained, because "the original" product defines the latest fashion trend; it's "what everyone wears." Luis checked the number 9 on the back and the size of the shirt, confirmed the correct last name of the player, and told the seller he would take it. He wanted to stay at the shop for a bit longer and browse through different models of the Boca Juniors' football shirts. They were all there: the formations of all Boca Juniors teams—each one with the exact details of each season—of the last 15 years and in all sizes. But there was no time. The game was about to start, and he and his son had to enter the stadium.

What is known as a "copy" or "counterfeit" implies a wide variety of possibilities in any of the three constituent parts of the intellectual property (IP) law—copyright, trademark, and patent law. The particular case of the garment industry, where the action of copying usually infringes trademark law, is not an exception in this regard. There are certain cases, such as the one of the Nike-branded Boca Juniors football shirt carrying the number 9, in which identical reproduction is praised. Those who manufacture identical products understand that potential buyers, because the products are identified with the names of players or specific positions in the field, or because they are conditioned by peer-group expectations, will want products that come as close to the original as possible. Thus, counterfeiters take into account the quality of fabrics, the characteristics of plastic identifications, the exact format of brand logos or the accuracy of the embroidery. In other domains such as the counterfeiting of coins, pieces of art, manuscripts, pharmaceuticals, or fashion accessories a similar logic is present. In the field of clothing, the production of exact replicas is particularly important when original pieces are exceptional and therefore "scarce," such as certain sportswear lines or haute couture items exhibiting very specific fashion designs. From the consumer's point of view, exact replicas often lead to consumer deception, although in many cases—as the above example shows—there is full knowledge about the copied nature of the product.

This chapter is not concerned with exact replicas but with counterfeits that are somehow similar. Copies that are similar hold a variety of possibilities that should be mentioned. While the counterfeited Boca Juniors football shirt previously mentioned has an equivalent in Nike's catalog, other counterfeited garments are only "inspired" by originals and consequently do not have a "legal" counterpart. In other words, if it were not for the fraudulent use of brand logos, the latter could probably not be considered copies. This last option, the reference or the use of brands, may also involve the use of altered versions of brand logos such as "Columbian," "Nikey," or "Leviz."

In this chapter I will refer to this nonidentical reproduction of items as "creative copies." The problem concerning either identical or similar copies has sparked numerous reflections in the field of law, especially regarding the question of how strictly intellectual property rights (IPRs) should be enforced and how different levels of enforcement positively or negatively correlate with innovation (Hilty; Hilty et al.; Raustiala and Sprigman). Meanwhile, anthropologists have been increasingly interested in practices, circulation, and the meaning of copies, while governments increasingly support strong IPRs and rigorous enforcement believing that unlimited IPRs will promote economic development. Some authors, for instance, analyze the relationships between IP regimes in the garment sector and the reproduction of structures of inequality and disenfranchisement of social groups (Thomas, *Regulating Style*, "Intellectual Property Law"; Luvaas). Other studies focus on the meanings that actors assign to copied products and how they evaluate the multiple forms of copies in relation to originally branded products (Crăciun, "Rethinking Fakes"; Lempert; Nakassis; Warkander). Adopting an economic sociology perspective, this chapter aims to contribute to this body of literature by analyzing the "copy" as a product resulting from the continuous interaction between informal clothing manufacturers and buyers. It will be argued that the interaction between both parties guides the production of the copy, which also means that the copy is not identical to the original because there is no intention of manufacturing an exact replica: it is a constant search carried out by informal clothing manufacturers to satisfy the buyers' imaginations and preferences. The creative copy is the result of a social relationship; the result of a continuous mutual adjustment of expectations. On the one hand, there are the garment entrepreneurs who are interested in interpreting and capturing potential customers' preferences by way of evoking colors, brands, designs, and fashion trends. On the other hand, there are the buyers who influence the manufacturing process by way of actively suggesting and communicating their preferences.

The analysis of creative copying as a sociological phenomenon is relevant for two fundamental reasons. First, as products that only partly incorporate elements of branded originals and that crucially integrate the point of view of potential buyers, creative copies are expressions of fashion. This is certainly not the usual point of view among scholars reflecting on the fashion phenomenon, probably because it is assumed that a "copy" does not involve any creative or innovative element. Such lack of creativity also extends to its producers, who are thought as only able to "copy" in a supposedly identical way. Second, the process of creative copying that takes place at the micro level is linked to social processes at the macro level, such as the local or global transformations experienced by the clothing industry. More specifically, the production of fashionable garments adapted to the tastes of customers is possible thanks to the worldwide emergence—especially in Latin America—of informal markets specialized in the wholesale of garments. By this I do not mean that processes of creative copying take place only in these marketplaces but that the latter specially foster the manufacture of creative copies.

In the first section of the chapter, I characterize La Salada as a one-product type of marketplace. After some conceptual clarifications and a brief methodological section, the chapter goes on to offer both a macro perspective in which I argue that the rise of garment-oriented marketplaces foster the manufacture of "creative copies," and also a micro perspective about the decisions and processes involved in the production of creative copies.

## On the Legality–Illegality Distinction

The argument presented in this chapter distinguishes between legality and illegality. A consequence of this decision is that I use the concept of sweatshop and not of "workshop," "family workshop," or "homework," all terms to be found in the literature. In the field of IP law, this means using notions such as counterfeiting or IP infringement. When I make the distinction legal/illegal, I refer to the compliance—or noncompliance—of certain actions with official norms. As Mayntz states, "There is no conceptual ambiguity about the distinction between legal and illegal properties of action if we define legal action as action in conformity with a legal norm, and illegal action as [action] that violates a legal norm" (2). This narrow definition of legality seeks to move away from broader notions of legality that implicitly or explicitly include moral components or socially accepted customs. Inversely, there is need to speak of legality only if an explicit state regulation prohibiting or regulating certain actions is absent.

There are two reasons supporting this conceptualization. First, a narrow definition of legality, one that only refers to the existence of norms, allows the legitimacy of these norms to be analyzed separately. In line with Max Weber, legitimacy refers to a subjective belief related to the validity of certain practices or normative order. Those who infringe IP laws, as described in this chapter, do so believing that using logos or copying designs are, for whatever reason, legitimate practices. Likewise, this legitimacy associated with certain practices, informal norms, or extra-legal authorities varies historically and across societies (Beckert and Dewey 7). This chapter describes a social field in which actions that can be considered illegal because they infringe IPRs enjoy social acceptance, a fact that explains the difficulties in enforcing laws as well as the high levels of creativity among those who copy. Pirates tend to be beloved characters who act outside the law and it is precisely that paradox that makes them attractive. The second reason for using the legal/illegal distinction is that it brings the problem of state power and social domination to the fore. As an expression of moral debates, private interests and public conversations, state definitions have an impact on society and they have therefore to be acknowledged—they are a social fact that, in turn, forces actors to make specific decisions regarding the business, to take risks, to hide, or to bribe state agents. Broad or narrow protections of IP, as mentioned in the introduction, may be the result of private interests' power, state's lack of autonomy, or IP conceptions that ignore consumers' rights. In any case, the hard job of dissecting which actions are legal and which are not shows us both the scope of state power to criminalize social groups, and how these states enforce, sometimes selectively, specific laws.

## Methodological Remarks

The research on informal garment production presented here is the result of seven months of ethnographic immersion in the La Salada marketplace in 2013 and 2019. During that time I forged many relationships with residents of the area, several informal workers in the market, municipal authorities, shed-market managers, and garment producers working outside La Salada and lenders at a micro-credit institution. All of this gave me a serious understanding of entrepreneurs' work and La Salada's role in the context of the Argentinian garment industry. Through snowball sampling, I came to spend a great deal of time with entrepreneurs, among them a Bolivian family who were the owners of a market stall at La Salada and responsible for its day-to-day operation. In total, I conducted 109 in-depth interviews with actors such a seamstresses, ironers, buttonhole makers, garment entrepreneurs, wholesale buyers, and other roles relevant in the context of the marketplace. When permission was given, the interview was recorded. Otherwise, it was transcribed afterwards.

## The Rise of Informal Wholesale Supply Marketplaces of Fast Fashion

The informal manufacture of fashion items adapted to a buyer's preferences by way of creative copying needs to be considered in the context of marketplaces understood as sites that facilitate encounters and continuous interaction between informal garment entrepreneurs and wholesale buyers. Since the beginning of the 1990s, a series of informal wholesale supply centers of garments manufactured in sweatshops emerged in Latin American and even European countries: the marketplace "Feira da madrugada" in Brazil (Vereta-Nahoum), the "Gamarra" marketplace in Peru, "La Salada" in Argentina (Dewey, *Making It at Any Cost*; Montero and Abalo) and "Macroloto 1" (Ceccagno) in the Italian city of Prato. What these marketplaces share and what distinguishes them from other similar economic spaces such as "Tepito" in Mexico or the Tehran marketplace is that these are single-product markets: they are specialized in the wholesale garment business. This specialization is not coincidental and should be understood as directly related to the fate of both the textile and clothing industries in each country. Since the mid-1980s, the development of export-processing zones and the reorientation of the global garment supply chain to Asian countries had a negative impact on local garment sectors, leading to the dismissal of thousands of qualified employees and leaving machinery and installations up for grabs. Since the mid-1990s, the conjunction of various factors, such as the influx of migrants and the availability of qualified workforce as well as an increasing demand of low-cost fashion items, stimulated the mushrooming of sweatshops at the outskirts of the aforementioned cities. These sweatshops would channel their production through the marketplaces mentioned above—locations that work as meeting points between sweatshop entrepreneurs and wholesale buyers who resell garment items in distant provinces or countries. In Argentina, according to the Argentinian Confederation of Medium-Sized Enterprises (CAME), more than 600 garment centers, or "Saladitas," resell items bought at the La Salada marketplace located on the outskirts of the city of Buenos Aires.

This local configuration of informal marketplaces surrounded by nearby sweatshops producing low-cost garment items is significantly different from classical accounts of sweatshop economies. There are two distinctive features of these successful economies that set them apart from constellations with migrant workers' participation in the garment industry (Bender and Greenwald; Bonacich and Appelbaum; Collins; Esbenshade; Green; Ross; Waldinger). First, as stated before, a significant number of sweatshops are closely linked to nearby wholesale marketplaces that nourish large routes of regional trade. Large amounts of low-cost garments are channeled through networks—reaching most of the Latin American Southern Cone and all countries of central Europe—that have emerged incrementally due to the actions of small entrepreneurs and traders. Second, related to this, these fast-fashion production centers are crucially disconnected from large retail firms and brands. This means that the implementation and monitoring of labor, health, and security regulations depends on domestic institutions, commonly nongovernmental organizations (NGOs) and state agencies, and not on multinational brands.

In Argentina, the demise of the textile industries, the rising unemployment, and the arrival of immigrant population during the 1990s had a direct impact on the area that now hosts La Salada, which subsequently underwent a dramatic change. La Salada covers 18 hectares of mostly flat land on the outskirts of the city of Buenos Aires and is dominated by the shed markets built to house the majority of the 7,822 market stalls that trade there. Being a single-product marketplace, nearly all the stalls sell garments: La Salada marketplace has become the focal point for a countrywide informal economy and is the primary provider of garments to the lower and middle classes in Argentina, as well as in neighboring countries. Three times a week, 200 long-distance buses and thousands of cars arrive at the marketplace to buy wholesale counterfeit garments branded with Adidas, Puma, Disney, and more. Even with the added cost of traveling across the country to reach the marketplace, the counterfeit goods are still cheaper than the originals; a testament to the success of La Salada's wholesaling approach.

## The Downstream Garment Entrepreneur

In the prevailing literature on the role of sweatshops in the garment industry, sweatshops are productive units working as providers of sewing services to legally constituted companies that are close to the end consumer. In other words, sweatshops are "upstream," i.e., they are somehow distanced from consumer markets and are therefore not in contact with end consumers. In this chapter, as stated earlier, I make the case of a different constellation. Informal marketplaces like La Salada create the necessary incentives for entrepreneurs to set up a sweatshop, to manufacture garment items, and to sell the production without intermediaries. There are several differences between the downstream entrepreneurs, typical at La Salada, and the upstream entrepreneurs, typical in accounts of the garment industry. For instance, a La Salada garment entrepreneur's job not only consists of delivering sewing services, cutting fabric, or assembling fabric cuts. Downstream entrepreneurs usually do not have a sweatshop specialized in the provision of outsourced services to other sweatshops. Quite the contrary, they become "downstream" because they themselves decide to take control over the entire production process of seasonal "collections." These decisions are, for instance, about outsourcing certain stages, such as sewing, assembly, ironing, or embroidery. However, what truly defines these entrepreneurs' position downstream in the market is their contact with end consumers, an aspect that influences the whole production process "backwards."

It is difficult to understand La Salada entrepreneurs' activity without taking into account the marketplace through which they channel their products. On the one hand, the frequent contact with buyers determines many aspects of the organization of their work in and outside their sweatshop. However, on the other, La Salada's offer of face-to-face contact with buyers and the possibility of bypassing market intermediaries have stimulated the emergence of a specific entrepreneur that fills a structural gap in the garment market. As I explain elsewhere (Dewey, *Making It at Any Cost*), entrepreneurs linked to the La Salada marketplace have been providing low-cost items of clothing to a section of the market that has been left untended by formally constituted companies since the early 1990s. By becoming the country's major commercialization center of low-cost garments, La Salada offered an opportunity to outsourcing entrepreneurs, who are traditionally linked to the formal garment market and multinationals by way of subcontracting. They were given the possibility of an upgrade: to reformulate their garment business in order to increase their profit margins. Reformulation meant switching from an outsourcing business model to what one now observes as the typical La Salada downstream entrepreneur; that is, the business model of only delivering sewing services was abandoned and in its place entrepreneurs took control of the whole production process, all the way through to commercialization through channels completely submerged in informality and illegality.

More specifically, what makes the job of La Salada entrepreneurs special is that they adapt their garment items to fashion trends by introducing fashion inputs. Such inputs appear towards the end of the production process and determine large parts of it. Entrepreneurs manufacturing children's caps, Adidas jackets, aprons decorated with Minions characters, women's clothing branded with the Akiabara logo: all these manufacturers make a constant effort to find inspiration in the information provided directly by buyers or gleaned from elsewhere. They are not interested in producing exact replicas, and "original" products serve as a point of departure; "originals" are templates to be recreated according to the demands, preferences, and fashion elements communicated by buyers or imagined by producers. In other words, what these entrepreneurs do is "understand how commodities get their meaning" (Aspers 132) in order for the added value (fashion input) to translate into better positioning within the marketplace. At this point we could observe that La Salada entrepreneurs contradict the extended assumption that this type of entrepreneur is only capable of producing copies; an understanding that denies their ability to collect and interpret information and act accordingly.

In the next section, I will show that this decoupling between the formal and informal markets originates in a variety of information-gathering practices developed by entrepreneurs in the marketplace. They "listen" to the demands, "read" the symbolic values of their buyers, and try to imagine the purchaser's point of view—that is, how they expect the item to perform (Beckert; Shackle).

## Interpreting Buyers' Ideas of "Fashion"

The new season was approaching and Pablo, the oldest son of a Bolivian family and self-made garment entrepreneur, was unable to identify the latest skirt worn by Las Leonas (the Lionesses), the women's national field hockey team. In the entire Conurbano, the metropolitan area close to the city of Buenos Aires, Las Leonas are a passion among women teenagers. "I don't know, I don't know," said Pablo, and continued,

> I've somehow lost track. I don't know what the newest model of the skirt is. But yesterday I watched the game, Italy against Argentina, the Las Leonas game, and I saw the uniform worn by the Italians … Puma, beautiful! I liked it very much! Puma. It was different. The problem is … you know. Here people like Adidas, everyone! Actually, it's women who like Adidas: *cumbieras* [women who like cumbia music] and girls who play sports. Women buy Adidas immediately! But with Puma, you have to swim upstream [*tenés que remarla*] … this is the problem. This is why I had to transform something from Puma into Adidas. I took the Puma pattern, but I put the Adidas stripes on it.

Pablo was inside the wire-mesh structure surrounded by the last of this season's models as he mentioned the production process along with clothing designs, brands, field hockey games, players, types of patterns and the preferences of specific social groups. The copying process turned out to be much more complex than I had imagined. He needed to decide which clothing item would define the next season—the period covering the end of the year when sales tend to be highest. A few weeks later, however, the new Adidas skirts were already lined up on hangers hooked onto the roof of the stall.

La Salada is the home of competition. With hundreds of shoppers coming in everyday from all over the country, it is crucial to keep up with not only the latest fashion trends, but also the quality of the materials, the colors, the brands, prices, and even transport possibilities for bulk purchases. If you want to be successful in La Salada you have to be able to satisfy a customer's every need. Thus, it appeared that offering something as apparently insignificant as last season's model of a hockey skirt could be reason enough for a customer to move on from Pablo's stall and find one that sells the latest model. During one of our short, casual chats, Pablo told me that some brand logos were more desirable than others. He explained this to me by letting me feel the texture of various fabrics and observe details like the seam or logo of garments. I could imagine that, in turn, his clients (also wholesale buyers) had clients of their own who expected the same in other parts of the country. Later, I also came to understand that this chain of expectations regarding the use and quality of garments were factors that compelled Pablo to improve his products. To be able to offer items that were considered "in fashion" Pablo had to find solutions to design and quality problems concerning his products. By plugging into this long chain of aesthetic expectations, Pablo's newly designed hockey skirt promised to reach new clients, diversify his product portfolio, and, most importantly, increase sales.

It is easy to assume that in a market like La Salada manufacturing *fashionable* clothes—products that carry symbolic meaning, social hierarchies, and feelings of belonging—simply means copying designs and brand logos created by established companies. But what does fashion actually mean to La Salada? How are the producers able to connect to the large number of new trends and tastes? Or, more generally, how are they sure that the designs they have envisioned for a new season will actually sell? In order to answer these questions, we need to examine a set of practices that are crucial for organizing production and identifying special niches.

Like Pablo, entrepreneurs in La Salada know that certain creative practices— broadly defined in the specialized literature as *counterfeiting* or *copying*— are crucial for increasing profit margins. This knowledge goes hand in hand with issues of brand reproduction, the diffusion of IPRs, and the way certain brands are appropriated (Coombe, "Tactics of Appropriation," *The Cultural Life*; Thomas, "Economic Regulation," *Regulating Style*; Nakassis) which consistently challenge the "copy/original" dichotomy and propose notions of style, bricolage, hybridity, and creolization (Crăciun, "Rethinking Fakes"; Hansen 372; Miller and Küchler; Polhemus; Thomas, *Regulating Style*). However, research in the field has kept silent on how buyers influence what is "in fashion" and *how* this form of individual learning is part of a greater process of garment production.

## *Practices of Monitoring*

If entrepreneurs in La Salada fail to interpret buyers' tastes in order increase their own economic possibilities, the market will penalize them and they will be excluded, as they would in any other market. Therefore, they must put a particular skill to use: the constant monitoring of the market. Monitoring refers to a series of practices whose main objective is to gather usable information. The decisions that sweatshop entrepreneurs make, and their level of success, are attributed to the quality and quantity of the information they collect. With the help of this information, entrepreneurs can construct their own "reading of the market."

There are two types of monitoring that are carried out by entrepreneurs both inside and outside the marketplace. The first type is carried out only during the three days a week that the marketplace is open. During these days, sweatshop entrepreneurs have the opportunity to "walk the market," i.e., to come into contact with customers, go through the aisles to keep track of what is being sold, check to see if models similar to their own are being sold, and verify the prices. The second type is employed outside the market and is based on information from the Internet and fabric shops. The latter can be monitored at all times and involves checking websites and social media, especially Facebook. The fabric shops are crucial sources of information and highly influence entrepreneurs' decisions. The interaction with sellers, fabric and textile suppliers, and also clients offers a unique opportunity to collect ideas for the new season. In general, monitoring practices can help sweatshop entrepreneurs expand their business opportunities and develop models that, depending on the results, can be used as templates for future production.

Monitoring fosters the development of a special sensitivity to novelty and to detecting what is different. Sweatshop entrepreneurs notice details in seams, accessories, buttons, and fabric textures with just one glance. But they are not the only ones with this ability; buyers have also developed this talent. The crucial fact is that the buyers and sellers know that they are both capable of noticing details, which is why details and small variations are so decisive. In short, the monitoring of competitors is intended to help develop "novelty" in the products; to create the idea that something is being changed while still maintaining low prices.

## *Monitoring Prices and Clothes*

Monitoring oriented towards finding a commercial niche means being able to identify opportunities. Thus, basic operations of comparing and identifying differences are vital. Once something is discovered, the trick is to specialize in it "so that everyone knows that that's what you do," as Matilde would say. Monitoring the marketplace every week adds one important aspect to the importance of counterfeiting, which is to check whether particular models or designs have already been manufactured or counterfeited by others, or have the potential to be manufactured. The monitoring process, in this sense, is closely related to the need for differentiation. For instance, if an entrepreneur sees that another one has counterfeited his model, they may try to differentiate their products by using different fabrics, though they will keep the same design since it is easier to change the fabric.

Sweatshop entrepreneurs carefully monitor the prices stipulated by the competition. This is the second aspect that really matters and that becomes a mandatory practice. Price monitoring is a standard strategic behavior upon which the business depends since La Salada is primarily a wholesale marketplace where demand tends to be inflexible. It also offers immediate indications for the reformulations of strategies. Going through the marketplace and scanning prices helps people like Pablo to evaluate the price–quality ratio of competitors' own products, to eventually reformulate Pablo's commercial strategy.

Because variation and change are not foreign to La Salada, sweatshop entrepreneurs find themselves constantly working on new ideas to keep up. Yet, sometimes this can also mean terminating a current product to release a new one that has better chances of increasing profits. Osvaldo, an experienced sweatshop entrepreneur found himself in such a situation. He told me about how he had to stop the production of tight-fit sweatpants because he was falling behind. "I was slacking off," he explained, "I made a very nice sweatshirt but it's not cheap, and that's why I'm already thinking of making a nice but cheaper sweatshirt."

The price is what matters. Like other entrepreneurs, Osvaldo wanted to unleash his creativity and produce clothing with "exciting" colors and "beautiful" seams, according to the common language of sweatshop entrepreneurs. But they cannot. At the end of the day the price of a model dictates its production. It is what controls trends and what will essentially attract customers. Thus, quality comes last. This is the reason why price monitoring is an essential feature and what fuels competition; it entails basing one's decisions on those of external forces. This allows little leeway for entrepreneurs but guides them past poor business decisions, or even helps to correct these. This skill soon becomes a habit and a vital practice for business continuity.

Although the price plays a decisive role in determining decisions and defining the dynamics within the three shed markets, visitors to La Salada may be surprised to notice that the prices of the garments are not displayed anywhere. Whoever wants to know the price of an item, whether buyer or entrepreneurs monitoring competitors, must ask. In most cases, it is possible to bargain. Prices can be modified using very pragmatic criteria like the quantity of items one wishes to buy or the prospect of future sales perceived by the stallholder. Prices may even be modified based on the client's "look," i.e., how wealthy they look. As a result, the profit margin is determined according to the specific situation established between the seller and the buyer.

## *Clients' Opinions about Fashion*

As already mentioned, with the exception of some imitations of jerseys or items worn by celebrities, there is no single product in La Salada that is an exact copy of an original design. Pablo's father explained to me what exactly goes into deciding which materials to use, what type of cut to try out, and which colors to incorporate:

> The clients tell you: [for example] Why don't you cut here or combine this with another color? People give you the ideas, because they don't always want the same! They don't want the classic, the typical Las Leonas skirt. You see, the classic one has the three stripes here. Look, people want us to put it another way, something that's out of the ordinary.

This type of situation makes sweatshop entrepreneurs refrain from manufacturing large quantities of garments, and instead produce small batches adapted to the current tastes of the customers, often at the expense of offering more elaborate designs. "We used to order embroidery," explains Matilde, who makes school aprons stamped with a Disney character,

> and we put a small butterfly on it to attract attention. But the mothers told me they wanted the old model, with the neckline like this and like that. [They wanted] always the same, always the same thing. But anyway, we would start doing that. They were telling me what they wanted.

These decisions reveal the true nature of La Salada: a marketplace for low-cost garments in which product differentiation based on adding details is valuable but subordinate to price.

Creating variation by using better fabrics or more intricate designs is almost impossible, not because of a lack of tools or knowledge, but because sweatshop entrepreneurs cannot risk making mistakes. By constantly monitoring, they stay updated and can react quickly when new trends or styles hit the market within the same season. When Pablo's sister Mariela told their father "people want tracksuits," the family reacted immediately to design new products. Trends can be driven by celebrities or famous athletes. In reference to Las Leonas, Pablo added that small talk with buyers was packed with constant references to celebrities or fashion trends led by television or clothing companies. The importance of reacting to the market is alluded to in Crăciun ("Rethinking Fakes" 852), whose interviewee Mustafa declared that his "branded jeans" manufacturing business "is based on a simple principle; that is, a prompt response to market demand." During a single season, these reactions can enable a continuous adjustment of expectations between sweatshop entrepreneurs and buyers in the context of certain fashions trends.

Exchanging perspectives about possible models, colors, or designs does not take place in a vacuum, but in the context of cultural scripts and understandings of demand. Thus, monitoring is also guided by culturally produced forms; ideas acquired by sweatshop entrepreneurs based on tastes and trends of "what women want" and "what the boys wear." Pablo's father Osvaldo knows how the pattern of women's trousers must be: "With good fit, with a good drape, like women want. They want it to be easy, a bit wide. A comfortable piece." The monitoring of competitors, prices, and other designs undoubtedly plays an important role in shaping tailoring decisions, but the search for a niche is also influenced by the ideas, tastes, and behaviors of the clients. On the other hand, the sales niche, i.e., the type of garment to be manufactured, is not something that is decided once and for all. The continuous monitoring of the marketplace serves to confirm or modify decisions.

### *Monitoring in the Internet and Fabric Shop*

Browsing the Internet for hours, especially between market days, is essential if a producer wants to offer customers new designs and products. The Internet plays a major role in offering new ideas, indicating trends, and helping producers create new products. Felipe explained,

> Now, you go to the Internet, you go to a site in Spain, you're looking for boys' fashion and you see what the trend is, you go to a site in England and do the same, you go to one in France and the same. Then you pretty much know the colors that can be used and the style of the clothes.

But the Internet alone does not lead to success. In the end, producers must rely on intuition and pay close attention to the design preferences and colors of the clientele in order the get the product right. Felipe almost fell into a trap that unfortunately caught many others when they saw that fluorescent colors were becoming fashionable in Europe.

> You looked on the Internet and everyone said: all of January and February will be fluorescent. No sooner said than done. It lasted those two months and not a bit longer. Anyone who bought fabric rolls [in that color] was stuck. I did only very little. It's not my style; I mean, the style of clothes that I manufacture doesn't work in that color.

Trends are also propagated by fabric shops. While standing in line or otherwise coming into contact with vendors in a fabric shop, sweatshop entrepreneurs receive valuable information about "what is coming out," i.e., what other producers are buying, and which trends are coming in from Europe. Each year, fabric wholesalers, especially those in the Once neighborhood, travel to fashion capitals such as Milan or Paris, or to textile and fashion exhibitions, to get acquainted with new trends and obtain catalogs exhibiting the designs and colors of the new season. On their return to Buenos Aires, these major fabric distributors operate as diffusers of trends. However, their suggestions concerning new trends and designs are reappraised by sweatshop entrepreneurs. Similarly, all the interviewees regularly visit sports stores in order to identify new models, look for colors, and gather ideas.

## Conclusion: Fashion and Uniformity

It was not until I walked down the aisles of La Salada myself, that I could understand and confirm what my interviewees had told me about the atmosphere of the market. I quickly realized that La Salada was a very family friendly marketplace—very female- and children-oriented. People would tell me that this was because "women change clothes a lot and therefore buy a lot," and that children regularly need a change of clothes "because they get dirty quickly."

During my walks through La Salada, it became clear that garments were characterized by uniformity in colors, designs, and brand logos as a result of the decisions made by manufacturers. The products were not "risky," mostly because the risk (the color or design) was taken by the companies who owned the brand. A Disney character printed on a shirt indicates the search for something that is more than a "plain model," but it is no longer a risk when the Walt Disney Company proves that items featuring this character are successful. In this sense, the practice of monitoring expresses a desire for differentiation among producers, although it is this same monitoring that leads to ideas being discarded and products exhibiting limited variation.

What surprised me even more was how the practice of copying, which is carried out in conjunction with a continuous monitoring practice, leads to a paradox reminiscent of Harrison White's observation that "the key is that producers watch each other within the market" (518). The paradox in La Salada is that stallholders are more likely to find an almost exact replica of an item at another producer's stall than in the store run by the brand they are counterfeiting. The reason for this is that a top-selling design counterfeited by another producer is a better guarantee of sales than the exact counterfeit of a branded item. Unlike the latter, the sweatshop entrepreneur's model is already adapted to the tastes of La Salada customers and has proven saleability in that commercial context. A similar strategy documented by Thomas (*Regulating Style* 91) is practiced in particular by manufacturers from the Maya community in Guatemala, who decided to copy brand logos simply because they do not know the tastes of the wider community; they believe that copying well-known brands is playing it safe. All of this highlights the importance of monitoring competition as well as how well certain models sell. "It's easy, we go through the whole marketplace and if someone has a good model, we do that. Because they also copy. Same as us. They copy, we copy. There is no code of behavior," said Pablo. There is in fact a code: counterfeit freely. Not only is the counterfeit of a counterfeit better because it is created in a way that is perceived to be "meaningful," but the modifications of each model lead the counterfeiters to believe that their products are worth more. What is most significant is that this dynamic culminated in shaping a market that is heavily adapted to its customers and is coupled to the formal garment market only in terms of price. In general, what drives these dynamics of creative copying is the continuous practice of monitoring exercised by almost 8,000 producers, which also incorporates influences from magazines, television, the Internet, fabric merchants, and the customers. The agency of the entrepreneurs resides precisely in the production of clothing that is a synthesis of these influences and not merely a copy of original designs from global corporations.

## Bibliography

Aspers, Patrik. *Orderly Fashion: A Sociology of Markets*. Princeton UP, 2016.

Beckert, Jens. "The Transcending Power of Goods: Imaginative Value in the Economy." *The Worth of Goods. Valuation and Pricing in the Economy*, edited by Jens Beckert and Patrik Aspers, Oxford UP, 2011, pp. 106–128.

Beckert, Jens, and Matias Dewey. *The Architecture of Illegal Markets. Toward an Economic Sociology of Illegality in the Economy*. Oxford UP, 2017.

Bender, Daniel E., and Richard A.Greenwald. *Sweatshop USA: The American Sweatshop in Historical and Global Perspective*. Taylor & Francis, 2013.

Bonacich, Edna, and Richard Appelbaum. *Behind the Label: Inequality in the Los Angeles Apparel Industry*. U of California P, 2000.

CAME (Argentinian Confederation of Medium-Sized Enterprises). "Mapa de la Argentina ilegal: hay 656 Saladitas en el país y 88.791 vendedores informales,"July 15, 2019, www.redcame.org.ar/contenidos/circular/Mapa-de-la-Argentina-Ilegal_-hay-656-saladitas-en-el-pais-y-88_791-vendedores-informales-.7579.html. Accessed December 15, 2019.

Ceccagno, Antonella. *City Making and Global Labor Regimes: Chinese Immigrants and Italy's Fast Fashion Industry*. Springer International, 2017.
Collins, Jane Lou. *Threads: Gender, Labor, and Power in the Global Apparel Industry*. U of Chicago P, 2003.
Coombe, Rosemary J. *The Cultural Life of Intellectual Properties: Authorship, Appropriation, and the Law*. Duke UP, 1998.
Coombe, Rosemary J. "Tactics of Appropriation and the Politics of Recognition in Late Modern Democracies." *Political Theory*, vol. 21, no. 3, 1993, pp. 411–433.
Craciun, Magdalena. "Bobbles and Values: An Ethnography of De-Bobbling Garments in Postsocialist Urban Romania." *Journal of Material Culture*, vol. 20, no. 1, 2015, pp. 3–20.
Craciun, Magdalena. "Rethinking Fakes, Authenticating Selves." *Journal of the Royal Anthropological Institute*, vol. 18, no. 4, 2012, pp. 846–863.
Dewey, Matías. "Domestic Obstacles to Labor Standards: Law Enforcement and Informal Institutions in Argentina's Garment Industry." *Socio-Economic Review*, vol. 16, no. 3, 2018, pp. 567–586.
Dewey, Matías. *Making It at Any Cost: Aspiration and Politics in a Counterfeit Clothing Marketplace*. U of Texas P, forthcoming 2020.
Esbenshade, Jill Louise. *Monitoring Sweatshops: Workers, Consumers, and the Global Apparel Industry*. Temple UP, 2004.
Green, Nancy. *Ready-to-Wear, Ready-to-Work: A Century of Industry and Immigrants in Paris and New York*. Duke UP, 1997.
Hansen, Karen Tranberg. "The World in Dress: Anthropological Perspectives on Clothing, Fashion, and Culture." *Annual Review of Anthropology*, vol. 33, no. 1, 2004, pp. 369–392.
Hilty, Reto M. "Economic, Legal and Social Impacts of Counterfeiting." *Criminal Enforcement of Intellectual Property. A Handbook of Contemporary Research*, edited by Christophe Geiger, Edward Elgar, 2012, pp. 9–23.
Hilty, Reto M. "The Role of Enforcement in Delineating the Scope of Intellectual Property Rights." *The Transformation of Enforcement: European Economic Law in Global Perspective*, edited by Hans W. Micklitz and Andrea Wechslerpp, Hart, 2016, pp. 227–243.
Isik, Damla. "Personal and Global Economies: Male Carpet Manufacturers as Entrepreneurs in the Weaving Neighborhoods of Konya, Turkey." *American Ethnologist*, vol. 37, no. 1, 2010, pp. 53–68.
Lempert, Michael. "Imitation." *Annual Review of Anthropology*, vol. 43, no. 1, 2014, pp. 379–395.
Luvaas, Brent. "Material Interventions: Indonesian DIY Fashion and the Regime of the Global Brand." *Cultural Anthropology*, vol. 28, no. 1, 2013, pp. 127–143.
Mayntz, Renate. *Illegal Markets Boundaries and Interfaces between Legality and Illegality*. MPIfG, 2016.
Miller, Daniel, and Susan Küchler. *Clothing as Material Culture*. Berg, 2005.
Montero, Jerónimo, and Eliana FerradásAbalo. "Sweatshop Workers in Buenos Aires: The Political Economy of Human Trafficking in a Peripheral Country." *Vulnerability, Exploitation and Migrants*, edited by Louise Waite, Gary Craig, and Hannah Lewis, Palgrave Macmillan, 2015, pp. 161–173.
Nakassis, Constantine V. "Counterfeiting What? Aesthetics of Brandedness and Brand in Tamil Nadu, India." *Anthropological Quarterly*, vol. 85, no. 3, 2012, pp. 701–721.
Polhemus, Ted. *Streetstyle: From Catwalk to Sidewalk*. Thames & Hudson, 1994.
Raustiala, Kal, and Christopher Sprigman. *The Knockoff Economy. How Imitation Sparks Innovation*. Oxford UP, 2012.

Ross, Robert J.S. *Slaves to Fashion: Poverty and Abuse in the New Sweatshops*. U of Michigan P, 2004.

Shackle, G.L.S. *Epistemics and Economics: A Critique of Economic Doctrines*. Cambridge UP, 1972

Thomas, Kedron. "Economic Regulation and the Value of Concealment in Highland Guatemala." *Critique of Anthropology*, vol. 35, no. 1, 2015, pp. 13–29.

Thomas, Kedron. "Intellectual Property Law and the Ethics of Imitation in Guatemala." *Anthropological Quarterly*, vol. 85, no. 3, 2012, pp. 785–815.

Thomas, Kedron. *Regulating Style: Intellectual Property Law and the Business of Fashion in Guatemala*. U of California P, 2016.

Vereta-Nahoum, André. "The Making of a Proper Marketplace: The Politics of Infrastructure in the Night Market (São Paulo)." *The Political and Cultural Economy of Popular Commerce: Gender, Inequality, and Materiality in Latin American Cities*, edited by Eveline Dürr and Juliane Müller, Lexington Books, 2019, pp. 87–108.

Waldinger, Roger David. *Through the Eye of the Needle: Immigrants and Enterprise in New York's Garment Trades*. New York UP, 1986.

Warkander, Philip. "'No Pansies!': Exploring the Concept of 'Style' Through Ethnographic Fieldwork." *Fashion Theory: The Journal of Dress, Body & Culture*, vol. 18, no. 3, 2014, pp. 233–250.

Weber, Max. *Wirtschaft und Gesellschaft: Grundriss der verstehenden Soziologie*. Mohr, 1956.

White, Harrison C. "Where Do Markets Come From?" *American Journal of Sociology*, vol. 87, no. 3, 1981, pp. 517–547.

# APPENDIX

## A Primer on Intellectual Property

*Juan Poblete*

In what follows I will describe first, the basic issues connected to the global expansion of intellectual property (IP) and second, what James Boyle calls the other sides of property: the concepts of public domain and the commons, as alternatives to the radically expansive global IP regime.

### The Basic Issues

Gilberto Gil, one of Brazil's most influential musicians, who served as its minister of culture from 2003–2008, stated in 2007:

> Digital distribution of intellectual property, if seen from the analogical era, represents a threat to business, security problems and a loss of social control. These perceptions of barriers to technology are but momentary setbacks which shall soon be resolved. It is more and more impossible to ignore the fantastic possibilities of democratizing access to knowledge that the digital allows. However, we must be ever vigilant as digital technology, like any other technology, can be used against individuals and society's interests.

As in the case of this book's Introduction, this quote was initially intended to be the opening epigraph of this Primer but was not allowed because Routledge policy is not to publish any epigraph quotes that are less than 150 years old to avoid legal problems, as they can be perceived as decorative and therefore deemed not fair use. The fact that the same quote can be included a few lines below where it was originally intended is a good illustration of how absurd IP regulations can be.

As German critic Walter Benjamin clearly saw in his pioneering essay "The Work of Art in the Age of Mechanical Reproduction," the new means of communication and reproduction that emerged during the first third of the twentieth century had not only the potential for thoroughly commodifying culture but also for radically democratizing its production and the access to it. With this process, capitalism begun its century-old trajectory towards information-rich commodities and further development of the technologies that allow their massified, and thus increasingly cheaper, production and reproduction. As Matthew David and Debora Halbert make clear in *Owning the World of Ideas: Intellectual Property and Global Network Capitalism*—from the photocopying machine to the latest 3-D printer and computer, i.e., from the capacity to reproduce texts to the ability to copy, at least potentially, almost anything—what has played out is capitalism's struggle to keep "global network society as global network capitalism" (93) despite the tensions and contradictions built in into such a system. The owners of IP are thus faced with a difficult task: making their protected products circulate as much as possible while controlling the socialization and reappropriation that necessarily happens as they expand (Rullani 103).

IP is constituted by three basic realms: copyright, patents, and trademarks. Additionally, there are trade secrets (the Coca Cola formula, for example), geographical indicators of origin (Champagne), plant seeds' rights (Monsanto), and industrial designs. As the sum of all these realms, "The notion of IP, then, embodies a number of crucial tensions" (David and Halbert 15) related to what they are meant or not to cover: "Copyright covers expressions, not pure ideas; patents cover manifestations of invention shown to be useful, original and non-obvious, not speculative inventions that cannot be 'seen' to work; trademarks cover recognizable signs, not general symbols" (7)

The first one of those tensions is between expression and idea. It is important because, depending on how strongly or weakly the distinction between these two concepts is drawn, any book about a group of Argentine and French friends living and chatting in Paris while they listen to jazz may infringe on the rights of Julio Cortázar or the heirs to the copyright for his novel *Rayuela* (*Hopscotch*). The second tension is between invention and discovery: does the patent holder own the technique used to discover something until then unknown, or the unknown thing itself? This is particularly important, as David and Halbert make clear, in the case of "the micro-world of particles, genes, and bacteria, [since] recent legal decisions have fundamentally blurred the distinction" (16). Next comes the difference between monopoly and free markets as already explained. Finally, there is the tension between creators and society at large, specifically how their respective well-being and rights are kept in balance, as will be explained below.

The central issue with the current global IP regime is that its unrelenting expansion is threatening its *raison d'être*:

> Such expansion can be seen across three dimensions—those of time, space, and depth. Expansion could, in principle, refer to coverage in terms of the duration of the protection afforded, the geographical reach such protection covers, and/or in terms of the depth of what is deemed protected (both in the kind of things that could be covered and how far one thing has to resemble another to be deemed an infringement of it). (David and Halbert 95)

The expansion in duration and geographical and material scope of IP has been tied to a series of multilateral agreements. They begin in the late nineteenth century with the 1883 Paris Treaty for the Protection of Industrial Property and the 1886 Berne Union for the Protection of Literary and Artistic Works, both administered by the predecessor of what is today the World Intellectual Property Organization (WIPO) based in Geneva. In 1995 the World Trade Organization (WTO) was created to replace the General Agreement on Tariffs and Trade (GATT). WTO created the Trade-Related Aspects of Intellectual Property (TRIPS) Agreement enforcing newly developed international IP standards. In 1996 WIPO generated the WIPO Copyright Treaty. In their expansive effort to impose globally a maximalist version of intellectual property rights (IPRs), developed countries not happy with the already overgenerous TRIPS, have begun pushing, first through free trade agreements (FTAs) and now even more globally, for what is known as TRIPs Plus demanding even higher protection for IPRs.

These multilateral entities and agreements with global ambitions are a key component of what could be considered, with David and Halbert, as the internally conflicted but highly productive political economy of global network capitalism:

> The establishment of the World Trade Organization (WTO) and its first act, the creation of the Agreement on Trade Related Aspects of Intellectual Property (TRIPS), set up a very particular ratchet that has been neoliberal globalization's governing principle ever since—on the one hand, the increased global regulation of IPRs and, on the other, the further global deregulation of labour. (1)

Trying to explain the contradictory but highly profitable process through which knowledge-based capitalism aggressively expands and feels threatened globally, David and Halbert note:

> In today's global network capitalism, IP has become more fundamental than ever for three reasons—the enhanced globalization, digitalization, and capitalization of the world—themselves the three key elements in today's global network capitalism. However, each of these elements is contradictory to the point of being paradoxical—at least in terms of the significance of IP. (2)

First, the authors speak of "neoliberalism's regulation that offers protectionism for the powerful and only uses market deregulation to discipline the poor" (104) The first part of the statement above refers to expanding IP regimes, while the second alludes to equally expanding and global outsourcing of production in order to minimize labor cost and levels of regulation affecting both. But these two globalizing moves turn out to be contradictory when it comes to their effects on IP. The first wants to ambitiously expand the rates of profit and levels of market control. The second, while seeking to minimize production costs, ends up making technology and know-how available to Third World manufacturers, who can then engage in their own parallel operations and dodge IP regimes.

The second paradox of global network capitalism when it comes to IP, relates to digitalization and is closer to Enzo Rullani's formulation above: "While digital content is formally protected for sale worldwide, digitization also makes content freely available to everyone everywhere" (4).

The third paradox connects to the contradictory nature of contemporary global network capitalism: "Strong IP suspends markets in the interest of protecting property" (5). IP regimes think of property as extending beyond the physical object to the right to make copies of that object, and now, centrally, intangible objects, creating a strong limitation in the functioning of markets, to the extent that IP regimes forbid competition and allow monopoly prices for the protected period. That is why IPRs have always had limitations in order to restore markets to their "normal" functioning after that period. But the nature of informational capitalism and its dependence on information-rich products have pushed it to extend the length, width, and depth of its IP protections. One side of free-world capitalism is attacking the other in the pursuit of as complete as possible market control and wealth accumulation. This is why Peter Drahos and John Braithwaite have spoken of "Information Feudalism."

Traditionally IP regimes have been defended as follows: "IPRs are manifestly balanced 'social contracts' between society and creators/inventors. Society extends 'quasi-property' protection to right holders as a reward/incentive for their efforts. In exchange, the creator/inventor's work becomes the common property of society when the protection runs out" (David and Halbert 9). IP property is quasi-property because in the interest of incentivizing creativity the creator is granted time-limited property rights, which when due allow the wider society to fully benefit by the incorporation of this creation into the public domain (more on this below). This is why Drahos and Braithwaite state:

> Intellectual property rights are, in essence, government tools for regulating markets in information. The problems of government capture [by the private interest of multinational corporations among other actors] that we describe in this book have led us to the view that there should be a presumption against the use of these rights rather than a presumption in their favor. (3)

As Vaidhyanathan, May and Sell, and Drahos and Braithwaite also do, David and Halbert's book critiques each one of those standard justifications for IP. In their view, for example, the contemporary copyright and royalties regime, whereby a company keeps the lion share of the profits a musical album produces, is defended as the only way to ensure that creativity and creators can have financial backing to flourish. Only by an expected return on investment would a record company front the money that will keep a creator able to concentrate for a year in their production. But the regime is such that if a company had given $1 million in advance against 15 percent royalties to a creator whose album eventually sells a million copies at $10 each, the company will make the following calculation: after production and publicity costs the company gets to keep 85 percent of the $6 million profit ($5.1 million). The artist nets $900,000 but still "owes" the company $100,000 from the $1 million advance. The artist is said to have failed to recoup the investment on their creation, even though the record company made more than $5 million on it. Instead of protecting the creative worker, the creative industries thus organized, David and Halbert contend, reproduce precarity and indebtedness in that sector (47–49).

Similarly, the current patents regime regulating, for example, the pharmaceutical sector, has pitted, for instance, national publics affected by AIDS, nation-states facing population health emergencies such as South Africa and Brazil, and the economic interest of companies that claim they can only innovate if their profits are highly protected. In what Shiva calls the neoliberal translating machine, Third World national issues of access to health and food become global issues of trade and IP (95). However, even under the current expansive patent regime, there are international provisions for the right of a country, faced with a matter of national interest, to respond to an emergency. For instance, a public health crisis can be dealt with by issuing compulsory licenses that legally allow a pharmaceutical company to produce drugs at a cheaper cost for which it does not have the patent or by allowing so-called parallel or gray-market imports from a country in which certain drugs, legally produced, are available at lower cost (Sell; WTO).

This situation has engendered a maximalist corporate position concerning the depth and duration of patents that is countered by a more flexible minimalist position held by those who prioritize access to medicine and public health under emergency or otherwise conditions. Additionally, pharmaceutical transnational corporations have strengthened their hand by using so called patent thickets—"overlapping patents that cover the same product or process" (Vaidhyanathan 54)—to prevent access to competitors, by extending protection to include not just the thing but the research tools that may allow any consideration of the thing and its properties, and by "evergreening" their patents through minor modifications to extend their duration. Equally important in this regard has been the progressive blurring of the separation between the idea or process patented as the blueprint for the creation of an object, and the object itself, as it has happened in the agricultural business area. Here transnational companies have managed to sell seeds that can only be used but not collected again or saved by the farmer at the end of the process.

In this process, pharmaceutical companies—which have invested millions of dollars in propagating a discourse that defends their right to profit on the grounds that it is the proper price for life-saving innovations—have managed to present themselves as life savers and guardians of the future while at the same time massively appropriating publicly funded research *and* claiming to be the only source of innovation. Mariana Mazzucato has given a vivid illustration of a similar issue and its ideological ramifications—pitting private creativity and state inertia—by studying, in a very different field, the case of the vast, foundational, and expensive public research that went into the creation of the patented iPhone (ch. 5)

This is why May and Sell conclude that in the current system of justifications for IPRs:

"Power manifest itself by constituting whose definition of efficiency is the guiding one and whose benefits are guarded or even expanded" (30). In a similar vein, Drahos and Braithwaite, considering that "intellectual property rights are justified using different kinds of theories such as utilitarianism, natural rights theory, and theories of justice," (15) suggest that the current globally expanding IPR regime fairs poorly in relation to all of them:

> A patent system that does not recognize the utility preferences of much of the world's population when it comes to disease can hardly look to utilitarianism (i.e. the greatest happiness for the greater number) for comfort. Claims that intellectual rights are natural rights akin to the right of liberty look implausible in a world where these rights are traded by corporate owners. A situation in which intellectual property rights are used to achieve massive wealth transfers to a small group of developed nations at the expense of other nations squares with no theory of justice we know of. (16)

## The Other Side of Property: The Public Domain and the Commons

Gilberto Gil stated in 2007:

> Multi-task networking, collaborative processes, sharing channels, possibilities of interference and multiple reproducibility, are first and foremost a cultural attitude that people are adopting more and more in their daily life, and which is having great impact in all walks of life. This cultural contemporary situation is as complex as was the construction of urban spaces, long ago … Although a few years ago virtual was considered not real, it is now one of our biggest realities. This new reality is forcing us to rethink the standards for intellectual property, registered patents, individual work and copyright.

You now know why this former epigraph is part of the main body of this chapter.

The other side of property, as James Boyle calls it in a 2008 book aptly titled *The Public Domain: Enclosing the Commons of the Mind*, is constituted by two key concepts: the public domain and the commons. While the concept of private property as in real estate property is broadly understood and valued both in concrete national contexts and globally, its opposite, what we could call forms of collective property that are held by the public in a commons that is broad and, ultimately, universal, is not. This is a problem for a fair and balanced system of IP because we live at a historic time in which private property, including its extension to IP, is expanding as global capitalism does, while the collective commons are contracting by the sheer force of the privatization and longer-lasting copywriting and patenting of more and more of the world. The public domain and the information commons need to be reconceived to take them out of their crippling state of conceptual underdevelopment and limited public understanding. We need, says Boyle, a movement capable of reinventing and defending them in the way the environmental movement has been mobilized to defend the Earth.

The public domain can be defined as "material that is not covered by intellectual property rights" (Boyle 38), either because it never could or because the rights to protection have expired. But this definition is too general and mostly negative. In fact, as both Boyle and Debora Halbert highlight, the public domain is not simply a repository of old knowledge but the basic ferment from which all new knowledge emerges. Boyle thus proposes that "the public domain is the basis of our art, our science, and our self-understanding. It is the raw material from which we make new inventions and create cultural works" (39). Advocating for a more granular and complex understanding of the public domain, Boyle points out that fair use, for example, i.e., the right to quote from the protected work in a review, is one of the "reserved spaces of freedom inside intellectual property" (Boyle 38). Halbert adds that we need to refine our understanding of the *public* within public domain. This requires linking the concept to those of public sphere and publics in order to ask: "What public, or 'people,' are served when discussing issues of the public domain?" (16). There are organized and unorganized publics. The state is an organized public and claims the right to know better about how to administer its properties, i.e., public property, and to speak on behalf of the people. Unorganized public "is the public at large" (18). Importantly, the organized public via the state is in charge of organizing the IP system so that private and public interests are protected and in balance, allowing for the time, extent, and exceptions regulating this regime (such as fair use). The unorganized public domain holds those works whose copyright has expired and that can, therefore, be used by anybody without permission or restrictions. Since this understanding of the public domain is the direct historical result of the limited protections granted by the copyright and patents regime, it is important to keep the interest of private protection and public access equally valued and considered. In order to effect this reconceptualization of such proper balance, Halbert suggest the need for thinking otherwise, exploring alternatives to the IPR regime and rethinking key concepts: instead of *falling into* the public domain, works could be thought as *freed into* it; instead of *IP* we could talk of "*a form of leasehold*"; instead of *a regime of private property*, IP should be thought of, following Marlin H. Smith, as quoted by Halbert, "as *a system of gatekeeping*, a regime for controlling how and when creative works are ceded—and elements of production returned—to the public domain" (38), which is the place from which they emerged in the first place, in the shape of a socially embedded form of authorship.

Analyzing the contemporary expansion of the IP regime Boyle has talked of a second enclosure movement. The first enclosure movement, from the fifteenth century on, in England first and then around the world, privatized the lands previously constituting the commons. In the words of economic historian Karl Polanyi, this first enclosure movement can be conceptualized as "a revolution of the rich against the poor" (qtd. in Boyle 44). Referring to the second enclosure Boyle adds:

> The argument of this book is that we are in the middle of a second enclosure movement. While it sounds grandiloquent to call it "the enclosure of the intangible commons of the mind," in a very real sense that is just what it is. True, the new state-created property rights may be intellectual rather than "real," but once again things that were formerly thought of as common property, or as "uncommodifiable," or outside the market altogether, are being covered with new, or newly extended, property rights. (45)

According to Boyle, there are two crucial differences between those two enclosures and they derive from the nature of their two main objects: land and information. First, unlike the enclosure of the commons' lands, the commons of the mind are generally nonrival (i.e., they can be used by multiple parties without affecting their quality) and nonexcludable (i.e., once in circulation, information tends to be shared at zero cost and does not lend itself easily to exclusions—charging for use, for example—originating in its creators). Second, while the enclosure of the lands may be arguably said (but not indisputably, as Boyle makes clear) to have increased productivity, that of information may have the opposite effect since the components of knowledge are smaller bits of information that can be combined in new and creative ways, but also now IP protected, making it impossible or too expensive for such combination to multiply. Because of that, the regime of IP before its current globalizing expansion was much more conservative, it was in fact, "braided" and had "thread a thin layer of intellectual property rights around a commons of material from which future creators would draw" (Boyle 50). IP law functioned, paradoxically, to protect the commons. Now, instead, IP wants to be everywhere and cover everything, becoming not the exception but the norm, and thus threatening innovation and the basic premise that "ideas and facts must always remain in the public domain" (Boyle 49)

A third and final difference between the two enclosures movements, according to Boyle, is contextual. It used to be very unlikely and often impossible for regular people to create or reproduce what had managed to earn copyright protection or earned a patent. Now, instead, not only is it technologically easy to generate affordable or zero-cost copies of many things, from texts to music, from objects to processes, but in many ways copying is part of the regular process of everyday knowledge dissemination.

In the context of a globally expanding IPR regime, this tension between private interests and properties on the one hand, and common or collective properties and the common good on the other, has generated the figure of the contemporary pirate, who infringes on the rights of IP holders by reproducing, without permission, discourses and goods that are protected by IPRs. But as we stressed in the Introduction to this volume, piracy is often in the eyes of the beholder, and is certainly context-dependent and situational. As Karaganis puts it:

> Media piracy has been called "a global scourge," "an international plague," and "a nirvana for criminals," but it is probably better described as a global pricing problem. High prices for media goods, low incomes, and cheap digital technologies are the main ingredients of global media piracy. If piracy is ubiquitous in most parts of the world, it is because these conditions are ubiquitous. (i)

More often than not, piracy is a nonoppositional practice in which commodities are produced, circulated, and consumed according to the same capitalist logic that governs the world of "originals" and brands ("Piracy is nonideological in that it does not represent a self-conscious political opposition to capitalism"; Larkin 298). However—because access to and regulation of knowledge are also not just widely extended everyday practices but also some of the key political issues of the present and the future—piracy as anti-systemic politics has also generated so-called pirate political parties, based on a platform of activism to fight "what they consider excessive copyright, surveillance systems, an intrusive technology systems" (Burkart; Vaidhyanathan 98).

As we saw in the Introduction, some states, such as the United States, which now lead the crusades against piracy and call others pirates, were themselves called pirates in their history, as they strategically privileged the needs of their own national development, instead of the demands of powerful international holders of IPRs. In the words of Balász: "The piggybacking of local industry on the intellectual products of more developed, geographically remote competitors is not an aberrant form of economic development—it is one of its basic features" (410).

As Lawrence Lessig states in *Free Culture: How Big Media Uses Technology and the Law to Lock Down Culture and Control Creativity* (2004): "Free cultures are cultures that leave a great deal open for others to build upon; unfree, or permission, cultures leave much less. Ours was a free culture. It is becoming much less so" (30).

In the war on piracy, free culture is often one of the first victims. Additionally, as Lessig reminds us, many of the big corporations that, inspired by the new "property fundamentalism," wage the current war on piracy, had their origins in a of form piracy, including "film, record, radio, and cable TV" (53).

This out-of-balance crusade on piracy follows the idea that "if value, then right" forgetting that the real value in the IP equation was historically creativity and that IP was simply an instrument to accomplish it by balancing individual benefit (profit) with public benefit (progress): "We have become so concerned with protecting the instrument that we are losing sight of the value" (Lessig 19). As an instrument, claims Lessig, IP has always been different than property in other domains: "Creativity depends upon the owner of creativity having less than perfect control" (119), i.e., having only a limited and reasonably expiring control. Both in the English and American traditions of IP development, Lessig highlights the same result: IP, unlike regular property that is forever, must be protected only for a reasonable period and then enter into the public domain to foster further creativity and progress. Instead, in the contemporary culture of IPRs hyperregulation, copyrights and protections are always extended and renewed, legitimizing a "piracy of the public domain" (220).

In US history, for example, copyright has been systematically extended. From the original 14 years plus potential 14 more, if the author still lived, in 1790; it went "to 28 plus 14 in 1831 and 28 plus 28 in 1909." It then followed the Berne Convention in 1886 and its revisions in 1948 and 1976 to go from life plus 50 to, following the Sonny Bono Copyright Extension Act, life plus 70 years of protection (David and Halbert 46–47).

As Debora Halbert states, the concept of IP itself may already be conceding too much to those who want to tip the balance from the historic compromise between private profit and public gain at the root of the system of copyrights and patents, to the benefit of owners of absolute IP: "Property is too often interpreted as being an absolute right (even though it is certainly not). To use the word property already skews the debate away from the complexity of balanced rights" (11).

In this new hyper-protected and everlasting new IP regime, most of the culture that is available is commercial protected culture, as works are prevented from entering the public domain. The prosecution-based legalistic culture of extreme IPRs—what Adrian Johns has labelled "the Intellectual Property Defense Industry" (498)—has been in charge of generating moral panics about the allegedly society-corrupting effects of piracy on individual and social morality, and threatening violators with the pains of hell. As Mat Callahan makes clear though, such campaigns have not simply and not even mainly tried to stop theft. Like a magician showing us one hand to trick us with the other, "the Intellectual Property Defense Industry" has had a hidden agenda with its moral panic efforts: "particular industries such as music, agri-business and pharmaceuticals, have unfolded strategies to increase profit and control at the very moment they are claiming to be victims of piracy" (Callahan and Rogers 246). As a result of this new war on piracy, the balance between available noncommercial free culture and commercial and IP-protected culture is permanently altered in favor of the holders of IPRs.

In that context, the lack of clarity on whether and what is still protected or not, and the threat of litigation, have a stifling effect on creators. Moreover, the concept of fair use—"the right to use copyrighted material without permission or payment when you make a work" (Aufderheide and Jaszi ix)—also is threatened as copyright is ruled by what lawyers call "strict liability," meaning that claiming ignorance or that you thought you were not infringing upon copyright or that you were providing a benefit for the public, are not acceptable forms of legal defense (Boyle 12). As Patricia Aufderheide and Peter Jaszi contend in *Reclaiming Fair Use: How to Put Balance Back in Copyright*, their effort "forms part of a much greater discourse in the United States and worldwide, critiquing the most stifling, confining features of copyright practice today. That discourse is variously called copyright reform, copyfighting, the copyleft, and advocating for a cultural/creative/intellectual commons" (10).

The concept of "commons" "is generally used to denote a resource over which some group has access and use rights" (Boyle 39) This happens often under certain conditions and may be restricted to specific forms of membership or wide enough to include a full society. In the more precise formula provided by David Bollier in *Think Like a Commoner: A Short Introduction to the Life of the Commons*, "a commons is *a resource + a community + a set of social protocols*" to govern access and rights to that resource (15).

The commons can also be thought of as an alternative to both, the private–public dichotomy—that opposes the interest of individuals to those guaranteed by the state—and the human–nature binary that counterposes our needs to the natural world seen as extractable resource. Instead, the commons and their proper management can include both "the common wealth of the material world" such as water, air, and produce, and "those results of social production that are necessary for social interaction and further production, such as knowledges, languages, codes, information, affects" (Hardt and Negri viii). The classical political genealogy of Hardt and Negri's central concept, commonwealth, may thus be already pointing to a potential overcoming of the current radical separation of the still-to-be-tapped commons and the always-expanding capital wealth. For Hardt and Negri, however, the opposite seems to dominate. Not just natural resources but also human/social resources are increasingly being exploited, mismanaged, and privatized through the expansion of new technologies protected by IPRs.

The Internet and new technologies, for example, have made the most of us not just as passive consumers but active producers and tinkerers, combining and slicing bits of culture as part of everyday culture in what could be conceived as the development of a cultural commons of almost planetary dimensions. Not surprisingly then these new technologies and spaces have become battlefronts in the so-called war on piracy and the reactions to it.

The privatizing and globalizing logic of contemporary neoliberal capitalism has then tested the strength and boundaries of concepts such as public domain and commons. When Western transnational companies attempt to appropriate indigenous knowledge that has been collectively produced and held, they question whether the concept of public domain can function interculturally between differently constituted IP regimes (David and Halbert 31).

Charging against the vocabulary of piracy, the criminalization of sharing, and the privatization of common knowledge in her pioneering 2001 volume, *Protect or Plunder: Understanding Intellectual Property Rights*, Indian activist and scholar Vandana Shiva denounced what, turning the tables, she termed biopiracy by patent-seeking transnational pharmaceutical companies using traditional knowledge to identify commercially exploitable plants in India:

> The properties of neem that make it useful as a biopesticide have been known and utilized in India for centuries. They were not an invention of the scientists, who have been granted patents for neem biopesticide. Such intellectual property rights are in fact intellectual piracy rights. To avoid such piracy, it is essential that the collective innovation of Third World communities be recognized. (7)

Shiva also provided a parallel view of Boyle's two enclosures movements, this time from the viewpoint of those historically colonized by European powers: "In the first colonization, the land of indigenous people was robbed from them. Through intellectual property rights and patents, the minds and bodies of indigenous people are being pirated; life itself is being colonized" (9). She calls this process "recolonization" because it is not only the appropriation of other people's goods and knowledges but also the naturalization of Western ideas of property and who has the right to claim it: "Patents are often viewed as tools for recolonization by the Third World but are viewed as a 'natural' right, as conquest was during colonialism, by Western powers" (12–13).

This process of recolonization, especially in the field of biopiracy, is possible through the use of historical strategies for the subjugation of Third World people, in particular the devaluation and translation into scientific terms of traditional knowledge, both of which lead in turn to their appropriation through patents. Creativity, knowledge and innovation, abundant in nature and in traditional communities, are thus privatized:

> Reclaiming the intellectual commons through asserting collective intellectual property rights represents the real model of equitable benefit sharing … Outlawing biopiracy and making patents based on the piracy of indigenous knowledge illegal is thus necessary for guaranteeing equity and sustainability. (68)

One of Shiva's conclusions is that instead of the Anglo and Eurocentric model of IP, with its built-in understanding of individual creativity and privately produced and owned knowledge, the rest of the world needs an embedded, people-centered, context-dependent understanding of IP. This would involve, for example, recognizing collective modes of creativity and knowledge production, as manifested in traditional agriculture in concrete local contexts and their seed selection and improvement process:

> The relationship of a community to its knowledge is integrally uncommoditized and communally "owned" and shared. The sum total of the communally owned knowledge which is of value (although not necessarily priced) is then more aptly described by the term "community intellectual rights." (127)

## Bibliography


Aufderheide, Patricia, and Peter Jaszi. *Reclaiming Fair Use: How to Put Balance Back in Copyright*. U of Chicago P, 2011.

Balázs, Bodó. "Coda: A Short History of Book Piracy." *Media Piracy in Emerging Economies*, edited by Joe Karaganis, Social Science Research Council, 2001, pp. 399–413.

Benjamin, Walter. "The Work of Art in the Age of Mechanical Reproduction." *Illuminations. Essays and Reflections*, Schoken Books, 1968, pp. 217–251.

Bollier, David. *Think Like a Commoner: A Short Introduction to the Life of the Commons*. New Society Publishers, 2014.

Boyle, James. *The Public Domain: Enclosing the Commons of the Mind*. Yale UP, 2008.

Burkart, Patrick. *Pirate Politics: The New Information Policy Contests*. MIT Press, 2014.

Callahan, Mat, and Jim Rogers, editors. *A Critical Guide to Intellectual Property*. Zed Books, 2017.

David, Matthew, and Debora Halbert. *Owning the World of Ideas: Intellectual Property and Global Network Capitalism*. Sage, 2015.

Drahos, Peter, and John Braithwaite. *Information Feudalism: Who Owns the Knowledge Economy?*New Press, 2002.

Gil, Gilberto. "Discurso do ministro da cultura, Gilberto Gil, em seminario sobre experiéncias acerca do tema cultura digital," December 14, 2007,http://cultura.gov.br/324387-revision-v1. Accessed December 15, 2019.

Halbert, Debora J. *Resisting Intellectual Property*. Routledge, 2005.

Hardt, Michael, and Antonio Negri. *Commonwealth*. Harvard UP, 2009.

Johns, Adrian. *Piracy: The Intellectual Property Wars from Gutenberg to Gates*. U of Chicago P, 2009.

Karaganis, Joe, editor. *Media Piracy in Emerging Economies*. Social Science Research Council, 2001.

Larkin, Brian. *Signal and Noise: Media, Infrastructure, and Urban Culture in Nigeria*. Duke UP, 2008.

Lessig, Lawrence. *Free Culture: How Big Media Uses Technology and the Law to Lock Down Culture and Control Creativity*. Penguin, 2004.

May, Christopher, and Susan K.Sell. *Intellectual Property Rights: A Critical History*. Lynne Rienner, 2006.

Mazzucato, Mariana. *The Entrepreneurial State: Debunking Public vs. Private Sector Myths*. Public Affairs, 2015.

Rohter, Larry. "Gilberto Gil Hears the Future, Some Rights Reserved." *New York Times*, March 11, 2007, www.nytimes.com/2007/03/11/arts/music/11roht.html. Accessed September 12, 2019.

Rullani, Enzo"Le capitalisme cognitif: Du déjà vu?," *Multitudes*, vol. 2, 2000, pp. 87–94.

Sell, Susan K. "The Geo-Politics of the World Patent Order." *Emerging Markets and the World Patent Order*, edited by Frederick M. Abbott, Carlos M. Correa, and Peter Drahos, Edward Elgar, 2013, pp. 46–60.

Shiva, Vandana. *Protect or Plunder? Understanding Intellectual Property Rights*. Zed Books, 2001.

Vaidhyanathan, Siva. *Intellectual Property: A Very Short Introduction*. Oxford UP, 2017.

World Trade Organization (WTO). "Fact Sheet: Trips and Pharmaceutical Patents. Obligations and Exceptions," September, 2006, www.wto.org/english/tratop_e/trips_e/factsheet_pharm02_e.htm. Accessed September 12, 2019.

# INDEX

For Product Safety Concerns and Information please contact our EU representative GPSR@taylorandfrancis.com
Taylor & Francis Verlag GmbH, Kaufingerstraße 24, 80331 München, Germany

www.ingramcontent.com/pod-product-compliance
Ingram Content Group UK Ltd.
Pitfield, Milton Keynes, MK11 3LW, UK
UKHW022017180926
475701UK00005B/893

* 9 7 8 0 3 6 7 4 2 3 9 9 5 *